CW00631696

BRAND VALUATION

BRAND VALUATION

SECOND EDITION

Edited by
JOHN MURPHY
Chairman, Interbrand Group

BUSINESS BOOKS LIMITED

LONDON SYDNEY AUCKLAND JOHANNESBURG

Copyright © John Murphy 1989, 1991

The right of John Murphy to be identified as the editor of this work has been
asserted by him in accordance with the Copyright, Designs and Patents Act
1988

Second Edition published in Great Britain in 1991 by
Business Books Limited
An imprint of Random Century Limited
20 Vauxhall Bridge Road, London SW1V 2SA

Random Century Australia (Pty) Limited
20 Alfred Street, Milsons Point, Sydney
New South Wales 2061, Australia

Random Century New Zealand Limited
9–11 Rothwell Avenue, Albany, Glenfield
Auckland 10, New Zealand

Random Century South Africa (Pty) Limited
PO Box 337, Bergvlei, South Africa

First Edition 1989

Typeset by ⋀ Tek Art Ltd, Addiscombe, Croydon, Surrey
Printed and bound in Great Britain by
Mackays of Chatham PLC, Chatham, Kent

British Library Cataloguing in Publication Data
A catalogue record for this book is available from the British Library

ISBN 0-7126-5020-2

CONTENTS

THE CONTRIBUTORS

David Andrew is founder managing director of Interbrand Pacific Pty Ltd, and is based in Sydney, Australia. Before joining Interbrand he was managing partner of Andrew Burbery Ireland, a marketing consultancy firm in Melbourne. However, the greater part of his career in marketing communications has been spent in advertising agencies – initially with McCann-Erickson, and subsequently with Ogilvy & Mather – with assignments in New York, London, Tokyo, Milan, Southeast Asia and Australia. He is an American and a graduate of Cornell University.

Michael Birkin is group chief executive of Interbrand, read law at University College London and qualified as a chartered accountant with Price Waterhouse. Before joining Interbrand he was personal assistant to Sir Mark Weinberg at Allied Dunbar. He is one of the architects of Interbrand's brand valuation methodology.

Tom Blackett is responsible for Interbrand's European operations. He trained in marketing with Unilever and has considerable experience in new product development and research. He worked for Inbucon Management Consultants before joining Interbrand in 1983.

Michael Bourke is an analyst covering the foods sector, and is employed by Panmure Gordon, the leading stockbrokers. He is particularly concerned with advising international investors on the merits of equity investments in the various European stock exchanges. He was previously employed in a similar role by Greenwell-Montagu and, most recently, by Prudential-Bache.

Before coming to the City in 1985, he worked for six years at the Ministry of Agriculture, Fisheries and Food as a fast-stream administrator. This involved a number of short postings in different divisions, culminating in a spell as private secretary to a junior minister. He has a BA in political science from Bristol University.

Alastair Brown is an assistant director at Hill Samuel working with Edward Buchan in the Smaller Companies Unit of the corporate finance division. He is a graduate of the School of African Studies and joined Hill Samuel in 1985 after qualifying as a chartered accountant with Ernst & Whinney.

Charles (Chuck) Brymer is a native of Kentucky and worked in broadcasting and with the advertising agency BBDO before joining Interbrand. He is president of Interbrand Corporation in New York and responsible for Interbrand's branding and design consulting operations in New York, Los Angeles and Chicago.

Edward Buchan is a senior corporate finance director at Hill Samuel which he joined in 1977, after qualifying as a chartered accountant with Deloitte Haskins and Sells. He helped found, and now heads, the Smaller Companies Unit of the corporate finance division which advises fast-growing companies, unquoted and listed, on financing and acquisitions.

Janet Fogg, a qualified trade mark agent, is managing director of Markforce Associates, the trade mark practice of the Interbrand Group. She is a member of The Institute of Trade Mark Agents in the UK and worked for two leading firms of chartered patent agents in London before joining Markforce Associates.

Paul Haftke is a director of Interbrand UK Ltd. He graduated from Sussex University with a BA in International Relations and subsequently obtained an MBA after studying at Cranfield School of Management and the University of Washington (USA). The early part of his career was spent in publishing, following which he worked in corporate and brand identity consultancy. He was with Addison Consultancy Group immediately prior to joining Interbrand.

Alfred King is managing director of the National Association of Accountants based in New Jersey, USA with special responsibility for all publications, research and management accounting practice activities. A graduate of Harvard College and of the Harvard Business School, he also holds a Certificate in Management Accounting. Before joining the NAA staff he worked with American Appraisal Associates and, latterly, with Valuation Research Corporation.

Gil McWilliam is an Assistant Professor of Marketing at London Business School. She previously lectured in marketing and product innovation at the Schools of Management of Imperial College London, and Cranfield Institute of Technology. Prior to joining academia, Gil spent several years in advertising as an account planner with J Walter Thompson, and latterly as a senior planner for Leagas Delaney Partnership. She consults widely throughout Europe on communications and branding problems. She is currently undertaking doctoral research in the field of branding typologies.

Martin Moorhouse is group chief accountant of Ranks Hovis McDougall. He was responsible for much of RHM's 'revolutionary' accounting policy for brands and was closely involved in the development, in conjunction with consultants Interbrand, of the methodology for brand valuation employed by RHM. He joined RHM in 1985, three years after qualifying as a chartered accountant with a small London firm, becoming group financial accountant in 1986 and group chief accountant in 1987.

John Murphy is chairman of Interbrand Group plc and founded the company in 1974. He is co-author (with Michael Rowe) of *How to Design Trade Marks and Logos* (Quarto, 1988) and edited *Branding: A Key Marketing Tool* (Macmillan, 1987). He has also written *Brand Strategy* (Director Books, 1990). He lectures widely on branding topics and is author of many articles on the subject.

David Nash is a chartered accountant and joined the Grand Met Board in December 1989, having previously held senior positions with Imperial Chemical Industries and Cadbury Schweppes. He is Chairman of Grand Metropolitan Finance and other group finance and holding companies and is responsible for group information technology systems. He is also a Fellow of the Association of Corporate Treasurers and a Council Member of the Science and Engineering Research Council.

Terry Oliver is President of Interbrand Japan and founded the company in 1983. He was born and brought up in London and trained at London University. He first worked as a journalist in London and Johannesburg and then moved to Tokyo some fifteen years ago. He studied Japanese at Rikkyo University and worked as a consultant with International Business Information Inc. prior to founding Interbrand.

Noel Penrose is a director of Interbrand and is based in New York. He is a chartered accountant and worked with Grant Thornton in the UK and with Price Waterhouse in Belgium. He held a senior finance position with GTE-Sylvania prior to joining Interbrand.

Raymond Perrier has a BA in Philosophy and Theology from New College, Oxford. Since joining Interbrand he has worked extensively in brand name and identity development with fmcg (fast-moving consumer goods), pharmaceutical and industrial companies both in the UK and West Germany. More recently he has been a member of the Interbrand brand valuation team assessing brands as diverse as whiskies and DIY products in European and North American markets. In particular he has conducted brand assessments for both licensees and licensors of some very well-known but previously undervalued brands.

Michael Renshall, a chartered accountant, is a partner in KPMG Peat Marwick McLintock in London. He was chairman of the UK Accounting Standards Committee from 1986 to 1990 and is Deputy Chairman of the Financial Reporting Review Panel. He received the CBE in the 1990 New Year's Honours List.

Paul Stobart is a director of Interbrand with special responsibility for strategy and group development. He read law at Oriel College, Oxford, and qualified as a chartered accountant with Price Waterhouse in London. Before joining Interbrand he was with Hill Samuel as an associate director in the Corporate Finance Division in New York.

FOREWORD
TO SECOND EDITION

In the nineteenth century most of a company's assets were 'tangible' – property, plant, stock, investments, cash, etc. A company's balance sheet was frequently therefore a proxy for its 'worth'. For much of the twentieth century, and particularly in the last 20–30 years, this has ceased to be the case. The 'intangible' assets of a company – its brands, copyrights, special distribution arrangements, licences, know-how, even its management skills – are frequently far more valuable assets than its tangible assets.

This fact has been particularly brought into focus in recent years by the large sums which have been paid for companies whose main assets are intangible. What has also been brought sharply into focus is that conventional accounting methods are not well adapted to dealing with 'intangibles': accountants are altogether happier when dealing with things they can touch.

A particular problem which has faced many companies is how to treat the 'goodwill' which arises on an acquisition. For example, if you pay £1 billion for a branded goods company, mainly to secure its brands, when its tangible assets are only £200 million, you have acquired goodwill, mainly in the form of brands, of £800 million. In most countries the acquiring company would be forced to amortize this goodwill element and, in the case of a 20-year amortization period, would have to write off £40 million a year against the profit and loss account. In Britain, however, (and in certain other countries) the company has a second option – to write off goodwill immediately against reserves – and this is the most frequently used method of treating the goodwill arising on acquisition in the UK. In this way the P&L account is preserved but the company's reserves are depleted instead.

Many acquiring companies, particularly those which have acquired valuable brands or other intellectual property rights, argue that either to amortize an asset which they strongly believe is not a wasting asset and thus to take a P&L hit, or to appear to have a weaker balance sheet post-acquisition by taking a write-off, are two equally absurd options and both are more or less disagreeable. It is from this that the practice in Britain of valuing brands and including them in the balance sheet has arisen.

In mid-1989 the London Business School, at the instigation of The Institute of Chartered Accountants in England and Wales, made a review of brand accounting for balance sheet purposes and concluded that 'the present flexible position [whereby brands could be included on balance sheets under certain circumstances] is potentially corrosive to the whole basis of financial reporting and to allow brands – whether acquired or home-grown – to continue to be included in the balance sheet would be highly unwise'. The report conceded, however, that 'brand valuation may be part of a useful internal management exercise. It may aid internal disclosure and visibility, and it may help both brand managers and senior management to gain a much deeper understanding of "brand equity"'.

Following the London Business School's report the Accounting Standards Committee tried, with mixed success, to encourage companies not to include brands on their balance sheets except in certain special circumstances but the situation was still largely unresolved when, in mid-1990, the ASC was replaced by the new Accounting Standards Board, a body which seems set to make enormous changes to British accounting practices but whose attitude to brand accounting is, at the time of writing, not yet known.

Many technical partners in accounting firms share the view that brands should be kept off the balance sheet but many others are horrified at the prospect of this new accounting treatment being prohibited, particularly when there is no prospect of any agreed, sensible standard for the treatment of the goodwill arising on acquisitions.

It is clear therefore that the brand accounting argument will continue to rage for some time, particularly in the context of the balance sheet. This book examines the issues involved, but goes beyond the rather narrow balance sheet arguments: once it is accepted that brands are valuable assets, whether or not you put them on the balance sheet, you must measure them, understand them and properly use and develop them. Indeed, a technique which was developed mainly in response to a need by companies to restore their balance sheets following goodwill write-offs has developed into a tool of considerable value in mergers and acquisitions, investor relations, fund raising, licensing and, in particular, in brand management and brand strategy development. Indeed, the stringency of accounting procedures is bringing to marketing and to brand management, areas which in the past have relied to a large extent mainly upon intuition, new analytical tools which seem certain to have a profound and long-lasting impact.

John Murphy
London
April 1991

Chapter 1

THE NATURE OF BRANDS

Tom Blackett

It is interesting to speculate whether it occurred to Frank M Robinson, when he decided to give his 'esteemed brain tonic' the name Coca-Cola, that he was contributing to the foundation of a rich tradition that would extend far beyond that most famous of products. The chances are that it did not, and that in branding his new product his intention was merely to distinguish it from the other sodas on sale at Jacob's Pharmacy in Atlanta, Georgia, and to find some way of protecting his invention from imitators. So exemplary is this lesson in sound commercial practice, however, that good branding remains an absolute essential of successful marketing. And so, no doubt, will it continue as long as society regards the principles of competition and free choice as fundamental to the creation of wealth and happiness.

Nowadays, of course, competition and choice abound and brands flourish. Brands – and in particular international brands – have never been so profuse or so pervasive of our lives. Countless millions of people throughout the world now breakfast on Kellogg's Cornflakes, tune in to a Sony Walkman on their way to work, sip Coca-Cola with their lunch, settle the bill with Visa, stop in at Hertz to hire a Toyota for the weekend, pick up a McDonald's on the way home, unwind with a Gordons gin, etc. This is no coincidence. Modern producers of goods and services understand the benefits of powerful brands. Accordingly, they spend fortunes on research, development, advertising and promotion in order to develop such brands and to maintain their uniqueness, appeal and value.

The notion of value cuts three ways. Value to the consumer is represented by the price he or she is willing to pay to obtain the satisfaction the brand is perceived to deliver. Value to the retailer, or supplier, is represented by the advantageous margins that strong brands provide and in the 'store traffic' that such brands help generate. Value to the producer is the reward of ownership, generally expressed in market share, sales revenue, profit, economies of scale, return on capital, security or cash flow, benefit to the balance sheet, etc. Brands, therefore, are genuine assets and, like other forms of asset, they can appreciate considerably as a result of careful management and development.

A strong mutuality of interest between the producer, the retailer and the consumer therefore underpins successful brands. But into the 'charmed circle' recently has stepped unbidden another party whose activities have elevated brands to an altogether different plane. This is the brand predator.

We have come a long way from Jacob's Pharmacy and the birth of Coca-Cola, to an era in which brands are regarded as tradeable assets, to be bought and sold, invested in and exploited, run down and revitalized. Brands are now highly sophisticated, frequently complex, pieces of marketing and legal property; to understand them better let us trace briefly their history.

THE DEVELOPMENT OF BRANDING

The word 'brand' is derived from the Old Norse word *brandr*, meaning *burn*, and it was by this method that early man marked his livestock. From the branding of his livestock he moved on to brand his works, and museums now have numerous early artefacts bearing their producers' marks. These range from Egyptian, Chinese, Sumerian, Greek and Roman gold and silver jewellery, to pottery, lead pipes, bricks and even foods.

There is evidence too that Roman producers would write and display simple messages to inform would-be customers of the quality and variety of their wares, where these could be obtained and for how much. Similarly, shopkeepers would display their names over their shops and many would use pictures depicting their goods. Thus a butcher would show a row of hams, a shoemaker a picture of a boot, and a tavern a crude picture of a vine. So even by the Roman era the true value of using one's distinguishing mark in trade was fully recognized. Once customers realized that one brand of product was better or worse than another, or that one shop offered service and goods of a higher quality than its competitors, they began specifying their preference by name – and branding was born.

The use of branding has, however, developed greatly in the last 100 years or so. The Industrial Revolution brought with it mass production, and the consequent development of advertising and marketing techniques made the selection of a good brand name highly important. In both America and Europe the rapid increase in population, expansion of the railways and construction of new factories brought with them a keen public demand for a wide range of newly available products. In fact, the greater the quality and variety of products, the greater became the demand for them. This resulted in the need for manufacturers to choose a brand name for their products that would be effective in as many ways as possible. It became no longer practical, in many cases, to rely only upon the manufacturer's name adequately to identify and distinguish the product; a brand name increasingly needed to be memorable, pronounceable, original and, frequently, directly or indirectly descriptive of the product it denoted.

By the second half of the nineteenth century, many countries had begun to operate legal systems which recognized the value of brands to both their manufacturers and consumers. They developed trade mark laws to clarify and impose restrictions on the sorts of names that could be protected by registration and which allowed brand owners to protect fully their existing brands. These laws benefited the trade mark user by allowing him, subject to examination, a monopoly on his brand name in relation to his goods; and they benefited the consumer by protecting him from imitation goods bearing the same or a similar name.

MODERN BRANDING

Most countries in the world now recognize that intellectual property – trade marks, patents, copyright and designs – is property in a very real sense, and confer rights on the owners of such property. And with branding now being applied widely to services, most developed countries have amended their laws to include the registration of service marks. Thus companies like American Express, Hertz and British Airways generally enjoy the same statutory rights in their brand names as companies like Heinz, Bic and Hoover.

The extension of branding to services is a relatively recent phenomenon, as is the deliberate branding of entire companies (corporate branding). Historically the world's classic brands have been built around tangible products delivering material satisfaction, which consumers buy repeatedly in units. Services, however, have no tangible shape or form, deliver satisfaction of a less definable character (and sometimes, like life insurance, arguably deliver no appreciable satisfaction at all), and are frequently irregular pur-chases.

Corporate branding has much in common with the branding of services because many service brands are corporate brands and are applied to a wide range of different products. Both have as their main aim the promotion of confidence and the reduction of uncertainty in the quality of what they offer. Both, therefore, rely heavily upon the image and personality they create for their brands to communicate these qualities to the marketplace.

Thus with the development of mass marketing and the extension of branding to services, the ways in which products and services are distinguished from one another have come increasingly to embrace non-tangible factors as well as such real factors as size, shape, taste and price. The qualities which consumers rely upon to choose between brands have become increasingly subtle and even, at times, fickle. Cigarette A may be virtually indistinguishable from Cigarette B yet outsell it ten to one; a fragrance costing £5 a bottle may be outsold by another with very similar physical characteristics but which sells at £50 a bottle.

Modern branding, therefore is concerned with assembling and maintaining the tangible and non-tangible elements of the brand in such a way that a differential advantage accrues. The art of successful branding lies in selecting and blending these elements so that the result is perceived by consumers to be uniquely attractive and influential on the purchase decision.

SOME IMPORTANT TRENDS

Over the last few years we have seen the application of branding techniques to a number of new areas and the growth of retailers' own brands is an interesting and important example. At one time, of course all the products sold in shops were the retailers' own (manufacturers had not yet learned that by branding their products they could 'talk' directly to the consumer and thus modify the power of the retailer) and, paradoxically, the growth of manufacturers' brands owes much to the inability of small corner shops and general stores to provide customers with the variety and quality of products they wanted.

In the last two decades, however, we have seen a gradual reversal of this trend with the balance of power shifting once more in favour of the retailer. In the UK, for example, where five or six grocery chains now account for around half the country's grocery sales, approximately one third of all their sales are of retailers' own brands. In the United States too the big grocery retailers are investing in own brand development and are beginning to sweep away the cheap-and-cheerful image that has for so long characterized such brands, and which has in recent years placed them at a competitive disadvantage.

Thus retailers' own brands are no longer the tacky generic products of the 1960s and 1970s; they are brands in their own right and are every bit as good – and frequently better – than manufacturers' brands. The signs, therefore, are that retailers' own brands will continue to grow in popularity at the expense of manufacturers' brands for as long as they continue to satisfy consumers' requirements for quality, value and variety.

Another area where branding is increasingly used is financial services. In the United Kingdom, the freeing-up of legislative controls on suppliers of financial services coupled, in 1986, with the provision of registration for 'service' trade marks, created an upsurge of interest in the use of branding. Many new suppliers with untested reputations entered the market bringing with them fresh and appealing new ideas for financial products and services.

At the same time many established suppliers began to introduce products and services into new areas. Those twin pillars of the UK financial services market – the banks and the building societies – for so long confined to 'mutual exclusion zones', began directly to compete with each other. Banks began to offer mortgages, insurance and more flexible saving schemes; building societies began to offer cheque book accounts, credit cards and electronic banking. Thus a need arose for branding to endorse, clarify and differentiate many of the new products coming upon the scene. This led to brands like Liquid Gold (a high interest bearing savings account from the Leeds Permanent Building Society), Capital Advantage (its equivalent from Barclays Bank), Vector, Orchard and Meridian (three 'life-style' cheque book accounts from Midland Bank), Leading Edge pensions from Abbey Life, etc.

Similarly, many manufacturers of high technology products have turned to product branding to help consumers understand the bewildering array of choice that is now available to them. Few manufacturers, however, have managed to emulate Steve Jobs' brilliance in naming his micro-computer Apple. Apple, at a stroke, rendered obsolete the decades of technical gobbledygook and industry jargon that had characterized computer branding and replaced it with the concept of the 'brand personality'. So as the purchase decision cascades downwards in organizations, and computer technology begins to encroach more and more upon our personal lives, the use of branding to demystify what traditionally has been the preserve of the expert is bound to increase.

In complete contrast is the market for pharmaceutical products. This is an area where names have long played an important role in helping to guide the selection and prescribing of medicines. Curiously, however, the pharmaceutical industry is perhaps the least sophisticated in its use of branding and only recently have drug manufacturers begun tentatively to use some of the techniques that have for some time been applied elsewhere. But while the use of branding – with the name, graphics, advertising and targeting working in concert to produce a well defined 'proposition' – is still in its infancy, the successful promotion of such 'wonder drugs' as Zantac and Tagamet has shown the industry how strong branding can help manufacturers reap the benefits of innovation.

HOW BRANDS SUCCEED

In psychology, the theory that the organized whole is something more than the sum of the parts into which logically it can be analysed, is referred to as *gestalt*. This seems a fitting way to describe modern branding. And it is from psychology that a great deal has been learned about how brands appeal. Jung, in his teaching on human psychology, gave the four separate functions of the mind specific names: thinking, sensation, feeling and intuition. Thus brands have four key ways in which they can be distinct from competition; some focus more on one type of appeal and some on another, so more than one model is needed to understand what makes brands successful.

Procter & Gamble, for example, has built a huge business on *rational* brands, brands which appeal to logic and good sense: Crest helps prevent cavities; Tide washes whiter; Flash Liquid dissolves grime on contact. Rational appeals also occur in other markets: the appeal of alcohol-free beer is fundamentally rational, as is the appeal of low-calorie tonic water and lead-free petrol. Many food, drink and fragrance-based products, however, appeal to *sensation*. Freshen-Up, a liquid-centre gum in the United States, offers a distinct sensation in the mouth with its mint flavour. But Pringles, the formed potato crisp, initially made little appeal to the senses – its flavour was boring and predictable, its shape and texture uniform, and consumers rejected the brand.

We react to brands with more than logic, however: we react with *emotion* and *intuition*. For over 20 years Martini has been supported with advertising based on the slogan 'anytime, anyplace, anywhere'. This slogan is now as much a part of the Martini brand as the name, the drink and the label and has formed the basis of a brand personality to which consumers respond with warmth and affection.

For an entirely different reason consumers respond to intuitive brands. Intuitive brands enable their users to make a statement about themselves; they react instinctively to them because such brands fit their lifestyles and aspirations. What, for example, is the difference between Miller Lite and Budweiser LA? Apart from minor differences both brands offer the same material satisfaction, cost about the same and are widely available. The main difference is that different people feel comfortable with different brands. So intuitive brands help consumers convey something about themselves to the world at large; such intuitive appeals are a tremendous asset for a brand.

THE REWARDS

The process of branding 'adds value' to the basic product; if the brand is successful the producer can frequently charge a premium and benefit from his or her ingenuity. Alternatively, the brand owner may choose to be rewarded by higher volumes, leading to economies of scale, or by the greater security of demand afforded by brands. Brands therefore are valuable to their owners because they represent a means to develop sales and profits which can, to varying degrees, be protected against competitive attack or trespass; brands are valuable to retailers, or suppliers, because strong brands can command higher prices and stimulate customer flow; and brands are valuable to consumers because they facilitate choice.

Brands therefore can acquire considerable value as long as they are kept in good repair by their owners and continue to offer consumers the qualities they require. Examples of UK brands which over the years have remained true to their promise are:

	Market	1933 position	Current position
Hovis	bread	1	1
Stork	margarine	1	1
Kellogg's	cornflakes	1	1
Cadbury's	chocolate	1	1
Gillette	razors	1	1
Schweppes	mixers	1	1
Brooke Bond	tea	1	1
Colgate	toothpaste	1	1
Kodak	film	1	1
Hoover	vacuum cleaners	1	1

These examples demonstrate that many good brands, for all their complexity of product and consumer appeal, are not only capable of surviving for extraordinarily long periods but are capable of maintaining their market position despite fierce competition and changes in fashion. How can this be? Let us take two examples, Coca-Cola and Kodak.

The Coca-Cola formula has remained much the same since the 1880s, but its image has been updated constantly to keep its appeal fresh and youthful. This factor alone has helped the brand retain market leadership in the teeth of competition from Pepsi-Cola and many retailers' own brands which offer a product of similar quality but at a lower price. Coke, therefore, has maintained its appeal by investing in and developing the non-tangible elements of its *gestalt*.

Kodak's products, on the other hand, have changed dramatically over the last 100 years. The brand had enjoyed continuous leadership and stability because it has been quick to adapt to changing technology and has exploited this to the benefit of the consumer. Kodak has done more than any other manufacturer to popularize photography. Through its investment in product development and its commitment to mass marketing, it has helped bring photographic competence to millions.

Thus brands offer a guarantee to consumers of quality and value; if this guarantee is honoured by the producer then consumers will reciprocate with their loyalty.

BRANDS AS ASSETS

Most brand owners now readily acknowledge that their brands are their most valuable and enduring assets. Despite changes of ownership and an almost suicidal neglect of product quality in the late 1970s, Jaguar Cars eventually recovered its market position and reputation, so much so that the business was eventually bought by Ford for £1·7 billion, a sum far in excess of the value of its tangible assets. Throughout this period the Jaguar name – if not, for a while, its vehicles – continued to enjoy enormous prestige and this factor alone probably contributed greatly to the survival of the company.

Similarly, The Claymore Scotch whisky, launched in the early 1980s by Distillers Company Limited as a 'price fighter' to protect its portfolio of world famous brands against the depredations of the UK retail trade, was DCL's only notable marketing achievement in that era. Since the takeover of DCL The Claymore has gone from strength to strength having been sold to the UK conglomerate Brent Walker and subsequently to Gallaher, and ironically has outlived several of its former, more illustrious stablemates which have disappeared from the marketplace.

The extraordinary resilience that good brands display represents a unique attraction to investors. Thus one of the main issues surrounding brands today is not so much how to create and market them, but how others perceive their success and, ultimately, their financial worth. Buying a major brand nowadays is often more attractive, and makes more financial sense, than building it up through marketing, advertising and promotion over a number of hard, risky, non-profit-making years. Brands are now increasingly regarded as tradeable assets of worth, and this has created an epidemic of acquisition fever, with major household names changing hands for staggering sums. For example, in a few brief months in 1988, almost $50 billion was paid for brands in just four deals:

- RJR Nabisco, the tobacco, drink and food manufacturer, was the centre of a $25 billion fight for control between its own management and various predators. Nabisco's European biscuits, crisps and snacks brands were later sold to the French food giant BSN for $2.5 billion by 'leveraged buyout' specialists Kohlberg Kravis Roberts, the victors in the takeover battle

- American food and tobacco giant, Philip Morris, bought Kraft, the maker of cheese products of the same name and a host of other brands including Miracle Whip toppings and Breyers ice cream. The price was $12.9 billion, four times Kraft's 'tangible' assets

- Grand Metropolitan, a UK food and drinks company acquired

Pillsbury for $5.5 billion – a 50 per cent premium on the American firm's pre-bid value and several times the value of its tangible assets

- Nestlé paid $4.5 billion, more than fives times Rowntree's book value, to acquire the York confectionery firm that makes Kit Kat, After Eight and Polo Mints

The reason why the prices paid for these businesses are so high is that, for all their intangibility in one sense, good brands produce profit streams that are highly tangible. Also, at least in the overcrowded consumer goods markets, it is extremely difficult to grow brands like Kit Kat, Winston cigarettes and Green Giant from scratch. So the value of such brands is twofold: first, the net value of future earnings; second, a premium for the sum a competitor would spend trying to create an equivalent brand.

Thus branded goods companies increasingly are the subject of takeover bids and this factor has contributed to the large number of companies now seeking valuations of their brands. In some cases these valuations are for balance sheet purposes. Companies that value their brands are able to present a truer picture of their real worth; not only does this provide useful information to analysts and shareholders, it also gives management a better tool to assess return on capital employed in a branded goods business.

KEY ISSUES

With the arrival of brands on the balance sheet branding has truly come of age. A practice which, one hundred years ago, was regarded as a useful way to help consumers recognize your product and at the same time stamp some ownership upon it, has developed into a sophisticated marketing technique and now enjoys enormously widespread application. But what does the future hold?

For a large number of brand owners two issues are likely to become increasingly important in the future: the 'coming together' of markets; and the high cost and risk involved in launching new brands. Let us consider the first of these issues – and in particular international brands.

While Professor Theodore Levitt's vision of the 'global village' has yet to materialize, the developed countries, whose inhabitants are the major consumers of branded goods, have shown in this century an enormous coming together of consumer tastes and expectations. The reasons for this are many and include improved communications, increased travel and greater language tuition in schools (particularly of English). The world is indeed a smaller place and international markets for standardized consumer products are rapidly opening up, with brands that are successful in one market increasingly likely to appeal on an international scale.

International brands like Kodak, Marlboro and Mercedes are immensely powerful by virtue of their universal appeal and the coherence of international brands makes it difficult for local brands to compete. The bigger companies, therefore, are keen to expand their brands internationally, using profits from one market to grow brands in another, eliminating weaker local brands as they go.

But while this form of 'commercial hegemony' may be entirely feasible for the large multinational companies, how can smaller businesses with more modest resources benefit from the wider opportunities that international markets provide? The answer frequently is through 'niche' marketing. Consumers throughout the world are becoming increasingly sophisticated and brands which offer a measure of exclusivity – or even eccentricity – are increasingly sought after and valued because such appeals are universal. Many niche businesses like Burberry, Crabtree and Evelyn, and Dunhill have developed successful international brands by nurturing a quality image and promoting this selectively to carefully chosen target consumers.

One of the key factors which will assist the international aspirations of all businesses is the planned dismantling by 1992 of tariff barriers between all member states of the European Community. This move, which, it is planned, will bring about a truly 'common' market, offers the single biggest opportunity ever likely to confront brand owners, European and otherwise. Satellite broadcasting has made pan-European advertising a reality, international distribution systems now exist and over 350 million consumers – a large proportion of whom are affluent – await the 'Euro-brands' of the future.

But companies have much to do to ensure that they grasp fully such an opportunity. American brand owners like Procter & Gamble, General Foods and Kodak, who have for long been a force in European consumer goods markets, and the skilful Japanese, excel at mass marketing. Such companies will be seeking to dominate those sectors where consumers expect uniformly high standards of quality and value, and where such standards can be achieved irrespective of the scale of production.

Let us next consider the development of new brands. As consolidation spreads throughout the consumer goods industries and leading brands become more firmly entrenched, the cost of launching totally new brands and growing them organically to major market share positions is becoming prohibitively expensive. It is also very risky – as many as 85 per cent of all new brands fail. Thus a strategy that many brand owners now pursue with varying degrees of success is that of *brand extension*.

Brand extension offers the brand owner the possibility of endorsing a new product with some or all of the qualities of an existing brand. He or she can thus enter a market more cheaply, establish the new product more quickly and increase the overall support and exposure of the brand. This strategy, safe though it may appear, is not without risk. By extending the brand to cover a new product the brand owner faces the possibility that all he or she is really doing is diluting the appeal of the existing brand. For example, in the UK in the 1960s Cadbury-Schweppes used its Cadbury name first on Marvel dried milk and then on Smash mashed-potato mixture. This helped establish the new products but over time proved damaging to Cadbury's image for chocolate confectionery. (The company has since sold off its non-confectionery interests and is taking steps to repair the situation.)

On the other hand brand extension has proved for many companies to be a remarkably successful strategy. It has reduced the cost and risk of new product launches, increased the exposure of brands and in many instances has helped revitalize old and flagging brands. It is apparent, therefore, that brand extension is entirely practical but needs to be treated with considerable care and skill.

CONCLUSION

At the start of this chapter we speculated on whether Frank M Robinson had the slightest inkling that he was helping to found a rich tradition when he coined the name Coca-Cola. It is interesting also to speculate whether the history of the twentieth century, when it comes to be written, will somewhere contain a paragraph or two about that essentially twentieth century phenomenon, the brand. We think it will. Recently the *Economist* (another strong, international brand with particular imagery and considerable value) reported that in the few years since the end of World War II, five times more 'wealth' has been created by human kind than in all of history up until that date. This explosion in wealth has seen, at least in the developed world, an explosion in consumer choice. Whereas forty years ago a British or American housewife might have performed all domestic cleaning chores with only three or four branded products, now she may have 20 or 30 specialist products for floors, baths, windows, stubborn stains, tiles, fabrics, toilet bowls, even chandeliers. Brands provide consumers with a means of shopping with confidence, even when faced with bewildering choice. They also provide the brand owner with massive benefits. It seems clear that the phenomenon of branding will survive and will continue to grow steadily in importance.

Chapter 2

THE BENEFITS OF VALUING BRANDS

Michael Birkin

Although the valuation of brands is still a relatively recent phenomenon, it is already clear that companies can gain a range of different benefits from brand valuation. In the UK the initial impetus for valuing brands came principally from the benefits that a company can derive from capitalizing the valuation on its balance sheet and this chapter discusses these benefits in some detail. However, brand valuation for balance sheet purposes has been adopted, in part at least, to avoid certain of the severe problems caused by anachronistic accounting rules and it is certain that these rules are now about to undergo a significant review following the setting up of the Accounting Standards Board (ASB) in 1990. Indeed, the ASB has already indicated that it will require more information on current use values of assets whether included on the balance sheet or not.

But irrespective of the accounting debate over the nature and purpose of the balance sheet, brand valuation has become an established practice with a variety of commercial applications and we shall look at these in turn.

MANAGEMENT INFORMATION

Branded goods companies usually acknowledge quite clearly that their most valuable assets are their brands, yet often the quality of their brand-related management information is unsatisfactory. Even in relatively sophisticated companies marketing and finance departments communicate poorly, a fact which has frequently led to brand managers carrying no real financial responsibility for their brands.

A brand valuation or 'brand audit' exercise can address this issue and set the scene for all brand-related decision making. Any brand valuation must look in detail both at current brand profits and at the likelihood of those profits continuing in the future. Thus all valuations inevitably consider the markets in which the brand operates, its positioning, trends, market share, strengths and weaknesses and so forth. Importantly, as all valuations normally take place on a comparable basis, detailed brand-by-brand comparisons result. The experience of recent years suggests that it is in the area of brand management and brand strategy development that brand valuation, evaluation and audit techniques will make their most important long-term contribution.

Brand strategy

A full brand valuation exercise will look at the brand's performance in both marketing and financial terms over an extended period of time, usually ten years or longer and, in an environment where brand managers often change every two or three years, can provide a unique overview of the success or otherwise of brand strategy vis-à-vis that of competitors.

The rigour of the brand valuation process also provides a reliable basis for the modelling of various 'what if?' options and the success or otherwise of these options can be quantified by forecast brand valuations.

Most importantly, however, an audit of a company's entire brand portfolio provides management with an unmatched foundation for strategy development – all brand-related data is organized in a comprehensive, quantified, comparable manner and all members of management can thus approach the strategy development process using a common, shared basis of knowledge. Brand strategy development, which is essentially a projective, visionary process can thus take place based on fact rather than hunch.

Resource allocation

The allocation of scarce marketing resources is a key issue faced by all branded products businesses as it is usually impossible for all brands to be fully supported at all times. Brand valuation helps in making decisions on whether to support a brand at all (some brands may best be 'milked' or even disposed of) and is also helpful in planning the allocation of marketing resources between brands. For example, management may have a choice between spreading the total annual budget across all brands or spending a larger amount on one or two brands, perhaps on a rotation basis.

There are no set rules as to which strategy is correct in any given situation but the basis for a decision rests on a thorough understanding of the nature of the brands themselves, the ways in which they interrelate with other brands within the portfolio, and the effect each alternative strategy has on the creation of brand 'worth'.

A full brand audit helps clarify these issues and there have been many instances where entrenched notions have been changed as a result of such an exercise.

Financial appraisal

Relatively few companies look at their brands as specific revenue-producing assets. Thus accounting may well be undertaken on a factory or production line basis and brand performance may well be obscured by being lumped in, for example, with own-label production. (See also Chapter 13 – Brand Accounting.)

This 'coarsening' of financial data inevitably leads to a lack of focus and to inappropriate brand-related decisions. Valuable brands may be used, for example, merely as training grounds for young executives with little management supervision, or the entire focus of the organization may be turned on to the newest, most glamorous brand and the strongest brands, on which the company's future depends, may be ignored and left to fend for themselves. Brand valuation has proved invaluable in financial appraisal and in helping to define brand strategies, measure performance and ensure that agreed strategies are consistently applied.

Brand extension

Brand valuation serves as a useful starting point for addressing many of the issues that have to be faced in determining whether a brand can sensibly be extended further. The key benefit of brand valuation is in 'crystalizing out' a clear, unequivocal profile of the brand, arriving at a detailed analysis of brand performance. It thus serves as a modelling tool for the exploration of various 'what if?' options.

International branding

The impending removal of trade barriers in Europe, the growth of satellite television and the opening up of Eastern Europe is leading (as will be discussed later) to renewed interest in international brands and the extension of national brands into new markets. Developing new international brands is an expensive and risky exercise, particularly in areas such as foods where the familiarity of local brands makes the prospects of any new brand decidedly uncertain. Brand audit has a useful role to play in improving the decision-making process for the internationalization of brands by identifying key strengths and weaknesses, highlighting the role of the product itself, the brand personality and the distribution system in brand success, and by helping to remove much of the subjectivity which so often surrounds such decisions.

MERGERS AND ACQUISITONS

During the 1980s companies began to pay particular attention to the inherent value of powerful brands, and this led to an unprecedented level of takeover activity involving major branded goods businesses. Figure 2.1 lists a few of the larger acquisitions in the period 1988-90 and the proportion of the purchase price which could not be attributed to tangible net assets.

Figure 2.1   Sample of brands purchased 1988/90

Vendor	Acquirer	Goodwill/ Consideration
Rowntree	Nestlé	83%
Pillsbury	Grand Metropolitan	86%
Trebor	Cadbury-Schweppes	75%
Verkade	United Biscuits	66%

In each of the above cases brands and their values were of central importance to the acquisition and the tangible assets of the acquired businesses – plant, stocks, freeholds, etc – represented only a small proportion of the value acquired. Indeed, it was Nestlé's takeover of Rowntree in 1988 that acted as the trigger for companies to find an acceptable brand valuation methodology.

The benefits of brand valuation in the mergers and acquisitions area are twofold:

- It can help in the identification of opportunities
- It can be an aid to price negotiations

Identification of opportunities

Companies embark upon the acquisitions trail for a number of reasons – competitive pressures, Stock Exchange pressures, availability of resources, the presence of an ambitious management team, etc. Normally companies start the acquisition process by drawing up, usually in conjunction with financial and other advisers, a set of acquisition criteria, for example size, management capabilities, price, market sector, technological base, geographical area, customer spread, labour relations record and so on. These criteria are used to evaluate and prioritize acquisition candidates so that the field is readily narrowed in a systematic, objective fashion. Often, however, even after an exhaustive process of this type, an acquirer in the branded goods area can still be faced with a choice between a number of prospective candidates and in such a case brand evaluation techniques can be used to determine the strength of a target company's brands, the prospects for extension or third-party sale, prospects for a given brand in the acquiring company's key market (if this is different from the brand's current market), distribution arrangements, customer base, vulnerability to competitive attack and, eventually, a brand's worth.

The need for strong and sustained growth, coupled with the risks and costs of new brand development, have also often led to such acquisitions being made at full prices and thus to a subsequent cutting of operating costs (and therefore of marketing budgets) in order to maintain or improve margins so as to justify the acquisition. Many acquisitive branded goods businesses have, as a result, extensive portfolios of brands but insufficient marketing budgets to support all their brands. This factor, coupled with the frequent need to 'offload' parts of the acquired business in order to reduce interest costs, may lead to an analysis as to which parts of the business, or which brands, no longer fit the portfolio. Thus, when acquiring a business, the new owner almost always acquires as part of the overall 'package' activities and brands which are not wanted. Thus merger activity in the branded goods industry has led to the growing practice of buying and selling brands and of periodically 'rejigging' brand portfolios, a process which seems bound to continue.

Brand evaluation can, in such circumstances, provide valuable evidence to management as to which brands are most suitable for divestment and which new brands (if they were to become available) would best fit the portfolio. The process of brand evaluation also reveals 'gaps' in the overall portfolio and suggests initiatives for closing these gaps.

Price negotiation

Negotiating the price of a business or brand is almost always a difficult process. In contested situations an opening bid can often be based on 'rational' grounds (eg earnings multiples or synergy benefits) but negotiations often move on to price levels which need to be justified by precise insights as to the value of the target to the acquirer, rather than more generalized indicators.

In such situations evaluation can play an important role. A brand valuation assessment, even with fairly limited data, can enable a potential acquirer to take an informed view as to how the brand will fit into his current portfolio, what are the extra benefits which can be earned, and thus whether he has the appropriate resources to make the brand work harder for the acquiring business than it does for the existing proprietor. A brand valuation may thus enable the acquirer to pitch his offer at a seemingly attractive price to the vendor but at a price which is nonetheless justifiable.

At the same time as enabling a suitable purchase price to be calculated, brand valuation can also serve to clarify the accounting issues which the acquirer will face after acquisition. In particular, it is beneficial to know what the brand valuation is likely to be, and therefore how much of the premium which the acquirer will be paying over net tangible assets will be accounted for by the brands.

The third key benefit to the purchaser of brand valuation is its assistance in putting together a financing package. Lending institutions are particularly prepared to supply funds where comfort is provided by strong brands; indeed there are moves afoot at present to use brands as actual security for borrowings or to assist in reducing coupon rates.

From the point-of-view of the vendor (or, in a contested situation, the defence) brand valuation has an equally important role. It is difficult to present one's brands as being 'valuable' without any idea as to what their inherent value in fact is. It also makes sense for all branded goods businesses which are vulnerable to hostile attack to undertake a brand valuation for defence purposes. This valuation should be undertaken on an 'existing use to the business' basis, as well as on the basis of the value of the brands to a third party. Clearly, it is a matter of judgment as to whether, and when, this information is released, but at least management should be aware of the 'hidden' values within their business.

Finally, there have been many instances when brand valuation has been used as a means of fixing a price when all parties have agreed that a sale will take place. In this context brand valuation, conducted by an independent third party, can be a valuable tool in arbitration.

With 'goodwill' (most of which will, in many instances, be attributable to brands) representing such a high proportion of current acquisition prices, it is important that all parties to a transaction understand the underlying values which fall under this nebulous and somewhat unsatisfactory heading. It is now rare for important transactions in the branded goods area to take place without some form of brand evaluation; indeed if such an exercise is not undertaken doubts may exist as to whether any premium paid can be justified or whether the management of the target company achieved the best price possible for shareholders.

INVESTOR PRESENTATIONS

It is important for any company to have sound communications with its shareholders and with the investment community. Although specialist analysts normally have a very full understanding of businesses in their sector, an understanding of the quality of a company's brands and an appreciation of the cash flows resulting from strong brands is frequently lacking. Clearly, those companies with strong brands would do well to demonstrate this fact to investors and emphasize the improved quality of earnings which result.

Thus a presentation of the strength of a company's brands should become a feature of all investor communication strategies, though the way in which the information is presented can be almost as important as the information itself. For example, merely saying to analysts that one's brand portfolio is worth, say, £100m is meaningless in itself – not only would there be doubt as to how the valuation was conducted but the analyst would not be in a position to make meaningful comparisons.

A more useful strategy may be to use the analysis to draw attention to the particular strengths and features of the brands as, arguably, the raw values themselves may be of less importance than the qualitative views of an experienced third party.

BRAND LICENSING AND FRANCHISING

Even though the licensing (or franchising) of trade marks is a common practice today, the setting of appropriate royalty rates is still largely subjective. Essentially a trade mark owner will ask for what he thinks is attainable. Brand valuation can, however, be used to provide a framework for the setting of royalty rates and, indeed, to justify higher royalty rates than may at first sight appear possible. Brand valuation can be used in a number of ways, for example, one can use the valuation simply to show to a prospective licensee what the asset is worth (and therefore the extent of the benefit which will accrue to him) or, perhaps more usefully, the brand valuation can be used to justify a royalty level using a royalty relief system. Royalty relief involves working backwards from the valuation and assumes that it represents the Net Present Value of future royalties that the company is relieved from paying through its ownership of the trademark. However, as any such calculation would show the full royalty rate that one would pay if the entire benefit and future capital appreciation of the brand were to accrue to the licensor, one would normally use this figure as a maximum and negotiate down from it.

A variation on this theme is that of internal brand licensing, an increasingly popular accounting measure for multinational groups which is discussed more fully in Chapter 9. By charging operating companies a commercially sound royalty for the use of trade marks and technical know-how, performance can be sharpened and, if handled in an appropriate fashion, group cash flows can be substantially improved. (See Figure 2.2.)

Figure 2.2

	Group HQ (Trademark owner) £m	Operating company £m	Total tax payable £m
Turnover	-	100.0	
Operating costs	-	(85.0)	
Initial taxable profit	-	15.0	6.0 (40%)
Royalty (say 5%)	5.0	(5.0)	
Revised taxable profit	5.0	10.0	
Tax actually payable	1.0 (20%)	4.0 (40%)	5.0
Saving			1.0

Clearly, the royalties charged have to be consistently applied and justifiable to the appropriate tax authorities. However, there can be no doubt that the operating company receives the benefit of the use of a valuable asset and should, as a matter of good business practice, be charged for this benefit. Also, operating companies are more likely to appreciate the value of corporate brands if they are charged for them.

BALANCE SHEET BENEFITS

Capitalizing the value of a company's brands on the balance sheet is a relatively recent phenomenon and the issue of whether or not the inclusion of brand values on the balance sheet is a good idea goes to the very heart of what a balance sheet is and what it sets out to do. The accounting purist's view of a balance sheet is that it is a simple statement, drawn up on an historic cost basis, of all the transactions of the business since its formation. It is not therefore in any way viewed as a statement of value, although in certain circumstances even the purist may approve of the revaluation of property assets when historic cost is clearly so divorced from any reasonable notion of value.

At the other end of the scale there are those who would like to change the basis of balance sheet reporting altogether by switching from an historic cost approach to one which values assets on an 'existing use' to the business basis. Under such a system all assets shown on a balance sheet would be periodically revalued on a consistent basis and the balance sheet would, therefore, be a proxy for a company's worth or value. Arguably, under such a system all assets capable of consistent valuation and revaluation should be included on the balance sheet; thus intangible assets should be included alongside tangible assets, especially in circumstances where the former are particularly valuable.

The UK's recently established Accounting Standards Board (ASB) is currently addressing this key issue (among many others) and will shortly be giving its view; it is quite possible that a compromise will be recommended whereby historical cost balance sheets will remain with current use asset values included as additional information to the Financial Statements.

However, within the context of a somewhat protracted and meandering balance sheet debate, brand valuation burst on the scene as a form of 'pre-emptive' strike by frustrated owners of valuable assets who had real balance sheet problems. Though brand valuation is just one of several initiatives which fundamentally challenge current accounting, albeit within existing rules, brands themselves have one key difference from many other intangible assets – they are identifiable, separable pieces of legal property which are increasingly bought and sold quite independently of the other assets of the business.

What, then, motivates companies to capitalize their brands?

Goodwill

Purchased goodwill is simply the difference between the price paid for a company and the value of the underlying net assets at the date of purchase. Current UK accounting rules (SSAP 22) require a company to account for purchased goodwill in one of two ways:

- By capitalizing goodwill as an intangible asset and depreciating the amount through the profit and loss account of the company over such period of years as the company and its auditors consider reasonable, or

- By writing off the whole goodwill amount against the reserves of the company at the date of purchase

Under either treatment it is clearly in the company's interest to minimize the goodwill figure. In the past the first approach has been rarely followed in the UK as the effect of it is to depress profits and hence earnings per share. However, this policy becomes much more attractive if part of the goodwill is properly attributed to brands that have been in existence for many years and which can be found to be appreciating in value rather than depreciating. Under such an arrangement a large part of the 'goodwill' element in the acquisition can be placed on the balance sheet and only the small 'rump' is depreciated.

If the latter policy is adopted (write-off against reserves) brand valuations can materially reduce the amount needing to be written off as the brand values are retained on the balance sheet; in this way acquisitive companies can maintain their balance sheet profiles. Figure 2.3 shows the balance sheet effect of valuing brands.

Figure 2.3   The balance sheet effect of brand valuation

	Company A	Company B	Enlarged company A (1)	Enlarged company A (2)	Enlarged company A (3)	Enlarged company A (4)
	£m	£m	£m	£m	£m	£m
Fixed assets	90	30	120	120	120	120
Intangible assets						
-goodwill			25	5		
-brands				20		20
Current assets	60	25	85	85	85	85
Current liabilities	(40)	(20)	(60)	(60)	(60)	(60)
Long-term liabilities	(25)	(15)	(85)	(85)	(85)	(85)
	85	20	85	85	60	80
Share capital	10	5	10	10	10	10
Reserves	75	15	75	75	50	70
	85	20	85	85	60	80

Notes

Company A purchases Company B for £45m paid in cash financing the acquisition through a long-term loan facility. The goodwill paid by Company A is £25m, being the difference between the acquisition price of £45m and the net assets of Company B of £20m.

(1) The goodwill of £25m is capitalized and will be depreciated over, say, ten years – a £2.5m charge against profits will be required each year.

(2) A valuation of Company B's brands shows that, of the goodwill paid, £20m can reasonably be attributed to brand values. The goodwill figure therefore reduces to £5m, a charge of £0.5m per year over ten years.

(3) The normal accounting approach is taken of writing off the goodwill amount to reserves. The enlarged Company A's balance sheet is therefore weaker than its pre-acquisition position.

(4) Brand valuation of £20m reduces the amount of goodwill to be written off to reserves to only £5m and therefore maintains a more reasonable asset profile for the enlarged group. Furthermore, there is no depreciation charge under this policy as the brands are not depreciated.

It must be said, however, that the brands being valued should be sufficiently strong that there are no grounds for depreciating these assets – declining brand values would leave the company with the same problem as it set out with as there would be a *de facto* depreciation as the depreciating asset would be identified at the periodic re-valuations and downward adjustments would be required.

Following the publication of the now defunct Accounting Standards Committee's ED 52 (in May 1990) fresh doubts arose over accounting for intangible assets (ie goodwill and brands). The draft suggested that all intangibles should be capitalized and amortized over a period not normally exceeding 20 years. This suggestion, however, received much criticism and was virtually overwhelmingly rejected by major UK businesses. It will be interesting to see how the response has influenced the thinking of the new ASB.

Gearing

It follows from any policy of writing-off purchased goodwill on acquisition that gearing ratios are inevitably adversely affected too. Despite the fact that many banks claim to lend primarily on the basis of interest cover, the reality has been shown to be quite different – gearing ratios are closely watched by lenders and, in any case, interest cover may be hard to prove. Therefore not to undertake a brand valuation exercise on the acquisition of valuable brands potentially puts a company in an inappropriately inflexible position.

Stock Exchange rules

The Stock Exchange stated in January 1989 that brands could qualify as assets when calculating whether a Class 1 circular is required to be sent to the shareholders of a company on the acquisition of another business, provided brand values were actually included in the balance sheet (a simple note to the accounts would not suffice).

Takeover rules in the UK require a company to issue such a circular seeking shareholder approval when the purchase price exceeds 25 per cent of the net assets of the acquiring company and the rule is intended as a protection for shareholders. However, it much reduces flexibility and responsiveness when making acquisitions, particularly in a competitive situation – vendors would clearly prefer to deal with an acquirer who can give a firm decision without the need to ballot shareholders – and the presence of a hostile shareholder on a company's register may make it impossible to get approval whatever the merits of the case without granting concessions to the hostile shareholder in other areas.

In recent years acquisitive companies who have taken goodwill write-offs have found that their net assets have been so reduced that

Class 1 circulars are required for even relatively small acquisitions. Clearly, the Stock Exchange class tests were never intended to be triggered in such instances and brand valuations can enable companies to preserve their balance sheets thus retaining flexibility. This single factor, and the specific Stock Exchange approval for it, has proved a key stimulus to companies to capitalize brand values on their balance sheets.

Borrowing capabilities

As has been discussed earlier, lenders are beginning to look at brands as assets on which to secure borrowings and, in certain circumstances, valuations can provide arguments for reduced coupon rates. Though this benefit is only starting to gain widespread acceptance, the fact that brands are separable and identifiable pieces of legal property is important to lenders.

Chapter 3

ALTERNATIVE METHODS OF BRAND VALUATION

Paul Stobart

This chapter sets out some alternative methods of asset valuation and explores the relevance of each to brand valuation. Before considering the alternative methods of asset valuation it is important to understand exactly what is meant by the term 'valuation': many definitions exist and a considerable number of books and papers have been written on the subject. For the purposes of this chapter, however, valuation is defined as the process of assessing the value now of all future benefits flowing from ownership of a particular property.

Several points of interest arise from this definition:

- Future benefits need not be monetary in nature. A collector of old history books may buy not for the future *economic* benefit that ownership of the books will bring but because the books will bring pleasure and satisfaction. Despite the lack of future economic benefit the books still have considerable 'value' to him

- This definition emphasizes the fact that value is dependent upon the characteristics of the owner and the purpose for which the property is being held. A winning Formula One racing car has great value to the sponsors and owners of the car. If the same car is owned by a private individual for use on a private circuit, it may have far less value. Indeed its value is, and must be, based on an entirely different premise. This is because the identity of the owner and the purpose behind ownership of the asset are entirely different in each case

- The more idiosyncratic the asset the more care needs to be taken in identifying the true purpose of ownership. As outlined above, the value of a Formula One motor car (a comparatively uncommon asset) can vary enormously depending on its owner and the purpose of ownership. On the other hand a ten dollar bill has an immediately recognizable and realizable value, at least in its home country, and will have the same value regardless of the characteristics of its owner or the purpose to which it is put

How, then, might intangible assets in general and brands in particular be valued?

INTANGIBLE ASSETS

Intangible assets are forms of property which, although they have value (since people are prepared to pay substantial sums of money to acquire them), do not have any physical substance. This is not to say that intangible assets are wholly amorphous or nebulous in nature. On the contrary, some intangible assets (and brands are possibly the best example) are highly distinctive. Marks & Spencer has built up a formidable reputation in retailing through sustained investment in management, staff training, promotional support and dedication to the pursuit of quality. Although this 'goodwill' may not have any physical substance, it is clear that the Marks & Spencer name (a piece of property to which its owner has very specific legal title) and all that it means to the consumer in terms of quality, reliability and value for money is worth a great deal.

Thus an intangible asset's lack of physical substance does not mean that it has no value. The difficulty lies in finding a way to calculate its value with precision when the nature of the asset itself suggests that the value will always be imprecise.

Because of this difficulty many people value the intangible assets of a business by assessing the value of all its assets, tangible and intangible, and then stripping out the value of the tangible assets; the balancing number is deemed to be the value of the intangible assets. Indeed, this is how accountants record the acquisition of one business by another, and the difference between the fair value of physically identifiable assets acquired and the price paid for the whole business is deemed to comprise the intangible assets or goodwill of the acquired business.

For many types of intangible asset there may be no choice but to adopt the above approach since it is impossible for some intangible assets to be separated out with any precision; management know-how, relationships with suppliers or customers, technical expertise and proprietary formulae would, for example, be difficult to separate out from the underlying business.

However, where it can be shown that the intangible asset *can* clearly be separated out, there seems no reason why a valuation of such an asset should not be undertaken provided it can be demonstrated that ownership of that asset generates quantifiable future benefits. In the case of a brand, as we shall see, it appears that the tests of valuation as set out above can be more than satisfied.

Let us look more closely at the characteristics of the brand name as an asset. A brand name is an intangible asset, the legal status of which is normally protected by virtue of its being a registered trade mark. Trade marks, if maintained properly, have no finite life and are freely transferable. A brand's strength in marketing terms can be protected by developing a brand's individual and distinctive equities such that a successful brand can command considerable consumer loyalty over a prolonged period of time. Indeed, strong brands could be described as a sort of annuity lodged in the mind of the consumer such that the brand will continue to attract consumers and be bought by them provided the brand's differential advantage is communicated clearly and consistently to consumers. It is this dependability of future income that gives strong brands their value.

Brands, therefore, are separable assets which generate a flow of future benefits. They would appear therefore to be capable of valuation, but how?

METHODS OF VALUATION

There are three generally accepted methods of valuing assets and the choice of valuation method depends on the nature of the asset being valued and the purpose behind ownership of the asset. Furthermore, a valuation can only be relevant to a particular point in time when a set of particular circumstances are known to exist. The three generally accepted valuation methods are **cost**, **cash flow** and **market**.

Cost

The cost approach to valuation involves assessing the value of an asset by calculating how much it would cost to obtain from an alternative source, the identical future benefits of owning the existing asset. One way to do this is to compute the cost of **reproducing** an exact replica of the asset; this cost is called the **cost of reproduction**. For a new asset, assessing this cost is often a straightforward exercise since all one has to do is find out the price of the new asset in the market (presumably the price you paid for it in the first place). For an old asset, however, the exercise is more complicated because of the difficulty of establishing the precise costs of reproduction of an asset which is perhaps outdated or outmoded.

In these circumstances, a more appropriate approach is to assess the cost of **replacing** the existing asset with an alternative which can provide the same future benefits. This cost is called the **cost of replacement**. It can be computed in two ways. The first is to identify the current cost of a similar asset and then adjust that cost for functional depreciation (the reduction in value caused by technical advances or improved manufacturing, sourcing and distribution techniques), physical depreciation (the reduction in value brought about by wear and tear through usage), and economic obsolescence, if any (the reduction in value resulting from the asset's economic viability becoming uncertain). The second way to compute cost of replacement is to identify all the individual costs required to bring an asset to the same current situation as the asset being valued. Again, an adjustment should be made to the resultant valuation for any economic obsolescence.

The cost approach works well for tangible assets like plant and machinery. Such assets can be readily identified and their cost profile can be quickly assessed. However, for assets not acquired for economic reasons the method is less appropriate. If we go back to our example of the collector of history books, it is clear that the value of the books lies not in the cost of printing and binding the books but in the pleasure that the ownership of the books will bring.

The cost approach also suffers from the fact that it takes no account of future benefits accruing to the asset. An asset could be valued at cost at a quite considerable sum and yet have no real potential of generating any positive cash flow in the future. As most of the rationale for owning brands is linked to the future benefits of such ownership, it seems clear that the cost approach is inappropriate for valuing brands.

The cost approach to valuing brands would also present practical difficulties. Assessing the costs of replacing an existing brand with another which has the same characteristics and future economic benefits would be an awesomely complicated, if not impossible, task. Trying to apply the cost approach to a brand such as Coca-Cola would involve the unenviable and, in all likelihood, impossible job of identifying all the costs ever incurred in the development of the brand since its inception and/or trying to assess how much it would cost to build another Coca-Cola from a zero base.

Cash flow

The cash flow approach to valuation ignores the costs of reproducing or replacing an asset but concentrates on the future cash flows to be derived from ownership of that asset. The future cash flows are discounted to what is called net present value by applying a discount rate which is intended to reflect the risk of the future cash flows being realized.

The purchaser of a Government bond, for example, may feel confident that annual interest payments due on the bond will be met as it is unlikely that the Government will go into bankruptcy. The discount rate would be low to reflect this confidence level. On the other hand, an investor who buys shares in a start-up high-tech company involved in a highly competitive industry will have an entirely different view about the risk of his or her investment and will demand a much higher return reflected in a higher discount rate.

Of course, not all assets are owned with the express purpose of generating cash – the collector of history books does not expect a flow of cash from ownership of the books yet, as we have seen, the books still have value. However, if the books were being acquired by a dealer in old books then the situation would be very different since the dealer would be looking to realize a sale in the future and, presumably, to make a profit in so doing. The value to the dealer could be calculated by computing future cash flows and making some assessment of the riskiness of the flows to that particular dealer (how easy it will be to sell the books, whether the dealer has other projects to which his money could be applied, the sort of returns the dealer demands from his investments, and so on). By discounting the future cash flows to their present value the dealer can assess whether the books he proposes to buy are good value for money. So, purpose of ownership is important in order to assess the appropriateness of the cash flow method.

Where the purpose of owning an asset is to generate cash flows, the discounted cash flow approach would, *prima facie*, seem to be appropriate. As the purpose behind brand ownership is normally to generate future cash flows, the discounted cash flow approach should be appropriate when valuing a brand. However, the following issues need to be addressed if such a valuation is to be attempted:

- *Quantification of future cash flows.* Although a brand is clearly capable of generating future cash flows the actual quantum of those flows could alter dramatically according to market circumstances wholly outside the control of the owner. If a new competitor were to enter the market with a superior product or if there were to be a long-term health or environmental scare then the cash flows from the brand could be severely damaged. Furthermore, it is often difficult to separate out brand-related cash flows from cash flows generated by efficiencies in other areas of the business such as the plant and machinery, distribution systems and/or management and marketing prowess

- *An assessment of the duration of the life of the cash flows is also required.* Due to its unique status in law a brand has no finite life yet it would be foolhardy to suppose that a brand had an infinite life. Again, changes in market conditions or lapses in brand husbandry may end a brand's life quite quickly

- *Some assessment of* risk *is needed to establish an appropriate discount rate.* Assessing risk is a complex process involving analysis not only of the brand's risk profile but also of that of the market in which the brand's cash flows are being generated. The inherent strength of the brand is a powerful indicator of how much risk is attached to its being able to generate cash. Strong brands are less risky than weak brands

Provided that a brand's cash flows can be separately identified, that the brand's likely lifespan can be estimated and that the riskiness of the brand's propensity to generate cash can be assessed with reasonable accuracy, then discounted cash flow techniques (or a variation on such techniques) provide a workable basis for brand valuation.

Market

The market approach establishes a value for an asset by identifying those values placed on similar assets in the market place. The residential property market is a good example of how the market approach to valuation works in practice. When putting a house on the property market the asking price is normally established by considering the prices of other comparable houses with an adjustment for the idiosyncrasies of the house in question. Looking at other market prices is a far better measure of value than attempting some assessment of the replacement cost of the house or of its future cash flows. (Replacement cost might, however, be relevant to an insurer who wishes to establish the cost of rebuilding a property destroyed by fire.)

The market approach requires the following:

- There must be a proper market in the assets being valued

- Transactions taking place in the market must be at arm's length

- The precise terms of transactions taking place must be known so that valid comparisons can be made

- The precise timing of the transactions should be known to allow proper comparisons

The market for brands and for branded goods companies has been dynamic in recent years and from the moment that Jacobs-Suchard first made a bid for Rowntree (a bid finally beaten by one from Nestlé) there has been a surge in interest in brands. The significant prices paid in the market for such properties have aroused considerable comment and multiples of 25 or 30 times earnings seem commonplace. The rationale for these high prices lies not simply in the attraction of brands as valuable marketing and legal properties but also in the potential financial benefits that ownership of the brand brings to the acquirer. The new brand owner may intend to obtain benefits from rationalizing production and there may be opportunities to extend the brand to new fields and/or new markets.

Above all, it is well known that buying an existing brand is a less hazardous practice than attempting to develop a new brand from scratch with all the risks and costs of a new product development programme. Major branded goods companies have often found that line extension and/or brand acquisition is preferable to new product development.

The difficulty of valuing a brand by applying the market approach is that every buyer has a different set of parameters regarding how much to pay for a brand or brand portfolio. The amount that a buyer might be prepared to pay can fluctuate widely according to the buyer's characteristics and purpose. Nestlé, for example, may well have outbid Jacobs-Suchard for Rowntree, not because it had deeper pockets but because its worldwide distribution system meant, quite simply, that it was *worth* more to Nestlé than to Jacobs-Suchard. Moreover, brands are not developed with a view to trading in them so the market approach does appear conceptually inappropriate. And, in any case, the market for brands, such as it exists, is full of inconsistencies and guesswork because the information that would facilitate comparable analysis is simply not available.

Other methods

Some observers have suggested that a brand's value should be based on its premium price over a non-branded equivalent product. The difficulty with this approach is that many brands are not priced at a premium and, in any case, very many brands do not have a generic, unbranded equivalent. Indeed, very many brand owners do not use brand strength to secure a premium but, instead, use the brand to provide massive, stable volumes and thus secure profitability through the economies which such volume provides.

Moreover, once a brand is established, the retailer may need to stock it to satisfy consumer demand and the brand owner can then push through other products under the same brand name benefiting from the stability and security provided by the umbrella brand. The Mars bar, a product which has no plausible generic equivalent, shows clearly how the process works. It is extremely keenly priced (a competitor recently reported that it could not produce an own-label equivalent at anywhere near the retail selling price of the Mars brand) and provides its owner with enormous volume. It is also reportedly an exceptionally profitable brand though, to the consumer, it has been and remains an outstanding bargain without any apparent hint of premium brand profit. It seems clear therefore that price premium is not a generally applicable method for valuing brands, though it does have applications in some circumstances.

AN ALTERNATIVE SOLUTION

A more practical approach is to value the brand in its existing use, that is ignoring any possible future changes in brand profile or any further exploitation of the brand by line extension or any other alternative use. This approach has the advantage that data on the brand in its existing use will be readily available for analysis. An assessment can thus be made of the brand's marketing strength, of its protectability at law and of its ability to generate cash flows. Moreover, there is a close relationship between brand strength and the predictability or quality of brand cash flow. Thus the stronger the brand, the more certain the brand owner can be that current cash flows will be maintained into the future. Hence, a brand might be valued on an existing use basis by applying a multiple to existing, maintainable brand cash flows, the multiple being derived from a detailed assessment of a brand's strengths. A strong brand would therefore command a high multiple, a weak brand a low multiple.

The range of multiples to be applied to brand cash flows or profits can be determined by a consideration of other capitalization multiples operating in the marketplace. Most stock markets, for example, value equity investments on a 'multiple of earnings' basis. The stronger the company, the higher the multiple, and vice versa. Similarly, in the fixed interest market, bonds have differing yields depending on the perceived 'strength' or risk of the issuer. A Government bond with inflation-protected cash flows has a high capitalization multiple, whereas a property company's fixed interest portfolio in the middle of a property slump has a high yield and a low multiple.

The theory behind the 'existing use' basis of valuation, together with an explanation of how this valuation process actually works in practice, is explored in more detail in the next chapter. It should, however, be noted that an earnings multiple system, dealing as it does with the potentiality for future brand earnings, is nothing more than a variant of the cash flow method of valuation.

CONCLUSION

Each of the traditional approaches to valuation has drawbacks when applied to brands although each method has applications in particular circumstances. What is clear is that whichever valuation method is adopted for a brand or brand portfolio, it must recognize the particular characteristics of a brand including:

- The fact that a brand is a specific, separable, transferable asset with no finite life and with clear legal title

- The marketing power of the brand and its ability to command consumer loyalty over prolonged periods of time

- Its ability to generate future cash flows

Of the three traditional valuation methods neither the cost nor the market valuation methods provide much assistance when valuing a brand except in very special circumstances. Discounted cash flow techniques provide a rather better solution though only when cash flows, brand lifespan and brand risk can be quantified with reasonable accuracy. An alternative approach, explored more fully in the next chapter, draws on some of the concepts used in the three traditional valuation methods, and especially discounted cash flow, but places them within the concept of 'existing use' thereby providing an altogether more appropriate solution for valuing these very particular assets.

Chapter 4

VALUATION OF TRADE MARKS AND BRAND NAMES

Michael Birkin

As we have already seen, trade marks and brand names are valuable intangible assets which, when established and used, are capable of producing revenue in their own right and which can be bought and sold independently of other assets and of management and employees. This chapter outlines a straightforward, consistent and applicable methodology for the valuation of brands for balance sheet and other purposes. This methodology was developed by Interbrand in conjunction with Ranks Hovis McDougall and has since been used by, among many others, Grand Metropolitan, United Biscuits, Nabisco, BSN and Lion Nathan. It has also been used in a host of applications besides the balance sheet including mergers and acquisitions, fund-raising, brand strategy development and brand licensing.

PROBLEMS OF VALUATION

The valuation of brands is a relatively new concept and although brands are bought and sold independently from other business assets, there is no identifiable market in brands as such. Brand valuation is therefore in part an art, not an exact science, and necessarily involves judgment. It also involves specialists in three quite separate and hitherto unrelated disciplines – marketing, accountancy and finance, and law. In order to conduct a proper valuation an unusual, even unique, blending of professional skills is therefore required. Also, any methodology must deal both with hard ascertainable factual information (eg market shares, sales and profits) as well as rather 'softer' qualitative information and skilled, professional judgment is needed in assessing brand strength and in determining brand-related profit.

Besides embracing different professional disciplines, any brand valuation methodology must, in order to win the support of auditors, investors and others:

- Follow fundamental accounting concepts
- Allow for revaluation on a regular basis
- Be suitable for both own-developed and acquired brands

FUNDAMENTAL ASSUMPTIONS

We define the value of a brand as encompassing the particular values attributable to the trade mark, logo, packaging and get-up, as well as to the recipe, formulation or raw material mix. In other words *brand value* embraces all the proprietary intellectual property rights encompassed by the brand. Thus for the purposes of evaluation we consider a brand to be an 'active trade mark' – a trade mark actually used in relation to goods or services and which has, through use, acquired associations and value.

The Interbrand methodology, when used for balance sheet purposes, deals with existing use and does not take account of any unrealized 'stretch' factors (eg line extensions or licensing). Nor is it normally concerned with the break-up value of a company's brands or with the valuation that, under different circumstances, a third party might put on them.

However, the methodology is sufficiently flexible that, for other purposes, a range of different valuation bases can be accommodated. We have, for instance, used the methodology to assess the value of brands to third parties using quite different distribution and overhead structures; to identify key initiatives which might be taken to improve the value of a brand; and also to determine the values which might be realizble for brands in the market.

ALTERNATIVE SYSTEMS

When developing an 'existing use' valuation methodology a variety of possible methods were explored.

Premium pricing

This system is based upon the extra price (or profit) which a branded product may command over an unbranded or generic equivalent. However, the major benefits which branded products offer to manufacturers often relate to security and stability of future demand and effective utilization of assets rather than to premium pricing, so premium pricing is rarely an acceptable method of brand valuation. Moreover, a strong brand which the retailer must stock due to customer demand also provides its owner with a platform for the sale of additional products and, at a practical level, it should be remembered as well that many branded products (for example most perfumes) have no generic equivalents and, in many instances (eg that of the Mars bar), it is difficult to conceive that a generically equivalent product could be offered at anything like as keen a price as the branded product. Furthermore, selling prices are often related to short-term tactical factors, a factor which makes it difficult to apply any methodology based solely upon this concept. Therefore the value of a brand clearly cannot be determined by premium pricing alone, though evidence of a strong price premium may well serve as a clear indication of brand strength and may therefore play an important part in a valuation.

Esteem

There have been moves, particularly in the United States, to develop brand valuation methodologies based principally on measures of brand recognition, esteem or awareness. Although the Interbrand methodology recognizes that awareness and esteem can be critical to a brand's success (and are therefore factors to be considered when assessing the overall strength of the brand), to build a model using as its corner-stone such 'soft' measures is inappropriate.

Historical cost

As balance sheets are traditionally drawn up on an historical cost basis it was necessary to consider valuation systems based upon the aggregate of all marketing, advertising and research and development expenditure devoted to the brand over a period of time. This approach was, however, rejected quite quickly: if the value of a brand is a function of the cost of its development, failed brands may well be attributed high values and skilfully managed, powerful and profitable brands with modest budgets could well be undervalued. Also, determining the historical cost value of most brands would be a near-impossible task.

Discounted cash flow

The concept of using discounted cash flow (DCF) techniques to achieve a brand valuation is attractive. Strong brands are, in effect, a form of annuity to their owners, so any system which can accurately assess the value of future cash flows is entirely supportable. The problem of DCF lies in its sensitivity: wide fluctuations can arise from relatively minor shifts in inflation and/or interest rate assumptions. This factor, coupled with the range of cash flows which can result from the differing brand development assumptions, means that DCF, although conceptually a strong system, has to be handled with care. Even when these difficulties can be overcome the valuer has the practical problem that he is generally given little time to complete the valuation and often has to satisfy auditors. In such situations modelling techniques using DCF can be hard to apply. Notwithstanding this, the Interbrand approach detailed below is closely related to the DCF approach and DCF techiniques are frequently used in conjunction with the Interbrand 'earnings multiple' approach.

INTERBRAND'S APPROACH

The approach most frequently adopted by Interbrand (and which is now, it must be said, most widely used by others) is an earnings multiple system, ie an appropriate multiple is applied to the earnings of the brand. Conceptually the system is sound (the arguments which support a discounted cash flow system apply equally to an earnings multiple system) and, practically, the system is robust, auditable and the valuation can be completed in a relatively short time frame, provided always that the requisite marketing, financial and trade mark legal skills are brought together. The system also has the real advantage that it is based upon hard, proven auditable data.

To determine a brand's value, then, certain key factors need to be determined:

- Brand earnings (or cash flows)

- Brand strength (which sets the multiple or discount rate)

- The range of multiples (or discount rates) to be applied to brand earnings

In addition, it is necessary of course to check whether or not the brand owner has, in fact, title to the brand and also the quality of this title.

BRAND EARNINGS

A vital factor in determining the value of a brand is its profitability or potential profitability, particularly its profitability over time. However, to arrive at a balance sheet value it is not enough merely to apply a simple multiplier to post-tax profits. Firstly, not all of the profitability of a brand can necessarily be applied to the valuation of that brand. A brand may be essentially a commodity product or may gain much of its profitability from its distribution system. The elements of profitability which do not result from the brand's identity must therefore be excluded. Secondly, the valuation itself may be materially affected by using a single, possibly unrepresentative year's profit. For this reason, a smoothing element should be introduced; generally, a three-year weighted average of historical profits is used.

The following issues must therefore be taken into consideration in calculating brand earnings:

- *Determining brand profits.* Since it is the worth of the brand to the business which is being valued it is important that the profit on which this valuation is based is clearly defined. For balance sheet purposes this profit must be the fully absorbed profit of the brand after allocation of central overhead costs but before interest charges. Taxation is, of course, also deducted, as will be explained later. For the purposes of evaluating the brand, interest costs are ignored since the basis of funding chosen for the brand is irrelevant to the brand's performance. (Were interest to be included in the calculation, the valuation could be materially affected by changes in corporate financing arrangements; as such arrangements are generally not brand-related they are normally excluded when determining profit)

- *The elimination of private label production profits.* The profits to which an earnings multiple is applied must relate only to the brand being valued and not to other, unbranded goods which may be produced in parallel with the brand but which are not sold under the brand name. These profits may be separately identified by the company through its accounting systems; alternatively, judgment may need to be exercised in assessing the extent of such profits based on production volumes, sales values or other acceptable methods. Insofar as 'allocation' is at the heart of much accountancy, the elimination of 'own label' profits has been found to be entirely feasible

- *The restatement of historical profits to present-day values.* Since historical earnings form the basis of the valuation these values must be re-stated to present-day figures by adjustments for inflation. This has the effect of ensuring that performance is reviewed at constant levels

- *The weighting of historical earnings.* A weighting factor is applied to historical earnings so as to determine a prudent and conservative level of ongoing profitability to which to apply an appropriate multiple. Thus once historical profits have been adjusted to present-day values a weighting factor must be applied to each year's brand profits which reflects the importance of those profits to the valuation. In many cases a simple weighting of three times for the current year, twice for the previous year and once for the year before that is used (see Figure 1). These aggregate earnings are then divided by the sum of the weighting factors used

- *Provision for decline.* There is a basic accounting rule that benefits should only be taken when they are earned, but that losses should be provided for as soon as they are known. This rule further implies that, in a brand valuation for balance sheet purposes, future brand profitability must be reviewed so as to see whether the profits on which the valuation is based will be maintained. Where the weighted average historical earnings are clearly below the forecast brand profits in future years, no provision for decline is necessary, provided of course that the

Figure 4.1 Weighting of historical earnings

	Earnings £000	Weighting factor	Weighted earnings £000
Year 1	545	1	545
Year 2	630	2	1260
Year 3	700	$\frac{3}{6}$	$\frac{2100}{3905}$
Weighted average earnings			$\underline{£651}$

forecast is reasonable and can be justified. However, it may be necessary to review the weighting allocation if forecast future earnings are significantly in excess of the weighted average profit value and are expected to remain at this level in the foreseeable future. It could well be, for example, that historical profits may have been depressed by factors now brought under control and it may be appropriate therefore to place greater reliance on more recent earnings when arriving at a valuation. Where, however, the weighted average earnings are greater than the forecast future brand profits, a provision for decline may be necessary to reflect the reduced level of future profitability

● *Remuneration of capital.* For the purposes of a valuation, to apply a multiple to all the profitability of a brand potentially over-values that brand. Not all the resulting capital sum can be attributed to the brand itself – some of it necessarily reflects the value of the other assets employed in the line, eg the distribution systems, the fixed assets, and the management. Or, put another way, if one fails to deduct a suitable return for the other assets employed on the brand there will, arguably, be double counting on the balance sheet.

Of course, the value of the 'other' assets will vary widely according to the industry concerned. Indeed, the situation can vary quite widely even within a single industry. Consider, for example, a company marketing two branded soft drinks, Brand X and Brand Y. Brand X is in normal retail distribution and competes with Coca-Cola, Fanta, Seven-Up and scores of other brands; Brand Y is sold through distributors who provide a door-to-door delivery service. Both brands may have identical profits yet their brand value will be quite different. Brand Y, for example, may derive little or none of its profits from its brand strength – the profitability of the brand may be exclusively related to its distribution system and the brand itself may play virtually no part in influencing consumer choice. Brand X, on the other hand, may represent a powerful consumer franchise and thus be a valuable brand asset.

There are several ways of identifying and eliminating earnings that do not relate to brand strength but the most frequently used system is that of charging the capital tied up in the production of the brand with the return one might expect to achieve if one was simply producing a generic. Such an assessment obviously requires analysis and judgment, but as a general rule the non-brand-related returns one would expect in an industry where brands play a relatively insignificant role (eg heavy engineering) will be greater than those where brands are critical to success (eg cosmetics or fragrances). Provided one is dealing with the current cost of assets a *real* return in the 5–10 per cent range is normal and can be used as a capital remuneration figure

- *Taxation.* The multiples we use are applied to the brand's post-tax profit figures. Therefore it is vital that all the reported earnings are collected on the same basis. A tax rate is normally applied which is the medium-term effective tax rate forecast for the company

All these factors must be carefully reviewed when determining brand-related earnings. An example of how they are applied is shown in Figure 4.2.

BRAND STRENGTH

The determination of the multiple (or the discount rate in the case of DCF valuations) to be applied to brand profit is derived from an in-depth assessment of brand strength, as it is brand strength which determines the reliability of a brand's future cash flow. The assessment of brand strength requires a detailed review of each brand, its positioning, the market in which it operates, competition, past performance, future plans and risks to the brand. The brand strength is a composite of seven weighted factors, each of which is scored according to clearly established and consistent guidelines. These key factors are as follows:

- *Leadership.* A brand which leads its market or market sector is generally a more stable and valuable property than a brand lower down the order. To score highly in the area of leadership a brand must be a dominant force in its sector with a strong market share. It must therefore be able strongly to influence its

Figure 4.2 Determining brand earnings

| | (£000s) | | | |
	Historic	Historic	Current	Forecast
Profit before interest and tax	500	540	570	600
Less profits from own label manufacture	200	210	220	225
Profits for the brand	300	330	350	375
Inflation compound factor	1.09	1.05	1.0	
Present value of profits for the brand	327	347	350	
Weighting factor	1	2	3	
Weighted profits	327	694	1050	
Three year aggregate weighted profits		2071		
Weighting factors total		6		
Weighted average profits for the brand		345		
Provision for decline		–		
Remuneration of capital		(100)		
Brand-related profits		245		
Taxation		(81)		
Brand earnings		164		

market, set price points, command distribution and resist competitive invasions

- *Stability.* Long-established brands which command consumer loyalty and have become part of the 'fabric' of their markets are particularly valuable and are normally afforded high scores

- *Market.* Brands in markets such as food, drinks and publishing are *prima facie* stronger than brands in, for example, high-tech or clothing areas as these markets are more vulnerable to technological or fashion changes. A brand in a stable but growing market with strong barriers to entry will thus score particularly highly

- *Internationality.* Brands which have proven international acceptance and appeal are inherently stronger than national or regional brands. Significant investment will have been incurred in the geographical development of such brands and they are less susceptible to competitive attack. They are, therefore, more robust and stable assets. Moreover, by no means all brands are capable of crossing cultural and national barriers so those that are must be considered as particularly valuable assets

- *Trend.* The overall long-term trend of the brand is an important measure of its ability to remain contemporary and relevant to consumers, and hence of its value

- *Support.* Those brands which have received consistent investment and focused support usually have a much stronger franchise than those which have not. While the amount spent in supporting a brand is important the quality of this support is equally significant

- *Protection.* A registered trade mark is a statutory monopoly in a name, device, or in a combination of these two. Other protection may exist in common law, at least in certain countries. The strength and breadth of the brand's protection is critical in assessing its strength. Indeed, if the legal basis of the brand is suspect it may not be possible to apply a value to the brand at all for balance sheet purposes.

When assessing brand strength a detailed audit should be conducted of each brand in conjunction with the marketing director or brand manager. A detailed questionnaire which gives all relevant brand information in a structured and comprehensive way is prepared and agreed. Packaging and TV and press advertisements are examined and inspection visits will normally be made to trade and retail outlets. Once a thorough understanding of the brand, its market, competitive factors, trends and so forth has been acquired the brand is scored on each of the above key factors. Normally the brand strength score would be discussed in detail and agreed with the brand owner.

Let us consider how four different brands might be scored:

Brand A   This is a leading international toiletries brand operating in a 'mainstream' and stable market sector. The brand has been established for many years and is brand leader or a strong number two in all major international markets.

Brand B   This is a leading national food brand which operates in a traditional and stable market but one where tastes are slowly changing with a move away from traditional products and towards convenience foods. The brand has limited export sales, and its trade mark protection, though quite strong, is based mainly on common law rights rather than registered rights.

Brand C   This is a secondary but aspiring national drinks brand launched just five years ago. The market is dynamic and growing strongly. The brand has been very heavily supported and much has been achieved. It is, however, still early days. The brand still has some trade mark registration problems in the UK and, even though non-UK sales are still minor, the brand name, 'get up' and positioning have all been developed with international markets in mind.

Brand D   This is an established but very small regional UK brand in a highly fragmented but stable market.

Based upon detailed brand-by-brand analyses, the scores attributed to each brand might be as follows:

Strength factors	Maximum score	Brand A	Brand B	Brand C	Brand D
Leadership	25	19	19	10	7
Stability	15	12	9	7	11
Market	10	7	6	8	6
Internationality	25	18	5	2	0
Trend	10	7	5	7	6
Support	10	8	7	8	5
Protection	5	5	3	4	3
	100	76	54	46	38

While these scores are hypothetical, they demonstrate the basic 'building blocks' from which an overall brand strength assessment can be derived. This method not only ranks brands in terms of strength, but it also allows brand-by-brand analysis and comparisons and highlights those areas where management could most readily direct its efforts to enhance brand strength and hence brand value. (In the case of Brand B, for example, two initiatives immediately present themselves. Firstly, management could consider 'leveraging off' the existing brand strength in a stable but relatively stagnant market to enter sectors of higher growth; secondly, if management were able to exploit the brand in overseas markets, the brand strength would be much improved.)

THE RANGE OF THE MULTIPLES

The strength of a brand is a direct determinant of the reliability of future income flows from a brand so the brand strength can be used to determine a multiple to apply to the brand-related profits. Thus the stronger the brand the greater the multiple. The relationship between brand strength and brand value follows a normal distribution and is represented by a classic 'S' curve such as that shown in Figure 4.3. The shape of the curve is influenced by the following factors:

- As a brand's strength increases from virtually zero (an unknown or new brand) to a position as number three or four in a national market the value increases gradually

- As a brand moves into the number two or weak number one position in its market and/or becomes known internationally there is an exponential effect on its value

- Once a brand is established as a powerful world brand its value no longer increases at the same exponential rate even if market share internationally is improved

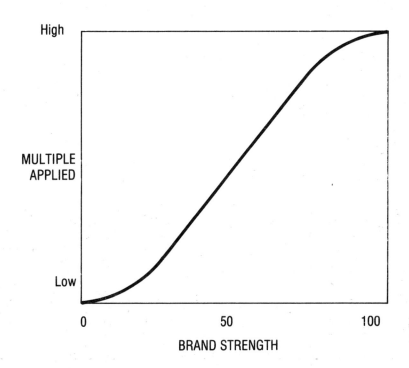

Figure 4.3   The Interbrand 'S' curve

Having determined brand strength and the shape of the 'S' curve the next problem is to determine the appropriate multiples. The bottom point on the curve is easy – a brand with no strength has a multiple of zero. But what is the multiple which should be applied to a notional perfect brand?

In fixing the multiples to be applied to brands the closest available analogy to the return from a notional perfect brand is the return from a risk-free investment. However, the perfect brand does not operate in a risk-free environment. Further, the return from a risk-free investment is capital free while part of a brand's earnings results from the capital employed in producing the product.

Allowances for these factors must be taken into account in determining the multiple to be applied for a brand operating in a real business environment. Thus the highest multiple that can be applied will be somewhat lower than that for a risk-free investment and may vary from business to business and industry to industry.

Moreover, other comparable multiples must be considered, such as those determined by current market conditions. The price/earnings (P/E) ratios of industries serving consumer goods markets provide one such indicator of the multiples that can reasonably be considered to apply to brands for balance sheet purposes.

Such P/E ratios, however, are an average for the sector as a whole and reflect both strong and weak brands as well as commodity and unbranded production. For example, the P/E ratio for the UK food manufacturing sector in March 1991 was around 12. Therefore the multiple at the high end of the brand strength scale should clearly be greater than the average P/E ratio of the sector in which the company operates and brands at the low end of the brand strength scale will be below this ratio.

Taking into account the risk-free investment analogy, sector P/Es, interest rates and values as determined by actual market conditions in fast-moving-consumer-goods sectors, we have determined that a maximum ceiling multiple of 20 is appropriate for balance sheet purposes, though this would be applied only to our notional 'perfect' brand. In practice, therefore, brands will be scaled below this multiple according to their brand strength.

It must also be remembered that the maximum multiple will vary from sector to sector and may also vary over time.

THE VALUATION CALCULATION

We have seen already how brand earnings are calculated and how brand strength scores are determined for different brands. Figure 4.4 shows how the valuation calculation is determined.

Figure 4.4 Determining the multiple

	Strength score	Multiple
Brand A	76	17.1
B	54	11.3
C	46	8.8
D	38	6.3

If each of the four brands described earlier had identical brand-related earnings of £164,000 then the brand valuation of each of the brands would be as shown in Figure 4.5:

Figure 4.5 Valuing the brand

Brand	A	B	C	D
Brand earnings (£000)	164	164	164	164
Multiple applied	17.1	11.3	8.8	6.3
Brand value (£ million)	£2.80	£1.83	£1.44	£1.03

This demonstrates clearly the greater valuation afforded to strong brands, even when brand earnings are identical.

SENSITIVITY ANALYSIS

Once the valuation calculation has been performed it is important to review the sensitivity of the key assumptions. The major assumptions which should be examined for their impact on the valuation are:

- The multiple applied
- The tax rate used
- The capital remuneration rate

If the valuation is shown to be particularly sensitive to changes in some or all of these assumptions it is sensible to adopt a prudent approach when valuing the brand, at least when this valuation is to be used for balance sheet purposes.

PORTFOLIO EFFECT

This methodology does not, of course, take into account the added value which might accrue from the portfolio effect of the brands owned by a company. The reason for this is that the financial benefits of owning brands operating in similar markets will already be incorporated in the individual profits of the brands. Since in this example we are essentially assessing the value of these brands to their current owner for balance sheet purposes, it is not appropriate to include an additional weighting for the extra value that a third party might place on the portfolio element.

OTHER VALUATION APPLICATIONS

This chapter has focused mainly on the technical aspects of valuation for balance sheet purposes, both of 'home grown' and acquired brands. There are, of course, many other situations where brand valuations can usefully be used and where the same basic method-ology can be applied. The assessment of the strength of the brand, for example, is unlikely to change greatly whatever the situation (and this is the area of the valuation process which normally requires the most detailed and time-consuming investigations) though attributable brand earnings and the appropriate multiple could vary considerably. (In the case of acquisitions, for example, synergy benefits could be identified and incorporated into the brand profits. Also it may be appropriate to include an acquisition premium.)

It should also be noted that even when the valuation is based upon notional royalty rates or upon discounted future earnings it is first necessary to identify brand earnings and review carefully the reliability of future income flows. In other words, the key elements of this methodology – the assessment of brand earnings and of brand strength – need to be followed whatever procedure is used to derive a valuation.

Chapter 5

ACCOUNTING FOR BRANDS – THE PRACTITIONER'S PERSPECTIVE

Michael Renshall

INTRODUCTION

Branding is not new, and the fact that brands may have considerable commercial value has long been recognized. In the past quarter of a century the importance of brands and branding has been increasingly recognized, and today considerable skill, effort and money are invested in their development and exploitation. The substantial sums which have been paid to acquire leading brands vouch for their potential.

Properly managed, brands serve to enhance a company's profile, improve its market share and hence sales and generally enable the branded product to command a price premium over unbranded competing products. All these factors serve to increase the company's profitability and thereby increase the value of the shareholder's investment. Brands are often an important economic resource of the company.

UK company accounts are normally prepared on the historical cost (or modified historical cost) basis. Assets are normally stated in the balance sheet at original cost (or alternatively current or replacement cost). It is a truism that under present accounting convention balance sheets are not statements of value. But it is the value of brands rather than their historic cost (if that could be known) that concerns users of financial statements. They know that the value of a brand is not related so much to its cost as to its ability to generate future cash flows. Certainly, when brands are appraised for the purpose of sale and acquisition this is likely to be the normal basis of evaluation. It is an approach, however, which comes close to the capitalization of future profits, a concept which makes conventional accountants deeply uneasy, not least because of its obvious uncertainty.

At the same time, one of the key factors for investors in making investment decisions is information to help them estimate the stream of future income that a company can reasonably expect to generate. Traditional financial reporting based on the concept of historical cost, in which assets are regarded as unexpired costs waiting to be absorbed in earning revenue, has been of limited use in meeting this need. Accountants, aware of how often commercial hopes are dashed in practice, have evolved concepts of prudence and conservatism in financial reporting which make them wary of bases of appraisal which would lead to assets being recognized and stated in the balance sheet at amounts which could, by their very nature, often be highly volatile and vulnerable to change.

There is thus a discrepancy between the type of information which investors find most useful – that which is indicative of future earnings –and the type of information which existing accounting convention focuses on: that is, cost-based information, which in itself says little or nothing about future prospects. Hitherto the financial community has tended to ignore intangibles in evaluating a company's financial position. There has been a general preference for real, tangible assets, and a scepticism about intangibles. The evidence of brands has undoubtedly forced a shift in these attitudes.

Brand accounting is a contentious area and divergent views are strongly held. This controversy arises because the issue extends beyond the identification of a suitable accounting treatment for brands (or intangible assets generally) to the nature of financial statements, their purpose and the matters which should be recorded in them. This chapter does not seek to support or attack any particular approach but concentrates on dealing, in the context of brands, with the main theoretical issues which must be addressed (Chapter 6 deals with the practical implications). The chapter also deals briefly with the way in which these issues have been addressed both in the UK and internationally.

DEFINITION

The term 'brand' in the accounting context is not defined and is generally used in a wider sense than that implied by the dictionary which regards 'brand' as synonymous with 'trade mark'. In the accounting context, a 'brand' includes all the tangible and intangible elements of a product which enable a company to achieve those advantages over competitors which lead to enhanced profits. These elements include a recognized 'brand name', a product or range of products, marketing and other specialist know-how, an established operation and trading connections and a recognized market position.

'Brand names', in the dictionary sense of 'brand' may be bought and sold as a 'bare right' without a related purchase and sale of the attributes of a brand. The accounting for purchased brand names (as with trade marks and similar items) is generally well understood and relatively uncontroversial. Problems arise when it is sought to attribute a value to intangibles for financial reporting purposes where that value is not corroborated by an arm's length sale and purchase transaction.

THE ISSUES

It is possible to deal with the recognition of brands in accounts in two ways: they may either be reflected as assets in the balance sheet or they may be recognized only by way of additional disclosure incorporated by footnotes in the accounts. The 'disclosure' route is uncontroversial and, providing the information disclosed is not misleading and does not conflict with the remainder of the accounts, this approach is unlikely to cause major problems. The approach of capitalizing brands and recognizing them as assets in the balance sheet can, however, create controversy which tends to revolve around four issues:

- Is it acceptable to recognize brands on the balance sheet?

- Is it appropriate to recognize both acquired and internally generated brands or should recognition be restricted to acquired brands only?

- Can brands be carried at either cost or valuation?

- Should brands be amortized?

Recognition

The difficulty surrounding the question of whether or not to recognize brands in the balance sheet is that in many cases brands, even when purchased, are not clearly distinguishable from other intangible assets, in particular goodwill. In order to identify whether or not a brand may be accounted for as a separate asset, it is therefore necessary to establish 'recognition tests'. A number of differing tests may be used; however, they will commonly include the ability of the asset to generate future economic benefits, the ability to be measured reliably and the ability of the asset to be disposed of separately from the business or its assets. Considering this latter test (of separability or identifiability) in the context of brands, the tests may be passed or failed depending on the circumstances. This may best be illustrated by considering the separability of a brand in two circumstances, firstly, in an enterprise where the branded good is the sole product and secondly, where it is one product amongst many brands.

In the first case, sale of the brand is likely to leave the enterprise with a bare manufacturing capability, with no product, customers or market position. While sale of the brand on its own may be commercially feasible, its disposal will effectively terminate the existing business. In accounting terms the brand is indistinguishable from the goodwill relating to the business and would be considered to be subsumed within it.

In the second case, the enterprise will remain a going concern if the brand is sold and indeed, if the brand sale is part of some strategic realignment, it may enhance the enterprise's value. Here, the brand is validly regarded as separable and might be recognized on the balance sheet.

The effect on accounts of capitalizing brands will vary depending on whether the brands are acquired or internally generated. If a newly created internally generated brand is capitalized, the effect is to increase profits by the costs of the brand which would otherwise have been charged against them and to strengthen the balance sheet by recognizing the brand. In future years, assuming that the brand is amortized, the asset will steadily diminish in carrying amount and profits will be decreased by the amount of the amortization. The effect is to defer recognition of the brand creation costs in the profit and loss account until later periods, matching them against the revenue which arises from the brand.

If the brand is long established but has not previously been recognized in the balance sheet, assuming the brand costs can be identified, recognition would normally be by way of a prior period of adjustment which increases retained profits and establishes the asset on the balance sheet. Future profits will again be depleted by annual amortization.

If, on an acquisition, it is considered appropriate to recognize acquired brands, they will be brought onto the balance sheet as intangible assets, and goodwill (being the difference between the fair value of the separable net assets acquired and that of the consideration given) is correspondingly reduced. There is no immediate effect on the balance sheet but future year's profits may vary depending on whether the useful economic lives of the brands are different from that of the goodwill from which they are separated.

In summary, the position depicted by accounts can be changed very considerably by the recognition of brands. In considering the question of whether or not to recognize brands, it is important not only to consider the changed position but also the effect on the restrictive ratios, percentages and limits which may be imposed by banking covenants, debenture deeds, articles of association and other agreements.

Acquired and internally generated brands

Brands may originate from two sources: either by acquisition from a third party or by creation within the enterprise. In the case of an acquired brand, it may either have been acquired by itself or as part of the wider acquisition of the shares or trade, assets and liabilities of a trading company.

When a brand is acquired by itself, the value at which it is brought into the acquiror's accounts will normally be its acquisition cost. In the case either of a brand acquired as an integral part of a larger acquisition or of a brand created within the enterprise, the initial carrying value is less clear. In accounts based on the historic cost convention, the 'cost' of an acquired brand is its fair value and appropriate methods of appraisal are available.

The position is somewhat less clear with internally generated brands. Typically, such brands have been created over many (sometimes scores) of years and complete and reliable accounting records are seldom retained for more than a few years. In these circumstances any 'cost' figure is likely to be arbitrary: difficulties arise in identifying the expenditure on the brand and distinguishing the extent to which this has added to the brand, maintained the brand or been used up. Capitalization of the asset may therefore fail on a recognition test such as 'reliability of measurement'.

Carrying at valuation

In most countries it would be normal to carry assets, including brands, at their historical cost. However, accounting practice in some countries, including the UK, permits the alternative of carrying certain assets at valuation.

Inclusion of brands at cost involves little uncertainty: providing it can be traced, the cost is certain and established by reference to historical transactions. However, unless there is a ready market in brands (which will seldom, if ever, be the case), any value used must stem from a valuation. Since by definition, no two brands are identical, a high degree of judgment must necessarily be applied in brand valuation. Whilst the characteristics of an adequate valuation may be debated at length, it is sufficient to note here that a basis of valuation is unlikely to be adequate for accounting purposes unless two suitably experienced and qualified valuers, provided with the same information, would produce broadly similar values. These will almost certainly depend on estimates of future income flows – an obviously judgmental issue, regarded sceptically by some but by others as no more uncertain than other valuation techniques.

Amortization

Most assets, including intangible assets, have a finite useful economic life. In order for accounts to reflect properly all the costs of enterprise, it is normal to reflect the cost arising from the progressive shortening of an asset's useful life (and hence decrease in value) by way of an annual amortization (or depreciation) charge. This enables the cost of the asset to the enterprise to be fully charged against the income and profits which its use enables the enterprise to generate.

The determination of amortization and its allocation to accounting periods stems from the consideration of three principal factors:

- The carrying amount of the asset
- Its expected useful economic life
- The expected residual value of the asset at the end of its useful economic life

In the context of brands, each of these factors is relevant.

A typical brand is established over a period of time, often many years, by way of careful development and enhancement through advertising and other promotional techniques.

If the enterprise wishes to retain the benefits of brand ownership (enhanced profitability etc), it must maintain the brand's market position and must perforce continue such 'brand maintenance' expenditure. In these circumstances, it may be possible to demonstrate that many brands have a very long (but arguably not infinite) useful economic life. Equally it is possible to argue that continued brand maintenance will progressively change the nature of the brand so that after a number of years, the brand has evolved into something different.

If properly maintained, the residual value may exceed the cost or present valuation of the brand and in these circumstances, it is difficult to demonstrate that amortization of the brand is necessary. Indeed, it is often argued that 'brand maintenance', which is frequently costly, takes the place of amortization, and that to charge amortization against profits in addition to brand maintenance expenditure would be unfair and would mislead a user as to the costs of the enterprise.

Equally, other brands, particularly if based on a 'fashion good' may have a short useful economic life and in these circumstances it may not be possible materially to prolong the life of the brand through brand maintenance. Whilst the actual life of the brand cannot be estimated with any certainty, its residual value is clearly small and annual amortization would be necessary.

It is not possible to generalize whether amortization is in theory necessary for brands as any conclusion reached will vary from brand to brand according to circumstances. However, simply as a function of prudence, and regardless of the approach to amortization, it is necessary to consider the carrying value of the brand whenever accounts are drawn up. To the extent that the brand has diminished in value below its carrying value and the diminution is not expected to reverse, the carrying value should be written down.

BRANDS IN THE UK

Existing legislation and generally accepted accounting principles (GAAP)

Financial reporting in the UK is underpinned by the provisions of the Companies Act 1985. This Act lays down rules which must be complied with in preparing a company's annual accounts. The overriding rule is that accounts must show a 'true and fair view' and in restricted circumstances the detailed rules may be overriden if by following them the accounts would cease to show this view.

The Act establishes 'historic cost accounting rules' which require fixed assets, the 'assets of a company which are intended for use on a continuing basis in the company's activities', to be included in the accounts at their purchase price or production cost. The purchase price or production cost, less the asset's residual value, must be reduced by provisions for depreciation so as to write off that amount over the asset's useful economic life. The carrying value must be further reduced for any permanent diminution in value. Where there is no record of an asset's purchase price or production cost, or such a record cannot be obtained without unreasonable expense or delay, the Act permits the value set out in the earliest available record of the company to be submitted.

The Act also permits 'alternative accounting rules' to be followed. These, *inter alia*, allow intangible assets to be carried at their 'current cost'; in most circumstances this would be considered equivalent to their market value. The increase from the previous to the new carrying value must be taken to a revaluation reserve on the 'share capital and reserves' side of the balance sheet; the uses of this reserve are prescribed by the Act. Depreciation and permanent diminutions in value are treated as under the historic cost accounting rules, substituting the 'current cost' for the purchase price or production cost.

Provisions of the Companies Act 1985 introduced by the Companies Act 1989 set out specific rules governing accounting for the acquisition of another undertaking. The Act requires that 'the identifiable assets and liabilities of the undertaking acquired shall be included in the consolidated balance sheet at their fair values as at the date of acquisition'. In this context 'identifiable' means the 'assets or liabilities which are capable of being disposed of or discharged separately without disposing of a business of the undertaking'. This is equivalent to the test of separability mentioned above and can be interpreted as meaning that when acquired as part of a larger acquisition and regarded as identifiable, brands must be identified separately from goodwill.

At present there are no accounting standards in the UK which deal explicitly with brands, although relevant principles are set out in various accounting standards. In particular, Statement of Standard Accounting Practice ('SSAP') No 2 identifies fundamental accounting concepts (notably 'accruals' and 'prudence') which must always be applied; SSAP 12 requires the depreciation of all fixed assets having a finite useful life and SSAP 22 sets out a test of separability, reinforcing the Companies Act test of identifiability.

Examples of disclosure

A survey recorded in *Financial Reporting 1990–1991: A Survey of UK Reporting Practices*[1] indicates that of 100 large listed companies surveyed, only six capitalized brands (in the previous year five of a sample of 100). 150 medium listed and 50 large unlisted companies were also surveyed and none of these capitalized brands in the year of the survey although in the previous year a similar number were surveyed and one per cent and two per cent respectively capitalized brands. It is not possible to identify the extent to which the remainder of the companies sampled have valuable brands but make no disclosure in their accounts.

At present there is a wide range of accepted treatments of the capitalization of brands. Two examples, Cadbury Schweppes and Ranks Hovis McDougall illustrate this diversity:

Cadbury Schweppes (1989 accounts)

Cadbury Schweppes capitalizes acquired brands at cost, without provision for depreciation, but reviews the value of brands annually and writes down the cost if there is a permanent diminution in value. The *Financial Review* on the subject of shareholders' funds, brand values, goodwill and borrowing powers explains the reasons for capitalizing acquired brands as follows:

> Historically we have written off goodwill arising on an acquisition consequently reducing shareholders' funds. Intangibles – goodwill and brand values – have not been recognized in the Balance Sheet. In 1989 the International Stock Exchange introduced new rules for assessing the value of the Company's assets in relation to acquisitions and disposals which eliminated the discretionary right of the Stock Exchange not to recognize the value of intangible assets unless they are shown in the accounts. This affects their assessment of the level at which circulars to shareholders, and possibly extraordinary general meetings, are required.
>
> Consequently, we have included in our Balance Sheet the values of major brands acquired since 1985 at cost. We have

[1]Published by the Institute of Chartered Accountants in England and Wales: Survey tables and examples by D.J. Tonkin.

decided that no amortization is necessary as our accounts reflect significant expenditure in support of these brands, principally by advertising and sales promotion. The values will be reviewed annually and reduced if a permanent diminution arises. Our auditors have reviewed the basis and calculations of the brand values included in the balance sheet and endorse this approach.

The issue of the accounting treatment of goodwill and its possible amortization, ie reduction in value over time, is unresolved but the debate continues. A significant part of the goodwill we acquire is in brand values which, providing they are supported, tend to increase in value. Revaluation of brands is therefore more relevant than a reduction in value on an arbitrary time apportionment.

The accounting policy on intangible assets is:

Intangibles represent significant owned brands acquired since 1985 valued at historical cost. No amortization is charged as the annual results reflect significant expenditure in support of these brands but the values are reviewed annually with a view to write down if a permanent diminution arises.

The notes to the accounts disclose intangibles as follows:

Intangibles	Group 1989 £m
Cost at beginning of year – as restated	104.3
Exchange rate adjustments	17.5
Additions	185.6
Cost at end of year	307.4

The restatement arises as a result of the change in accounting policy on intangibles.

Ranks Hovis McDougall

Ranks Hovis McDougall capitalizes both internally created and acquired brands and carries them at their current cost. The 1988 *Chairman's Review* explained the decision to capitalize as follows:

In order to recognize the great importance of our brands, we have taken the opportunity this year to include them in the balance sheet. The figure of £678m has been shown as an intangible asset. I would emphasize that this only recognizes the value of the brands as they are currently used by the Group and does not take account of their future prospects or, indeed, their worth in the open market.

BRAND VALUATION

The 1989 *Chairman's Review* explained the movement in brands:

> A review of the Group's brands has led to an increase of £62m to £740m in the balance sheet 'current cost', of which £27m relates to brands acquired during the year.

The accounting policy set out in the 1988 accounts was as follows:

> Until the end of the current financial year intangible assets (including brands) have been written off to reserves. With effect from 3 September 1988 brands, both acquired and created within the Group, are included at their 'current cost'. Such cost, which will not be subject to amortization, will be reviewed each year.
>
> The accounting treatment of additions to goodwill is considered, as previously, on an individual basis and elimination against reserves has been selected as appropriate for the current year.
>
> The prior year figures, including reserves, have not been restated because of the impracticality of establishing a meaningful cost of all brands previously acquired; the Group results of the previous year are unaffected. An amount has been transferred from revaluation reserves in respect of the estimated cost of brands acquired in the last six years.

In 1989 the policy was summarized:

> Brands, both acquired and created within the Group, are included at their 'current cost'. Such cost, which is reviewed annually, is not subject to amortization.

The 1989 accounts contained the following note:

	The Group 1989 £m	The Company 1989 £m
At 3 September 1988	678.0	-
Additions	27.1	-
Disposals	(1.1)	-
Revaluation	36.0	-
At 2 September 1989	740.0	-

The Group has valued its brands at their 'current use value to the Group', in conjunction with Interbrand Group plc, branding consultants.

This basis of valuation ignores any possible alternative use of a brand, any possible extension to the range of products currently marketed under a brand, any element of hope value and any possible increase of value of a brand due to either a

56

special investment or a financial transaction (e.g. licensing) which would leave the Group with a different interest from the one being valued.

The current debate

In January 1989, the Accounting Standards Committee released its provisional views on accounting for intangible fixed assets, with special reference to brands (Technical release TR 738). The technical release indicated that where acquired brands or other intangibles were separately identifiable and their share of the acquisition cost could be identified with reasonable certainty, they should be recognized on a company's balance sheet. The ASC took the view that there is a rebuttable presumption that such intangible assets have a limited useful economic life and hence a policy of providing for depreciation or diminution in value was considered necessary. However, the ASC also indicated that, in view of the uncertainties surrounding the derivation of the value at which brands and similar intangibles should be recorded, it believed the practice of incorporating such assets in the balance sheet should be discouraged. If useful to users, information on intangible assets should be disclosed in the notes to the accounts.

On the same day that TR 738 was released, the London Stock Exchange formally changed its rules on which assets could be included in the net asset 'class test'. The class tests are used to determine whether capital transactions are of sufficient size to require the notification or approval of shareholders. In the past, the rules required that goodwill and other intangibles be excluded from the calculation; following discussions with interested parties it was determined that intangible assets (including 'purchased goodwill, brand values, newspaper and magazines titles') could be included in net assets, provided they were included in the audited accounts. The Stock Exchange also indicated that such intangible assets could be treated either as depreciating or non-depreciating provided they were written down appropriately when there was a permanent diminution in value.

In February 1990, the Accounting Standards Committee superseded TR 738 with TR 780 which was revised and reissued in May 1990 as Exposure Draft (ED) 52 – *Accounting for Intangible Assets* to a proposed accounting standard on the subject.

ED 52 proposed three tests, all of which must be passed before an intangible fixed asset may be recognized in the balance sheet. Summarized, these are:

- The intangible asset's historic cost must be determinable

- Its characteristics must be distinguishable from goodwill and other assets

- Its cost must be measurable independently from goodwill, other assets or earnings

The ED noted in respect of the third test that in order for the test to be passed in the case of acquired intangible assets (that is, where cost is fair value), 'there will normally need to be an active market in intangible assets of the same kind independently of the purchase and sale of businesses or business segments'.

The ED considered the application of these criteria to brands and concluded that for accounting purposes the term 'brand' is synonymous with goodwill. Brands are therefore regarded as being subsumed within goodwill and should not be accounted for as separate assets. The ED does note, however, that information about brands may be relevant to users of accounts, and that if so additional information about the enterprise's brands may be disclosed.

This conclusion provoked controversy, not least amongst those enterprises which, for good reason, capitalize brands.

BRAND ACCOUNTING IN THE UNITED STATES

Accounting practices in the United States follow similar principles to those in the United Kingdom, although there are a few significant differences. As a general rule, accounting in the US is much more 'rule based' than in the UK: UK accounting standards tend to take the form of statements of broad principles and objectives, those in the US provide detailed guidance and are often industry-specific.

US accounting practice distinguishes between 'identifiable' and 'unidentifiable' intangible assets and prescribes differing treatments depending on the date of acquisition of the asset. Both identifiable intangible assets (for example, patents, trade marks and franchises) and unidentifiable assets (for example, goodwill) may be acquired from others or developed by the enterprise. A distinction between the two is that identifiable intangibles may be acquired singly whereas unidentifiable intangibles cannot.

The accounting treatment of intangible assets acquired before 1 November 1970 is largely irrelevant for present purposes. Intangible assets acquired on or after that date are dealt with as follows: Intangible assets acquired singly are recorded at cost or, where identifiable and acquired as part of a larger acquisition, at their fair value. If acquired as part of a larger acquisition, identifiable intangibles must be recorded separately and the carrying value of unidentifiable intangibles is determined as the excess of the purchase price over the fair value of identifiable net assets acquired, in the same way that purchased goodwill is in the UK. When developed internally, identifiable intangible assets are normally written off against profits but may, in limited circumstances, be capitalized at cost. The costs of developing, maintaining or restoring assets that are not specifically identifiable cannot be capitalized and are written off against profits as incurred.

The cost of capitalized intangible assets is written off against profits, normally on a straight line basis, over the intangible's useful life which is restricted to 40 years. Any unamortized cost is written down as appropriate to reflect any permanent diminution in value.

Internally created brands may not normally be recognized in accounts and their costs of creation must be written off immediately. The cost of acquired brands must be amortized and the amortized cost cannot be revalued. The accounting treatment required for brands is therefore the same as for goodwill although a marginal difference might arise if the brand was separated from the goodwill and assessed as having a different useful life. The difficulties of justifying the separation of brands and establishing their fair value outweigh the marginal benefits and there is therefore no real incentive to do so. In practice US companies do not recognize brands separately.

BRAND ACCOUNTING IN THE EUROPEAN COMMUNITY

Historically, accounting practices within Europe have developed separately, though practices in some countries are closer to those of the UK than in others. With the advent of the European Community, a slow process of harmonization of accounting practices commenced. This process is largely through Company Law Directives and the First, Second, Fourth and Seventh Directives are now generally in force and have established minimum standards throughout the Community. In the future, the process of harmonization will be aided by the newly established Consultative Forum of Accountancy, an advisory body to the European Commission.

Despite this process of harmonization, there remain substantial differences in accounting practice. It is not within the scope of this work to explore these differences in detail, but the main practices adopted by the United Kingdom's principal European Community trading partners in accounting for goodwill, brands and trade names are summarized in Figure 5.1. (See also Figure 11.1 in Chapter 11.)

INTERNATIONAL ACCOUNTING STANDARDS

The International Accounting Standards Committee is an international body supported by the accounting institutions of over 70 countries. The Committee publishes International Accounting Standards (IAS) intended for use world-wide in the preparation and presentation of accounts. Few enterprises prepare their accounts solely in accordance

Figure 5.1 Accounting treatment of goodwill, brands and trade names in various European countries

	United Kingdom	Germany	France	Netherlands	Belgium	Italy	Spain
Goodwill							
Treatment in accounts: asset/eliminated	(1) Optional	(2) Optional	(2) Asset	Optional	Asset	Asset	Asset
If optional, most common treatment	Eliminate	Either	N/a	Eliminate	N/a	N/a	N/a
If an asset, amortization required/optional	Required	Required	Required	Required	Required	Required	Required
Maximum amortization period (years) (4)	None	40	40	None	5	10	10
Typical amortization period (years)	20–40	15	20	5–10	5	5	10
Internally generated goodwill recognized	No	No	No	No	No	No	No
Brands							
Accounting method: within goodwill/separate/ disclosure only	Optional	Goodwill	Optional	Optional	Optional (3)	Optional	Goodwill

If accounted for separately:

Recognition of acquired/ internally generated brands	Both	N/a	Both	Acquired only	Both	Acquired only (5)	N/a
Carried at historical cost/ valuation	Either	N/a	Either	Cost	Cost	Cost	N/a
Amortization required	Optional	N/a	Optional	Optional	Yes	Yes	N/a
Maximum amortization period (years) (4)	None	N/a	None	None	N/a	None	N/a
Typical amortization period (years)	–	N/a	10–25	5	3–5	–	N/a
Trade names Accounting method: within goodwill/separately/ disclosure only	Optional	Separate	Optional	Optional	Optional (3)	Optional	Separate

	United Kingdom	Germany	France	Netherlands	Belgium	Italy	Spain
If accounted for separately:							
Recognition of acquired/internally generated trade names	Both	Acquired only	Both	Acquired only	Both	Acquired only (5)	Acquired only
Carried at historical cost/valuation	Either	Cost	Either	Cost	Cost	Cost	Cost
Amortization required	Optional	Yes	Optional	Optional	Yes	Yes	Yes
Maximum amortization period (years) (4)	None	None	None	None	N/a	None	None
Typical amortization period (years)	-	-	10–25	5	3–5	-	5–10

(1) Accounting practices in the Irish Republic are essentially the same as in the UK
(2) For group accounts – slightly different rules apply to goodwill in company accounts
(3) Either as an asset or written off through the profit and loss account
(4) If 'none', over useful economic life
(5) Registration costs only recognized as internally generated assets

with IAS though these standards do form the basis of national standards in some countries and others ensure that local standards conform, as a minimum, to the requirements of IAS.

There is no international accounting standard dealing specifically with the subject of intangible assets and appropriate international practices have to be developed from the principles set out in the IAS *Framework for the Preparation and Presentation of Financial Statements*. Broadly, assets, which may either be purchased or produced by the enterprise, are recognized in the balance sheet when it is probable that future economic benefits will flow to the enterprise and the asset has a cost or value that can be measured reliably. Amortization should be charged against profits if the value of the asset to the enterprise decreases through time and the carrying value should be reduced for any permanent diminution in value. Assets may be revalued, and on acquisition, assets are recognized in the accounts of the acquiror by reference to a test of 'identifiability'.

CONCLUSION

The debate about accounting for brands has highlighted a fundamental problem about the generally accepted accounting treatment of fixed assets. The historic cost convention regards fixed assets as unexpired costs, carried forward to be expensed in due course against the revenue they will earn. The balance sheet is stressed not to be a statement of value. But intangible assets, and brands in particular, represent an earnings capability of which the historic cost, even if ascertainable, is of limited or little use to the users of financial statements without further information about attributable earnings and prospects. The indications are that the Accounting Standards Board wants to move towards making the balance sheet more meaningful to users. They do not promise an early answer to the question of goodwill and intangibles, but one senses a tendency towards reform.

Chapter 6

ACCOUNTING FOR BRANDS – AN INDUSTRY PERSPECTIVE

David Nash

Grand Metropolitan is an international brand-owning company operating in three sectors, food, drink and retailing. It ranks, by market capitalization, in the ten largest UK companies and in the 30 largest in Europe. Its portolio of brands includes many of the world's leading names including the best-selling vodka in the world (Smirnoff), the leading US vegetable brand (Green Giant), the second biggest hamburger chain in the world (Burger King) and the world's largest chain of eye-care stores (Pearle). It was also the first UK company to include in its balance sheet the value of the brands it had acquired.

This chapter sets out the reasons why brands have become so important to business; the progress of GrandMet to its current position as one of the largest brand-owning companies in the world; and the case for including brands in the balance sheet. It demonstrates that brands are potentially more valuable to a company than its most sophisticated manufacturing plant or automated production line.

THE DEVELOPMENT OF BRANDS

The theory of brands and branding has generated a great deal of media discussion in recent years, initially in the marketing journals and more recently in the accountancy and business press.

In the past, companies typically produced a single product; the company name and the product name were identical and the little advertising that was undertaken was aimed solely at promoting knowledge of the product and stating its attributes. This contrasts dramatically with the situation today where many companies produce a wide variety of products and have a large range of advertising media available. Advertising is more targeted, with each of the brands a company owns being marketed in a distinctive way to enhance its consumer franchise by building a relationship with the consumer.

The building of an emotional relationship between brand and

customer is the other change that has occurred; in the 1960s as the UK started to enjoy greater affluence, consumers were able to consider not only their immediate *material* needs when making a purchase but their *emotional* needs as well. Previously, price allied to performance had been the key criteria in most consumers' decision-making. Now there was a move towards the purchasing of items that were not simply utilitarian but which made a statement about the purchaser – even if the item in question was a soap powder.

Advertising became increasingly aimed at creating the right image for the product, encouraging the consumer to aspire to it or to adopt it as an essential part of daily life. Persil is a good example of this trend – it used an advertising campaign that projected the image that any housewife who took a pride in her family would have to buy Persil. Advertisers eagerly welcomed the new media available to them through television and the improved printing techniques that led to the proliferation of colour magazines. These made their messages more persuasive than the newspapers and bill boards to which they had been previously restricted.

Other changes concern the way in which advertisements convey their messages to the consumer – a glance at the adverts of the 1960s reveals how stark they were compared with today's offerings. Huge sums are now expended in market research, copy-writing and in shooting a commercial so as to ensure that it appeals to the consumer in precisely the right way. These developments within the advertising industry, allied with greater affluence, have been key stimulants for the growth of brands. Brands are now central to consumer choice – what teenager would have been without Reebok trainers in 1990? We have also seen a new appreciation from the brands' owners and managers of the worth of their brands, and though the costs of sustaining a brand have significantly increased, so too have the potential rewards from successfully managing a powerful brand, a fact which is clearly reflected in the profit and loss accounts of leading brand owners and in the prices paid to acquire major brands.

GRAND METROPOLITAN AND BRANDS

Formed as an hotel company in 1962 by Sir Maxwell Joseph, GrandMet expanded through the 1960s and into the 1970s as an entrepreneurial property company capitalizing on Maxwell Joseph's talent for spotting under-valued property assets. During this period GrandMet moved from being purely an hotel company to embrace pubs and breweries, dairies, dance and bingo halls, betting shops and many other property-related activities.

The high interest rates of 1974/75 proved difficult for GrandMet as the company had to bear the weight of the substantial borrowings accumulated in building its property portfolio. As a result, it diversified from its concentration on property and proceeded to build a geographically balanced portfolio of businesses and a number of companies were acquired in both the UK and the USA. A further review in the mid-1980s sought to identify the Group's key strengths and it soon became clear that many of its most successful businesses were within the branded products sector and that its ability to manage and develop brands was the Group's principal competitive advantage. Management perceived that ownership of a successful brand meant an almost guaranteed profit stream for the foreseeable future; brand ownership frequently ensured that the profits earned per unit of sales were significantly higher than from a similar non-branded or generic product. Whilst other aspects of business management – such as cost control and technological leadership – were important to success they were unlikely to influence the Group's long-term profitability in the same way that a leading brand could.

The Group therefore focused on a strategy of building and supporting its brands on an international basis. This was achieved through a process of 'decluttering' whereby businesses that were not branded or which did not have the benefit of, or potential to become, premium brands were sold off. This left GrandMet, at the beginning of 1987, with a portfolio of good branded businesses but relatively modest borrowings. The stage was now set for the concentrated drive to become a leading international branded goods Group.

THE ACQUISITION OF HEUBLEIN

The first major step along this route came in 1987 with the acquisition of Heublein, a major US drinks company, from RJR Nabisco. Heublein was started in 1875 by Andrew Heublein and his sons in Hartford, Connecticut. One of its earliest products was bottled cocktails but the company soon expanded its range, adding its own products as well as imported wines and spirits. Innovative marketing helped the company grow rapidly. Its greatest coup came in 1939 when it paid $14,000 together with a small ten-year royalty, for the Smirnoff vodka brand. This once-proud brand had, prior to the Russian revolution, graced the tables of the Tsar and his court as the biggest-selling vodka in the country. Heublein's marketing skills were used to establish vodka, and Smirnoff in particular, as the favourite spirit drink of the American people. By 1987 Smirnoff was also the best-selling vodka in the world selling approximately 14 million cases per annum, and was second only to Bacardi in all spirit brands worldwide. Heublein also owned Popov vodka, the second-ranking vodka in terms of sales, Dreher brandy, Heublein cocktails and, as a worldwide agency brand, Jose Cuervo tequila.

From a commercial viewpoint the logic of the acquisition of

Heublein by GrandMet is clear: the addition of the Heublein brands and North American distribution network to those of GrandMet created significant synergy benefits and thus fully justified the price paid, a view which was not only held by the company – the day after the deal was announced the *Financial Times* reported that 'Analysts . . . warmly welcomed the Heublein acquisition' and that 'The Heublein acquisition was seen in the City yesterday as good for Grand Metropolitan'.

ACCOUNTING FOR BRANDS

In conventional accounting terms, however, the Heublein brands acquired by GrandMet were worthless. Whilst property, plant, and other tangible assets could be attributed a value, generally applied practice dictated that brands should not be valued.

In January 1988, GrandMet published its first set of accounts following the acquisition. Because the Heublein brands were not valued, £565m of the £800m paid for the company was written off as goodwill, and though this write-off was made against reserves rather than as a charge to profits, it meant that balance sheet net assets fell substantially and hence gave the impression that £565m of the company's money had been wasted.

The problem facing the directors of GrandMet was whether the consolidated balance sheet truly and fairly presented the assets of the Group. The balance sheet complied with generally accepted accounting principles in the United Kingdom (UK GAAP) but it failed to recognize the Group's most valuable assets, its brands. Indeed, the situation seemed analogous to the impact of off-balance sheet finance: the balance sheet of a company using off-balance sheet finance may comply fully with UK GAAP and yet it may fail utterly to reflect the true nature of the assets and liabilities of the company. In such a situation it is appropriate to reflect the substance of such transactions rather than their precise legal form; in other words, it may be appropriate to include them on the balance sheet. Thus, while a strict interpretation of UK GAAP might perhaps mean that brands should not be included on the balance sheet, the directors were not convinced that the accounts presented a true and fair view unless brands were included. In the first set of accounts published after the Heublein acquisition, conformity won the day, but the Board of GrandMet were left pondering a number of questions:

- Was the money spent on Heublein lost or at least irrecoverable?

  The answer here was clearly no. Not only were the brands already contributing significantly to the profitability of the Group but they were also saleable. Unlike goodwill and certain other intangibles that are inextricably linked with the other assets and systems of the business, brands could be sold separately. This is most easily demonstrated in licensing agreements where brand rights to particular territories are sold, and there is no reason why a worldwide brand could not be sold in the same way. (In practice, of course, the assets used in producing the brand are usually sold along with the brand – normally however, this is to avoid the vendor being left with idle assets rather than because the assets are an integral part of the brand)

- Would the inclusion of Heublein at its cost be a radical departure from standard accounting practice?

  Again the answer was no. Whilst on consolidation goodwill was written off and only the value of the tangible assets was included in the Group's balance sheet, within the individual accounts of the acquiring company this was not the case. Here the acquired company is included in the parent's balance sheet as an investment at its cost unless its current value has permanently declined to a level below that cost. In the case of Heublein the changes wrought by GrandMet since acquisition had added to its value rather than detracted from it. It was therefore worth more than was originally paid and no write-down would be necessary. (In fact, Heublein was acquired by a US company and there is no requirement to produce the separate accounts of a parent company in the US. Therefore no accounts were prepared in which Heublein was included as an investment; but this does not alter the principle involved here.)

- Although brands were not normally valued by UK companies, was the valuation of brands specifically disallowed by UK accounting standards?

  Once again the answer was no. Indeed, careful reading revealed that the Accounting Standards appeared to *require* brands to be valued. SSAP 23 stated that following an acquisition a company should value 'all separable tangible and *intangible* assets acquired'. Though the italics are ours, it appears indisputable that intangible assets should be valued.

- Did the valuation of brands breach the historic cost convention under which accounts are drawn up?

  Again, no. Following an acquisition all assets acquired are valued at their market value and this is deemed to be the price the acquiring company has paid for them. The difference between the sum of these values and the price paid is goodwill. Valuing brands on acquisition would in fact be attributing a cost to them in the same way that a cost is attributed to manufacturing plant. They would then be carried at cost in the balance sheet.

The result of this period of consideration was a realization by the Board of GrandMet that their instinctive feeling that brands should be included in the balance sheet was correct. Not only did their obvious value make a persuasive argument for their inclusion in the balance sheet, but their capitalization was consistent with UK accounting principles.

In deciding on a value for each of the acquired brands GrandMet already had a brand valuation model which it used in acquisition appraisal. The key to this model was the assessment of the commercial advantage the brand offers to its owner. This is best expressed in terms of the premium profit it can generate. This premium profit is the additional or improved profit that can be generated in excess of that which could be earned by a generic equivalent. The premium is not necessarily due to a higher sales price per unit but could also be the result of a greater volume of sales, greater certainty of sales or some other similar factor.

In other words the premium element does not necessarily mean more, it may mean better. It is then necessary to attach a monetary figure to the premium profits and accumulate it for a number of years into the future; these sums are then discounted at an appropriate rate to produce a current value for the brand. (Such techniques are discussed more fully in Chapter 3.) Working alongside our auditors, Peat Marwick McLintock, this model was fine-tuned to ensure that it provided valuations of sufficient integrity and prudence to include in the balance sheet.

An announcement was issued in August 1988 stating GrandMet's intention to value its brands and setting out the key principles to be applied. It was decided to incorporate not only brands acquired with Heublein but other recently acquired major brands. A cut-off date of 1 January 1985 was selected and a total value of £608m arrived at, a sum which appeared in the September 1988 accounts.

As with any innovative idea the reaction from analysts was cautious, but most of them welcomed this step towards the provision of greater clarity in accounts and rightly forecast that others would follow.

THE ACQUISITION OF PILLSBURY

The next major step in GrandMet's metamorphosis from a property company to a branded products company was the acquisition in the United States of Pillsbury in January 1989. The price paid of $5.8 billion was a large one but the brands acquired were a mouth-watering proposition for both consumers and GrandMet!

Pillsbury's origins date back to 1869 when Charles A. Pillsbury acquired a 50 per cent interest in a small Minneapolis flour mill. Within 13 years The Pillsbury Flour Company was the largest flour producer in the world. During the next decades a volatile wheat market gave the company financial problems, but despite this it continued to expand, adding a wide range of prepared dough and oven-ready products. The Pillsbury brand was extended to accommodate many of these new products and became a major, broadly-based brand. Other products like pizza and gravy powder were added later and major acquisitions continued with Burger King in 1967, Green Giant in 1978 and Häagen-Dazs in 1983.

Although one of the reasons for the takeover of Pillsbury by GrandMet was GrandMet's belief that it could significantly improve the management and direction of Pillsbury, the brands were very strong indeed: the Pillsbury brand, for example, was the undisputed leader in the United States with 80 per cent of the market for prepared dough products; Green Giant was the leader in the processed vegetables sector of its home market and had a significant share of a number of overseas markets, particularly France, Canada and the UK, and was sold in over 50 countries. Häagen-Dazs is a super-premium ice cream brand which had over 60 per cent of the US super-premium market and, despite its concentration on superior quality (and price), was second in the total US ice cream market. Jenos pizzas held the leading position in the (admittedly fragmented) US pizza market; and Burger King was the undisputed number two in the worldwide hamburger restaurant market. (Burger King, it must be said, was perceived externally as the worst casualty of the errors and lack of direction of previous management; nonetheless, with 6,000 stores in more than 30 countries, it was a major competitor for McDonalds, the market leader.)

Once the acquisition was completed these major brands were valued using the same criteria as those applied to the Heublein brands, and a value of £1.9 billion was attributed to them. This valuation did not, however, include all of the Pillsbury brands: a number of strong but less important brands were not included due to their smaller size.

Following this acquisition, GrandMet's balance sheet at 30 September 1989 demonstrated the importance of brands to the Group:

	£bn
Brands	2.7
Other assets	6.9
Liabilities (mainly debt)	(6.7)
Net assets	2.9

Without brand capitalization the balance sheet would have shown net assets of only £0.2bn, a situation which would have been absurd.

RATIONALIZATION OF BRAND VALUES

With brands worth £2.7bn included in the balance sheet, GrandMet carried the largest balance sheet brand value of any UK company. However, the fact that brands are of such substantial value is demonstrated both by the prices at which they change hands and their value to their owners. (Chapter 7 gives details of the acquisitions of branded goods companies, the prices paid and of the price/earnings multiples.)

It must also be emphasized that there is a wide gulf in value between leading brands and those lower down the rank order. The price tag attaching to a brand increases exponentially with quality and strength and the prices paid for top brands reflect the considerable difficulty of creating from scratch a brand of world renown. Despite significant advertising investment and product development expenditure, most new brands will fail to achieve the status of fully-fledged premium brands. (These failures are, by their very nature, not well known since it is invariably an inability to achieve public recognition that dooms the putative brand.) One example of such a failure, however, is Quatro, a canned soft drink brand introduced by GrandMet in the mid 1980s. The product was good and scored well in blind tastings against other soft drinks. The advertising campaign was modern and vibrant, well-liked by consumers and backed by a substantial investment. Yet with all this going for it the brand failed because, competing in a market dominated by the likes of Coke, Pepsi, Fanta, Sprite and Seven-Up, it was unable to attract sufficient recognition to build a relationship with its consumers.

Building premium brands is very difficult but a host of 'near brands' exist that fall somewhere between a commodity product and a true premium brand. Whilst they are in an expanding market and the economy is robust such brands can do quite well, but when trading conditions become more difficult, due, for example, to the arrival of new competitors or to an economic recession, they frequently fail to maintain their performance. These 'near brands' do not typically have the pedigree or customer loyalty of premium brands, even though they may be familiar to consumers. The value of such brands is necessarily suspect since their future ability to earn premium profits is subject to significant risk.

All the brands included on the GrandMet balance sheet have well-established pedigree and a leading market position. Their stability is further demonstrated by their performance since acquisition: in every case we have seen either volumes increase, market position consolidated or the brand franchise expanded. This growth in the strength of the brands has driven profit growth in excess of the market average, ensuring a positive contribution from the brands even after the financing costs of their acquisition. They, more than any other factor, will ensure the future profitability of the Group.

AMORTIZATION

This superior performance indicates that the value of the brands has appreciated. GrandMet has not, however, used the increased value for balance sheet purposes, but has retained the brand on its balance sheet at what is effectively the price that was paid to acquire it, a policy which is consistent with the way in which production plant is valued at acquisition but not revalued thereafter. Conversely, however, it is also necessary to ensure that the brand has not declined in value. The standard accounting methodology to deal with a decline in value over time is a systematic depreciation charge to write down the asset over its remaining useful life, but though this works well with wasting assets like plant and machinery it is inappropriate when the market value of the asset is increasing and where its value is not diminished, in any way, by the passing of time. Not only would such an approach be illogical, it would also be extremely difficult, if not impossible, to determine the life over which a brand should be written down since, provided it is well managed, it does not have a determinable life. Under such circumstances a more appropriate method of ensuring that any diminution in value is reflected in the accounts is to carry out an annual review of the value of the brand. Any shortfall in the value would then be written off for balance sheet purposes and charged to profit.

This approach has been decried by some commentators as a wish to have one's cake and eat it – the company has benefited from increased asset values and yet has avoided a depreciation charge. This argument, however, ignores the significant expenditure on maintaining a brand. The only way a brand can retain its market position is if its owners commit considerable resources to advertising, marketing and product development. A failure to provide the necessary funds will result in a deterioration in the brand's relationship with its consumers such that they no longer perceive it in the way they formerly did, either because the product can no longer compete technically or because its image has become tarnished. As a result the premium profits earned by the brand, and hence its value, will decline. Conversely, if sufficient resources are committed to maintain the brand and, in addition, a depreciation charge is made, the profit and loss account will have suffered two charges in respect of that brand even though the brand itself is worth as much, or more, than previously. Since the profit and loss account is intended to match the revenues earned by a company and the costs incurred in generating those revenues, there is a clear mismatch in charging two portions of cost for only one stream of revenue.

Furthermore, under the system adopted by GrandMet, management does not escape the threat of a depreciation charge since the possibility of a write-down exists if a brand's value declines. Such a write-down would be a visible sign of management failure and, as such, would be a much better indication of management performance than an annual depreciation charge that is unrelated to the commercial realities of the brand's performance.

CONCLUSION

The capitalization of brands has found favour with many large companies who understand the importance of brands to their businesses. It has also been positively received by all the major accountancy firms. However, it is not without its detractors. The now defunct Accounting Standards Committee produced an exposure draft which attempted to prohibit the capitalization of brands and some commentators have voiced concern that brands are too esoteric and uncertain to warrant inclusion on the balance sheet.

This reaction is a natural one within a profession which is, quite rightly, conservative in its outlook. However, there is a need to recognize the changing nature of economic activity and react positively to this. Property revaluation, for example, which at one time was unheard of, is now seen as a central part of accounting for property assets due to the rapid increase in property values. It is now right, we believe, to react to the rapid increase in brand values.

Problems remain, however, with the inclusion of acquired brands on the balance sheet. First, there is the anomaly between this treatment and that adopted for homegrown brands. There seems little logic in two otherwise identical companies reporting radically different asset values simply because one has acquired its brands and the other has grown them from scratch. This anomaly is, however, caused by the rules governing acquisition accounting in general and applies to both tangible and intangible assets.

The second problem with the capitalization of brands is the lack of an agreed methodology, though most parties currently valuing brands appear to be using the same basic principles and, as far as it is possible to judge, reaching similar conclusions on value. However, there is a need for a more formalized structure, possibly along the lines of that used by the Royal Institute of Chartered Surveyors for property values.

The level of interest in brand capitalization which has already been demonstrated will ensure that, given time, formal procedures will develop and remove what is, effectively, the last barrier to the general acceptance of brand valuation. Properly applied, brand valuation will add considerably to the usefulness and integrity of financial statements without sacrificing the all-important principle of prudence that is essential for widespread acceptance.

Chapter 7

BRAND VALUATION AND ITS ROLE IN MERGERS AND ACQUISITIONS

Edward Buchan and Alastair Brown

INTRODUCTION

Has the increased prominence given to the Brand Valuation debate since 1988 affected the question of how much one company is willing to pay for another? The answer, unsurprisingly, is elusive and is perhaps most fairly expressed as 'probably'.

The concept of a value attributable to brands is nothing new – indeed it has existed in the takeover arena for many years. For example, in 1978 Allied Breweries would probably not have paid a price for J. Lyons, regarded by many at the time as high to form Allied Lyons, nor would Hanson Trust have paid £2.3 billion for Imperial Group in 1986, nor ultimately would Kohlberg Kravis Roberts have paid nearly $25 billion for RJR Nabisco, without in each case the acquisition of pre-eminent brands.

Takeovers have not, however, been driven purely by the desire of the more sophisticated consumer product companies to build market share by acquiring portfolios of strong brand names. They have also been driven by the belief of certain acquisitive groups that there has been a failure by stock markets to recognize the true economic value of certain companies possessing strong portfolios of brands.

Since the £2.5 billion bid for Rowntree by Nestlé in April 1988 the media prominence given to the importance of brands has jolted into action not only stock markets, but also those companies with less-developed awareness of brand values. In the case of stock markets we have seen an increased consciousness among investors of the potential value of brands with, in some cases, a re-appraisal of the worth of companies with exceptional portfolios of strong brands (see Figure 7.1). Equally, many companies have made a major push to increase investor awareness of the quality (and therefore value) of their brand portfolio. This heightened awareness of brands and the impact this has on mergers and acquisitions is considered in this chapter.

THE DEVELOPMENT OF BRAND AWARENESS IN MERGERS AND ACQUISITIONS

The notion of a value attributable to brands in the takeover context is nothing new. The perceived benefits of owning a portfolio of brands has been evident for many years to management running brand-rich consumer product companies, in particular those in the food and drinks sectors which have grown to become the major players on both national and international stages. It goes without saying that the motivation for these companies to grow through acquisition has frequently arisen from the strategic requirement to establish leading positions in their chosen markets by controlling strong national or international brands; and the obvious corollary of this strategic requirement is that the brands which are acquired have a worth quite separate from the tangible assets shown on the target company's balance sheet.

Consumer product companies know that it can take many years to establish a successful branded product capable of generating premium profits and cash flow; and the investment to reach this state of happiness will have fallen over several financial periods under a medley of accounting headings – manufacturing plant, research and development, advertising expenses, management costs and so on – little of which will be identifiable in a company's accounts. Balance sheets prepared on the historic costs basis will therefore largely be not more than a snapshot of past expenditure, and the correlation between balance sheet values and profit and cash flows can become increasingly obscure where assets, both tangible and intangible, have relatively long lives.

Until recently no attempt was made by acquiring or disposing companies (other than newspaper publishers) to put a value on their brands and stock markets and investment bankers were generally content to let any premium paid to net tangible assets fall into the nebulous accounting category of 'goodwill'. Changes in the perception and financial treatment of this premium to tangible assets have, however, begun to be more widespread and this development has arisen for both conceptual and technical reasons. Conceptually, many companies have found it increasingly unacceptable for their balance sheets to show little indication of the value of the company, and technically, the erosion of balance sheets by the conventional requirement to write off goodwill on acquisitions has left some companies looking over-geared. These issues are discussed in detail elsewhere in this book and we will not dwell on them here save to say that the technical aspect has probably been at least as influential as the conceptual in driving the debate forward in the mergers and acquisitions area.

The change in the perception and financial treatment of brand values by companies which are active in mergers and acquisitions is best illustrated by examples of transactions that have occurred in Europe and the United States (see Figure 7.2).

Europe

Ranks Hovis McDougall

The publication of RHM's 1988 accounts incorporated, for the first time in the UK, an independent valuation of the company's brands. The context of RHM's brand valuation is important to an understanding of the reasons the company had for breaking new ground.

Goodman Fielder Wattie, the Australian baking group, acquired a 15 per cent stake in RHM in 1986 from S & W Berisford and was widely believed to be preparing for a bid. The bid eventually came in 1988, representing a prospective multiple of 15.5 times RHM's 1988 earnings, but was referred to the Monopolies and Mergers Commission. The remarks made by RHM in the company's defence documents are indicative of the role that brands had to play in the battle to win the hearts and minds of RHM's shareholders during the course of the contested bid. These remarks should be viewed in the context of RHM having produced a list of the keys to its success and placed the company's brands as the second item after management, demonstrating clearly the importance it attributed to the brand portfolio:

> RHM owns a number of strong brands, many of which are market leaders, which are valuable in their own right, but which the stockmarket tends consistently to undervalue. These valuable assets are not included in RHM's balance sheet, but they have helped RHM build profits in the past and provide a sound base for future growth.

In amplifying the factors supporting the value of its brands the company explained:

> RHM has a broad portfolio of well-known brands around the world.
>
> RHM recognises that brand support and development are critical in generating sustained growth in earnings. The money invested in brand advertising alone amounted to £98 million over the five years ended 5th September, 1987.
>
> Consumers are generally prepared to pay a premium price for brands that have earned their recognition and loyalty, resulting in higher margins for the manufacturer. RHM's expertise has enabled it to give to a commodity product such as salt a strong brand name, Saxa, with the associated margin benefits. Many of RHM's brands are dominant. Such brands are

very hard to attack, given the risk of investing large sums in trying to develop a new brand from scratch. For example, notwithstanding repeated challenges, Bisto has been a dominant brand and a major earner for 78 years.

RHM has strong brand names overseas, as well as in the UK, and has the financial resources to develop these further. RHM's brand expertise is illustrated by the outstandingly successful Mr. Kipling, in which RHM has invested nearly £50 million over the 5 years ended 5th September, 1987 and which since its creation in 1967 has:–

– achieved a 36 per cent. share of the UK branded packaged cake market
– increased sales to almost £100 million in 1986/87
– contributed a very high proportion of RHM's total packaged cake trading profits which were £17 million in 1986/7

GFW has failed to offer you full value for RHM's brands.

All the points emphasized above in relation to the quality and support of the RHM portfolio were designed to increase shareholder awareness of the issues which influence the value of a brand portfolio. What is particularly important, however, is the priority given to brands (and implicitly their values) in the takeover defence and the comprehensive litany of facts dedicated to a matter which hitherto was generally relegated to a minor role in the takeover drama. In the Avana/Robertson Foods battle in 1982, for example, the famous Golly brand of jams and marmalades was almost ignored by the press, which focused only on current year's earnings. (Robertson Foods was taken over by Avana, which was subsequently bought by RHM.)

Following the referral to the Monopolies and Mergers Commission of the bid from Goodman Fielder Wattie, the predator was left with a hostile 29.9 per cent holding in RHM with the observers on the touchline keenly anticipating the next move. When it came, the publication of the independent valuation of the brand portfolio represented not only a new addition to mergers and acquisitions strategy but also brought about a rapid and very significant increase in the brand consciousness of stock markets, analysts and investment bankers.

The aggregate of RHM's net tangible and intangible assets following the brand valuation amounted to £0.98 billion, against the £1.78 billion price tag of the Goodman Fielder Wattie bid and the brand valuation was clearly not intended therefore to represent the worth of the business on a takeover. In which case what was it intended to represent? The answer can probably be most readily supplied from the text of RHM's own 1988 accounts:

In order to recognise the great importance of our brands, we have taken the opportunity this year to include them in the balance sheet. The figure of £678m has been shown as an intangible asset.

I would emphasise that this only recognises the value of the brands as they are currently used by the Group and does not take account of their future prospects or, indeed, their worth in the open market.

Jacobs Suchard/Philip Morris

June 1990 saw the revival of European takeover activity with the acquisition of Jacobs Suchard by Philip Morris for SFr5.4bn. This was the largest takeover in the European food sector since Nestlé's £2.5bn bid for Rowntree in 1988. Whilst representing a more modest price earnings ratio than the Nestlé Rowntree bid, it clearly demonstrated the continuing importance of market share and brand names, and the increasing concentration of the world's food industry in the hands of a few companies. In addition both Jacobs Suchard and Philip Morris were outside the European Community and were perhaps concerned by the implications of the emergence of the Single Market, and the dominant presence therein already held by Nestlé and Unilever.

LVMH/Pommery & Lanson

In December 1990 the continued interest in the value of luxury brands was amply demonstrated by Louis Vuitton Moët et Hennessey paying BSN FF3.1bn for the champagne brands Pommery and Lanson. This represented an exit multiple of nearly 39 times Pommery and Lanson's earnings after taxation, and gave LVMH 24 per cent of the world's champagne market. Moët was at the time the world's largest champagne group, with the acquired brands occupying third place behind Seagram, who owned Mumm and Perrier Jouet. BSN admitted that they had been unable to achieve the market position that the Group required for their main products, namely first or second place. LVMH, on the other hand, believed that they could improve the Lanson and Pommery brands' profitability by distributing them within their existing champagne sales network. They also believed that this would protect the images of the brands.

Within three months, LVMH had sold Lanson on to a privately-owned French group, Marne et Champagne, for FF1.6 bn. In a single move Marne became the world's second largest champagne producer after LVMH. It was a good example of using a brand to enhance sales and image, since Marne was effectively acquiring the right to put Lanson labels onto its own, rather more obscure champagnes.

The United States

The US has witnessed some of the largest takeovers involving groups with national and international brand portfolios. Major deals in recent years include:

OFFEROR	OFFEREE	PRICE
Philip Morris	General Foods	$5.6bn
Philip Morris	Kraft	$13.1bn
Kohlberg Kravis Roberts	RJR Nabisco	$24.5bn
Grand Metropolitan	Pillsbury	$5.8bn

Accounting practices in the US, however, have caused technical problems for US public companies acquiring businesses for sums substantially in excess of the value of the tangible assets. Unlike the UK where goodwill (defined as the excess of purchase consideration over tangible net assets acquired) can be written off against reserves, depreciated over a period of time, or valued in the form of, for example, brands or copyrights and carried without an obligation for amortization, US public companies are required to amortize goodwill over a maximum of 40 years. So although a predatory UK company can have its balance sheet radically affected by writing off goodwill on acquiring a company, there need be no impact on the P&L account.

For the US acquiror, however, the requirement to charge goodwill depreciation through the profit and loss account means that reported earnings can be reduced following an acquisition. This accounting technicality has helped favour the leveraged buy-out (LBO) in acquisitions of brand portfolio groups, since initially cash flow is more important to the success of an LBO than disclosed profit because of the high level of debt servicing. Another consequence is that US acquisitions of brand portfolios have frequently been followed by divestments to reduce the purchase goodwill and hence the goodwill depreciation charge against profits.

RJR Nabisco

The realization of the hidden value of brands using the LBO was perhaps epitomized by Kohlberg Kravis Roberts' $24.5bn bid for RJR Nabisco (manufacturer of Winston and Salem cigarettes, Planters peanuts, Fig Newton and Oreo cookies amongst many other consumer brand names) in November 1988. In the year that followed there was much reshuffling of businesses amongst the key US and European food and drinks manufacturers.

- In June 1989 BSN acquired Nabisco Europe for $2.5bn, and within a month had disposed of the Smiths and Walkers Crisps brands to Pepsico, the world's largest crispmaker, for $1.4bn

- In September 1989 Polly Peck announced the $875m acquisition of Del Monte's fresh fruit business from KKR. One reason for the acquisition, besides consolidating Polly Peck's position as the third largest fruit distributor in the world, was the use of the brand name to enhance their margin on existing products

- In the same month a management team announced their intention to acquire the Del Monte processed food business for $1.475 bn. The investor Group included Del Monte senior management, Citicorp Capital Investors and Kikkoman Corporation (the involvement of the Japanese is discussed in more detail below). The European juice and tinned fruit business was subsequently sold on to local management in April 1990 for $375 m

- In October 1989 Nestlé acquired three of RJR Nabisco's confectionery businesses (Baby Ruth, Butterfinger and Pearson) for $370m

- In March 1990 Britannia Brands, a joint venture between BSN and an Indian industrialist, Rajan Pillai, paid $180m for RJR Nabisco's Asia-Pacific businesses

In addition to the more substantial transactions, a significant number of smaller disposals were also made by KKR of peripheral RJR Nabisco businesses throughout the period. By the end of March 1991 approximately $6bn had been raised from the sale of these businesses, and RJR Nabisco is currently reducing its financing costs by the issue of equity and large tranches of cheaper debt. Within five years or so it is anticipated that RJR Nabisco will have paid off its debt altogether.

Japan

Over the last few years the comparative strength of the Japanese economy has facilitated extensive outward investment. In order to minimize foreign resentment the Japanese approach has generally been low-key. Nevertheless, some prominent brands have been acquired in both Europe and the USA. For example, in February 1989 the Mitsubishi Corporation acquired the Princes/Trex brands from Nestlé for approximately £50m. The transaction came at a time when the Japanese were beginning to fear that Europe would be closed to outsiders after 1992, but it was not widely reported due to sensitivity surrounding the death of Emperor Hirohito.

In September of the same year the Kikkoman Corporation was behind the management buyout of Del Monte's processed foods business from RJR Nabisco, although characteristically they declined to give details of the quantum of their subscription for the $1.5bn raised. Kikkoman had held the marketing rights for the Del Monte label in Japan since 1963 and wanted to broaden its association with the brand. The traffic has not been entirely one way, however, and coincidentally the first foreign organization to take a controlling stake in a Japanese company was the ill-fated Polly Peck, which had previously acquired Del Monte's fresh fruit operations. Polly Peck purchased 51 per cent of Sansui Electric Company, the hi-fi manufacturer, and said at the time that the most important asset being acquired with Sansui was the brand name.

Japanese clothing companies have also been prepared to pay handsome prices in order to acquire premier Western brands. In April 1990, Renown Inc, which had previously been unknown in the European retail market, acquired Aquascutum. This had been preceded by the acquisition in December 1989 of the West German men's fashion group Hugo Boss by Leyton House, a Japanese private company. Most recently, in February 1991, Sankyo Seiko made a £65m recommended cash offer for Daks Simpson in order to establish a presence in the market for premier branded goods.

The accounting position is that, as in the USA, goodwill has to be capitalized rather than being written off against reserves, but in Japan it then has to be amortized over the much shorter period of five years. However, purchased brands can be capitalized and do not have to be amortized at all, and so the overall accounting environment is probably not markedly more hostile to potential acquirors of brands than it is in the USA. Given this, it is not surprising that the growth in brand value awareness appears to have had a similar effect in Japan as elsewhere.

SECTOR CONSIDERATIONS

When most of us think of brands we think of consumer products ranging from food and drink, to toiletries, to household cleaning items. It is fair to say that most of the discussion surrounding brand valuations in takeovers has focused on companies manufacturing or distributing such items. The influence of the brand valuation debate, however, extends beyond these consumer products and into, *inter alia*, media and communications, home improvements and textile manufacturing. Intangible assets in the media and communications sector share a number of characteristics with brands and are discussed more fully in Chapter 10.

What is clear is that the importance of intangible assets in takeovers is not confined to consumer goods companies, but exists in any situation where the characteristics which are important to the value of a brand are present.

In this way, the pharmaceutical sector, which had seen relatively little merger activity in recent years until the merger of Beecham with SmithKline Beckman, has now also witnessed the US$20bn takeover of Bristol Myers by Squibb: an increasing number of takeover bids may be made in this sector in the future as predators seek to capture the drug/medicine portfolios of other companies.

Similarly, clothing manufacturers and retailers may also seek to add to their portfolio of brand names by strategic acquisition. Indeed, developments such as Renown Inc's acquisition of Aquascutum and Sanyo Seiko's recommended offer for Daks Simpson show that this process has already started.

Perhaps the most recent illustration of the widespread importance of brands is the agreed merger of Williams Holdings with Yale and Valor. Williams is an acquisitive industrial holding company which operates through two broad divisions: industrial and military products and consumer and building products. Many of the company's activities are far removed from the food and drinks sector, where the brand debate started, and yet part of the rationale behind the offer was that: 'it has long been Williams' policy to invest in businesses with strong brand names and large market shares'.

It is important, therefore, for the investment banker as well as the marketing strategist to be alert to the potential for the added value of brands in any set of relevant circumstances, not merely those that have been widely publicized to date.

MARKET CONSIDERATIONS

Surprisingly, most major takeovers witnessed an exceptionally large premium being paid over the pre-bid price to secure victory – 'surprisingly' because it might be reasonable to have expected the increasing number of takeovers in the food and drinks sector to have led stock markets to two conclusions:

- That major restructuring of the global food and drink manufacturing industry was underway as companies attempted to achieve sufficient critical mass to compete effectively in an increasingly international market place

- That a significant element influencing the bid premium which a predator might be prepared to pay was the perception of the quality and durability, and therefore value, of the brand portfolio

Investors might reasonably have been alert to the potential for bid activity in the consumer goods sectors and reflected this in the market valuations attributed to those companies which, for one reason or another, were likely to be vulnerable to those groups aggressively building, or seeking to build, a strong presence in quality brand names.

There are, however, several reasons why stock markets have to date generally failed to reassess significantly the value of companies with brand portfolios.

First, an act of faith would be required to build into a share price a premium to reflect the possibility of a bid without having any indication of when or from whom the bid might come. Of course, the identity of one or more possible bidders could be the source of speculation, but the same thing can be said about virtually any company in any sector and investors (as opposed to arbitrageurs) are generally not inclined to buy shares in a company on any other basis than the fundamentals of anticipated future profits, cash flows or tangible assets.

The second, and probably more important reason for the absence of any major 'correction' in stock market values is the absence, until recently, of any objective yardstick to measure the value of brands in the same way that a company's other owned assets are valued.

Even with the emergence of a yardstick in the form of an independent valuation undertaken by specialists, the small number of companies which have disclosed details of any brand valuation in their published accounts has generally done little more than put a corporate toe in the water as they have valued, with the notable exception of RHM, only acquired brands. On the basis of the small number of companies disclosing any details at all of brand values it is probably premature to draw any firm conclusions about whether or not brand valuations have moved markets, insofar as the share price of a company has moved significantly following publication of a brand valuation.

What can be said with a degree of certainty, however, is that the increased prominence given to the role of brands in mergers and acquisition means that the concept of a brand value, which has been one of the fundamental factors influencing consumer product companies seeking to grow by acquisition, is now firmly embedded in the consciousness of investment bankers.

Another important factor influencing the ability of stock markets to attribute value to a brand portfolio is that brands seem to be worth different amounts to different people. Clearly, the Rowntree portfolio of confectionery brands was worth much more to Nestlé than the valuation ascribed before the bid by the stock market. A major reason for this phenomenon is simply that Nestlé believed it could extract greater profits out of the Rowntree portfolio than Rowntree itself had been able to. In addition, the cost to Nestlé of building a significant portfolio of brands – the cost not only of product development and marketing, but also management time – would have been immense. It would also have carried a significant risk.

Equally important, however, is the fact that most investors underestimated Rowntree as a company possessing a high quality brand portfolio. The main reason for this oversight was that although the company had developed its portfolio of branded products effectively it had failed to emphasize to the investment community with sufficient force the commercial benefits which its brand development strategies would bring. The result of this failure was that Nestlé paid a premium of over 124 per cent to the pre-Suchard 'dawn raid' price and won control.

So where does this leave the investment analyst and corporate financier? In some difficulty, would be the straightforward answer. Without access to the marketing strategies of those groups seeking to build brand portfolios it is not possible to gauge with any accuracy the extent to which company X believes it can improve on the profits of company Y simply by exploiting more efficiently the brand portfolio. Of course, the stock market can draw its own conclusions about a company's current worth by analysing its margins and return on capital compared with other companies in the sector, but it is only the marketing entrepreneur who can tell you whether a brand portfolio is producing the returns that it should.

Accordingly, in the absence of a brand valuation which suggests an undervaluation by the investment community, it is probably fair to say that stock markets will continue to have difficulty valuing consumer product companies on any other basis than that of their anticipated future earnings and will leave potential predators to determine whether or not the market has done its sums correctly. After all, it is generally only the predator's belief in its superior brand management, and consequent enhancement of profits, and the opportunity an acquisition presents in contrast to building a brand brick by brick, that enables it to justify to its shareholders a high price for a brand portfolio.

Finally, in considering brand awareness in mergers and acquisitions, it is important to assess the pros and cons to a company of undertaking and publishing a valuation of all or part of its brand portfolio. Clearly, if a company believes the stock market has failed to appreciate the value of its intangible assets in the shape of its brand portfolio, an independent valuation can bring to investors' attention the 'hidden' assets owned by the company. If the resulting aggregation of tangible and intangible assets results in a figure suggesting that the current stock market valuation is too low, the share price might be expected to rise and, if it does, the company will have achieved its objective of obtaining a re-rating of stock market worth.

One of the potential pit-falls of publishing brand valuation details, however, is that although the valuation provides an effective benchmark to underpin the share price, it can also set a ceiling on the share price in the minds of investors. If, therefore, the brand valuation has undervalued the company's brands it can not only limit any potential increase in a company's share price, but also, more importantly, undermine the company's negotiating position in the face of an unsolicited approach from a predator. Moreover, a published brand valuation may even serve, in effect, as an invitation to hostile interest from third parties and thereby achieve the opposite aim from that sought.

The moral of the story is therefore to exercise a degree of circumspection before publishing brand valuation details – at the time of writing no company has yet published a brand valuation during the course of a takeover.

THE FUTURE

The Lex column of the *Financial Times* had the following to say on 7 June 1989, after the announcement by French food conglomerate BSN of its acquisition of Nabisco Europe:

> The price paid by BSN for Nabisco Europe revives issues dormant since the Rowntree deal. Perhaps the Europe-wide consolidation of the food industry is reality after all. Perhaps, too, the yawning gap between stock market and industry valuation of brands is overdone. BSN seems to be paying 27 times prospective earnings, more even than Nestlé paid for Rowntree; while United Biscuits – the closest parallel to Nabisco Europe, and a vastly strong company – is on a multiple of 12.
>
> But like Nestlé, BSN is paying twice: once to get the brands, and again to deny them to others.

While being wide of the mark in suggesting that the brand value issue had been dormant since Rowntree's acquisition by Nestlé, the observation that a huge gulf continues to exist between the value attributed to consumer product companies by industry predators and by stock markets is amply illustrated by the bid premia which have come to characterize merger activity in the food and drinks sector.

Lex's comments also underline the fundamental importance of brands to corporate strategy in an increasingly international consumer market: companies wishing to establish leading positions in their chosen markets need leading brands to fulfill their objectives, and if a competitor controls the leading brands it is an uphill struggle to displace it.

The importance of the role of brands in the takeover arena has been tacitly recognized for many years by consumer product companies, and increasingly by stock markets, with the result that brand values have become more and more a central issue in determining price.

The corollary of the growing importance of brands has been the

Figure 7.1 Movement in share price of companies with strong brand portfolios

Company ordinary shares	Price at 13/3/ 88	Current price (Spring 1991)	% change	% gain/loss on industrial index	% gain/loss on market index
Cadbury Schweppes	260p	385p	+48.08	+12.66	+12.51
Dalgety	293p	383p	+30.72	− 0.54	− 0.68
Grand Metropolitan	482p	804p	+66.92	+27.00	+26.83
Guinness	312p	911p	+191.99	+122.16	+121.85
RHM	323p	321p	−0.62	−24.39	−24.49
Reckitt & Coleman	815p	1524p	+86.99	+42.27	+42.08
Unigate	273p	315p	+15.38	−12.21	−12.33
United Biscuits	265p	380p	+43.40	+9.10	+8.95

Source: *Datastream*

Figure 7.2 Recent brand transactions in the food and drinks sector

Purchaser	Company acquired	Some key brands acquired	Cost	Date
BSN	Nabisco Europe	Smiths, Walkers, Belin, Saiwa, Ritz	$2.5bn	Jun 89
Pepsico (US)	Smiths/Walkers Crisps	Smiths, Walkers, Jacobs, Huntley & Palmer	$1.4bn	Jul 89
Polly Peck International	Del Monte Fresh Fruits	Del Monte	$875m	Sep 89
Allied Lyons	Dunkin Donuts Inc	Dunkin' Donuts	$325m	Nov 89
Allied Lyons	Whitbread Spirits Division	James Burrough Buckingham Wile Atlas Peak vineyards	£545m	Dec 89
American Brands	Whyte & Mackay	Claymore, Haig, Crawford's	£160m	Feb 90
CPC International	Smithkline Beecham brands	Ambrosia, Marmite, Bovril	£157m	Apr 90
Philip Morris	Jacobs Suchard	Tobler, Toblerone, Milka, Night and Day, Carte Noire Jacques Vabre	SFr 5.4bn	Jun 90
LMVH	BSN's champagne brands	Pommery, Lanson	FF 3.1bn	Dec 90

corresponding growth in the importance of their accounting treatment. In the United Kingdom the Institute of Chartered Accountants has recently published Exposure Drafts attempting to bring the amortization of goodwill into compulsory effect (by disallowing the option of immediate write-off against reserves).

This would move the United Kingdom towards the position in the United States. Similarly, the Institute's proposals to encourage the amortization of any capitalized brands, although currently ignored, may render the practice of capitalization of brands less attractive if such treatment becomes a legal requirement in the future.

However, whilst the debate over accounting for brand valuations may not have reached its conclusion, the role of brand value in takeovers, whether expressed or implied, has been firmly established and is here to stay.

Figure 7.1 illustrates the generally strong performance of the major food companies with quality brands during the period following the resurrection of the brand factor in takeovers. The uplift cannot, of course, be attributed entirely to brand values since the food manufacturing sector has enjoyed a relatively buoyant time on the back of the high level of corporate activity in the sector as companies have sought to take positions in domestic and international markets.

The only significant exceptions to the outperformance of the companies in Figure 7.1 against the market are Ranks Hovis McDougall and Unigate. The former's last set of interim figures was disappointing, mainly due to exceptional restructuring costs, whilst the latter's non-food businesses were largely responsible for the group's poor performance.

Chapter 8

IS BRAND VALUATION OF ANY USE TO THE INVESTOR?

Michael Bourke

'THESE ARE GDP GROWTH PLUS A BIT STOCKS'

The external investor has two main weapons in his arsenal: the information available to him and his experience. Later in this chapter we shall consider the quality of information and how it is used, but first let us consider experience.

Most companies that exploit brands have been around for a long time and, particularly in the United States and the United Kingdom, have sought external capital via the Stock Exchange many years ago. So external investors have had a long time to get used to their characteristics, and have quite a wide range of tools with which to assess how much variability is introduced by different management styles, etc. The phrase 'These are GDP growth plus a bit stocks' – a quotation from a senior international fund manager – is a good summation of this collective experience. Investors know that companies with brands are good, sensible investments, but also know that their capacity to surprise in the short-term is limited.

Consequently, the external investor tends to value these businesses by reference to the prevailing interest rate on money, plus or minus a bit according to his perception of economic and financial trends and the qualities of the individual company. Typically, a portfolio of equity investments will include some brand-driven stocks but it is unusual to find investors who deviate significantly from market average weightings when deciding what proportion of their money to allocate to this area.

This approach is not wrong and there is plenty of powerful statistical analysis to demonstrate this fact. One of the longest running time series in the UK is the FT Actuaries All-Share index which measures the price performance of a large sample of quoted UK companies, and sub-divides this sample by sector. Figures 8.1 to 8.4 show the price performance over the past 20 years of four of these sectors, relative to the UK market. Two – food manufacturing and brewers and distillers – are sectors where brands are important. The other two – electricals and oils – are sectors where technological innovation and commodity prices are the key driving forces.

Figure 8.1 FTA food manufacturing relative to FTA All–share 25/3/91

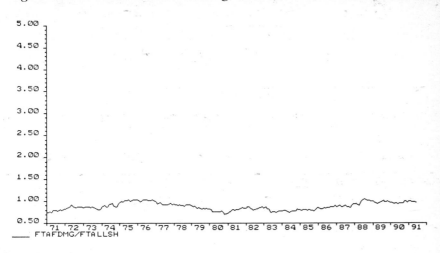

Source: *Datastream*

Figure 8.2 FTA brewers & distillers relative to FTA All–share 25/3/91

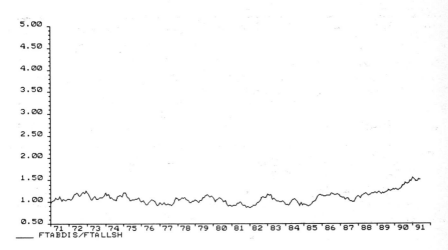

Source: *Datastream*

Figure 8.3   FTA oils relative to FTA All–share   25/3/91

Source: *Datastream*

Figure 8.4   FTA electricals relative to FTA All–share   25/3/91

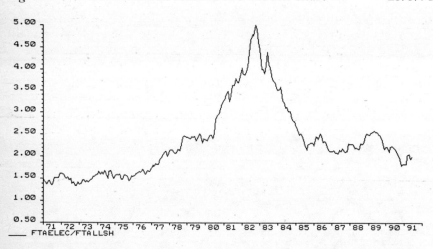

Source: *Datastream*

The relatively flat profiles of the two branded sectors show how closely capital returns for this sort of business correlate with average market returns. By contrast the oil sector shows clear boom or bust characteristics, as does the electricals sector for rather different reasons. When sectoral time series are plotted for other equity markets, such as New York, a not dissimilar pattern is shown (Figures 8.5 to 8.8 show US sectoral time series for two branded sectors, food and soft drinks and for largely unbranded sectors, oils and electricals.)

'GOOD BRANDS ARE A BETTER INVESTMENT THAN THE BEST REAL ESTATE'

In the 1980s there were definite signs that this close correlation between the return on brand-driven investments and average market returns was beginning to break down, principally because of corporate activity by other brand-driven companies, and by organizations dedicated to arbitraging the gap between open-market valuations and corporate valuations of the shares of brand-driven companies. For a variety of reasons, including strong economies, ready availability of capital, and a growing reluctance to take the risk of trying to grow new brands from scratch, M&A activity in branded businesses boomed. We look below at two examples of brand-driven takeovers from this era: the takeover of Rowntree by Nestlé and the takeover of RJR Nabisco by Kohlberg Kravis Roberts.

In the past year M&A activity has waned with weaker economies, particularly in the Anglo-Saxon countries. Interestingly, however, there is as yet little sign that the inflation in the asset value of brands has been reversed. This suggests that the quote at the head of this paragraph from a board member of a leading US food company remains as valid today as it was when it was first made three years ago.

Figure 8.5   S&P foods relative to S&P Composite Index   10/4/91

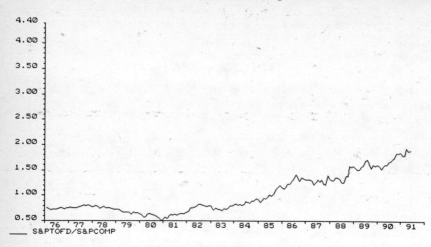

Source: *Datastream*

Figure 8.6   S&P soft drinks relative to S&P Composite Index 10/4/91

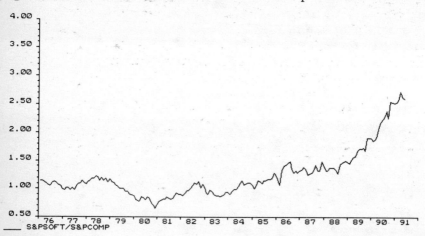

Source: *Datastream*

Figure 8.7   S&P oils relative to S&P Composite Index   10/4/91

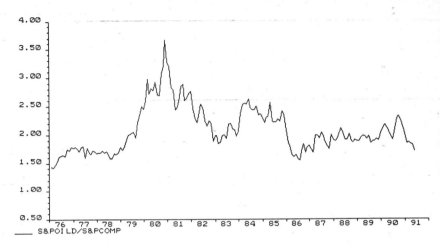

Source: *Datastream*

Figure 8.8   S&P relative to S&P Composite Index   10/4/91

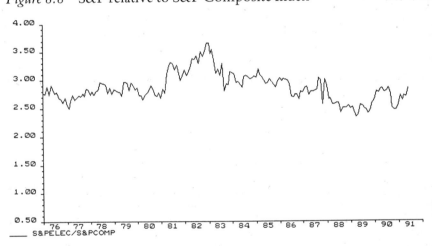

Source: *Datastream*

'I SOLD ALL MY ROWNTREE AT £6.30, BECAUSE THAT WAS A FAIR ECONOMIC PRICE'

The takeover of Rowntree by Nestlé in 1988 is perhaps one of the clearest examples of how different investors apply different valuation criteria to the same assets. Figure 8.9 covers the period when the bid was taking place, and shows the changes to the share price resulting from the main news items during the bid. Two points are worth emphasizing. The first is the wide gap between the first clear indications of bid activity and the final agreed take-out price. £10.75 represented approximately a 150 per cent premium to Rowntree's pre-bid trading value – way above the 50 per cent premium that is the Stock Market's rule of thumb for ceding control to a predator. The second related point is the amount of stock which was sold at prices well below the final, agreed, valuation. By the time the Rowntree board recommended shareholders to accept Nestlé's offer, over half the shares were already held by Nestlé themselves, or by Suchard, the competing bidder. The quotation at the head of this Chapter, from a senior UK fund manager, sums up why. Two different valuation criteria were at work here.

As a company, Rowntree dated back to the last century and its main brands date back to the 1930s. Its earnings potential and average growth rate were well-known and for a fund manager with several thousand quoted UK vehicles to choose between, £6.30 was indeed a fair economic price in market conditions at the time.

However, Nestlé and Suchard were not operating in such a liquid market. Both wanted to rival Mars as world leaders in the confectionery industry. Both had existing confectionery businesses which were constrained by exactly the same factors as Rowntree faced – the mature nature of the confectionery market and the longevity of brands, which meant that organic growth was slow and extremely expensive, with no certainty of success. To attain a quantum leap in size it was essential to buy, and there were only four possible choices in the world – Cadbury and Rowntree in the UK, Hershey in the United States or the other Swiss business. Otherwise it was a case of looking for smaller companies, with strengths in a particular niche of the market. Suchard and Rowntree had exploited this route successfully in the past, but there were fewer and fewer suitable businesses around.

The attraction of Rowntree lay in that multi-purpose word 'synergy'. In branded goods, size in a particular market place is extremely important, because it allows the large corporate and marketing overhead to be spread over a much larger sales base. When two competitors agree to merge, considerable savings can be made by amalgamating head offices and sales forces, and by extracting extra, volume-based, discounts from suppliers of goods and services – almost everything from raw materials to packaging

Figure 8.9 Rowntree share price 1988

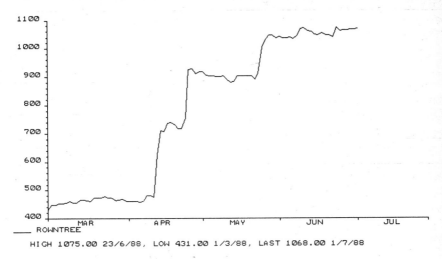

HIGH 1075.00 23/6/88, LOW 431.00 1/3/88, LAST 1068.00 1/7/88

Source: *Datastream*

and advertising is less expensive per unit if the volume is increased.

One branded goods company we know routinely works on the basis of an average saving of 7.5 per cent of sales through extracting synergies from complementary acquisitions. Given that the average operating margin in branded goods is around 8–10 per cent, it can be seen that such savings may nearly double the profit that can be extracted from a business. And because brands give a great deal of protection against competition, such savings need not be whittled down by competition.

It was the existence of such synergies, we believe, which led both Nestlé and Suchard to target Rowntree. Apart from its core business in the UK (Where Rowntree rivalled Mars and Cadbury for market leadership, whereas both Suchard and Nestlé had a limited presence) Rowntree had a string of confectionery subsidiaries in Europe which were not large enough to deliver double-digit operating margins on sales – but added to the Suchard or Nestlé businesses in those countries, real economies of scale were possible. Other confectionery companies did not offer the same scope for savings, and consequently the price that could potentially be paid for such businesses was much lower.

'THE SHAREHOLDERS WON'

The world's largest takeover to date, of RJR Nabisco by Kohlberg Kravis Roberts (KKR), is another example of the difficulties of brand valuation, or of how valuation depends on the perspective of the bidder. First mooted at $75 per share, or $17.3 billion, the bid advanced in leaps and bounds to finish up at $109 per share, or $25.1 billion.

Unlike Rowntree, where synergistic benefits from the merger of similar branded businesses was envisaged, the bidders for RJR Nabisco were shell corporations put together by Wall Street investment banks. Several different vehicles were proposed of which two, one created by Shearson Lehman and several RJR executive directors and the other by KKR, survived to the final round of bidding. With little equity injected by their partners, these vehicles were almost wholly dependent on the amount of debt they could borrow against the RJR assets they hoped to buy. Since this sum was constrained by the amount of interest which the business could afford to meet, it might be asked just why there was a difference of **nearly $8 billion** between the first bid and that which finally succeeded. Other writers on this event have suggested that the answer is simply greed on the part of the participants, and this is no doubt part of the story.

However, simple greed on the part of already very rich men, with a lot to lose, seems to me to be an inadequate explanation on its own. The wide variation in valuations was surely due to the difficulty in deciding just what intangible assets like brands are worth. The bidders all approached the problem in the same way, by effectively ignoring the tangible assets in the business and concentrating on the future streams of cash flow which the brands were expected to generate. There are two big differences between their approach and the dividend discount approach of the traditional investor. The first is that cash flow applied to pay interest is tax-deductible in the United States, whereas if it is allowed to flow to the bottom line and used to pay dividends it is heavily taxed. The second is that when you're thinking about borrowing up to the chin to finance a buyout, you think very hard about the amount of cash flow which will be generated!

It is interesting that with minds focused in this way, the two last bidders for RJR Nabisco eventually came up independently with blind offers which were so close that the committee of independent directors who were acting to advise shareholders judged the bids essentially even in monetary terms. The final price was some 60 per cent above the highest price at which RJR Nabisco stock had ever traded, and was well in excess of twice the pre-bid share price. The quotation at the head of this section, from Ross Johnston, former CEO of RJR Nabisco and leader of the losing consortium is apt in the circumstances.

RECONSIDERING OLD CERTAINTIES

It is against such a background that external investors need to consider how to value brands and in doing so we may consider a quotation from Francis Bacon's *The Advancement of Learning*:

> 'If a man will begin with certainties, he shall end in doubts, but if he will be content to begin with doubts, he shall end in certainties.'

Quite simply, the old certainties that allowed external investors to feel reasonably sure of the value of their investment in a branded company are breaking down rapidly under the pressure of different valuation systems and different economic pressures. So the external investor's experience is a less reliable guide than in the past to valuing scarce assets such as mature brands. Instead one has to look harder at publicly available information.

It is my experience as an analyst that external investors pay a great deal of attention to any information which has an influence on the profit and loss account of a branded goods company, but spend less time on information which bears upon the balance sheet. Some investors are increasing the amount of attention they devote to the cashflow statement, which provides a link between movements in the balance sheet and the profit and loss account, but this trend is not yet well-established in the UK.

Concentrating on the profit and loss account is, as an investor's historical experience shows, quite an efficient way of discounting the future stream of dividends which an asset can earn, and consequently of arriving at the net present value of a stable stock like a branded goods company to an external investor. But a balance sheet should, at least in theory, tell him a great deal more about the underlying value of the assets themselves, and offer at least some clues to what it might be worth to someone else. An ordinary share in a company, after all, offers three things – a right to any dividends that are declared, a right to any share of assets after liabilities in the event of liquidation and the right to vote in certain circumstances. The latter two rights are all too often overlooked simply because liquidation of quoted companies is rare, and voting rights are only rarely critical.

However, to an external investor, if not to the company itself, takeovers have the same effect as a liquidation – stewardship of the assets is transferred to other hands and a payment is made representing the valuation of the assets over liabilities to the other party. The only difference is that the shareholder always has a say in the matter through the exercise of his vote, with the other party needing to win the approval of the requisite number of shareholders. In a contested takeover both the existing management and the bidder will usually provide additional information to help shareholders to make up their minds; oddly, however, it is only in a few asset-driven areas, such as property shares or investment trusts, that the defence will tend to use an asset revaluation as a cornerstone of its case.

The main reason for this is not coyness on the part of the management, but the poor quality of data in the balance sheet as a result of existing accountancy conventions. The overriding weakness of historical cost accounting – that it takes no account of inflation – remains a lee shore for the accountancy profession, despite various attempts at reform and the adoption in the UK at one time of current cost accounting as an optional statement in the annual report.

Current cost accounting has now all but disappeared from view, partly because inflation rates have declined but to a considerable extent because piecemeal company-led reform has removed its worst inequities. These days revaluation reserves have spread well beyond property companies, and are found in a large number of asset-rich retail and industrial concerns. Depreciation of freehold land is practically unknown, and of freehold buildings it is extremely rare.

The treatment of overfunded company pension funds in the accounts has also been reformed recently, because contribution holidays had become so widespread. None of these measures provides a complete remedy for the effects of inflation, but their net effect has been sufficient to ease the strain caused by balance sheets which bore little relationship to current market worth, because of the effects of inflation.

But other objections to balance sheets prepared under the historical cost convention have grown in importance. Two particular related areas of concern have been the treatment of goodwill on acquisition and the treatment of intangible assets. While related, we think it is best to keep these two concepts separate. This is because goodwill arising on acquisition can quite easily be dealt with within the constraints of the historical cost convention, as several UK companies have recently shown, by choosing to capitalize the amount involved. Indeed, it is standard practice to do so in the United States, and to amortize the amounts involved, usually over 40 years. The difficulty is how to deal with intangible assets, when no transaction has taken place to put a value on those assets.

Current accounting conventions do not lend themselves comfortably to capitalizing assets when no transaction has taken place. However, to avoid the question entirely is to drive a coach and horses through the basic purpose of a balance sheet. For a branded goods company, intangible assets are frequently the most important assets of all. In such cases trying to assess whether the management is achieving a satisfactory return on equity, or even whether the business is prudently capitalized or not, is quite impossible without assigning a valuation, either explicitly or implicitly, to the brands.

Brands are of course only one form of intangible asset. But they have features which make prudent valuation possible – they are detachable from the other assets in the business; they have property rights recognized in law; and the stream of earnings they produce is fairly reliable. These characteristics should allow brands to be valued with at least the precision that is accorded to property valuations, the other great exception to historic cost accounting. Valuing brands in this way would make it much easier for external shareholders to assess the performance of management i.e. whether they are effective stewards of the shareholders' capital.

Management which is making good use of its assets, and growing the asset base, would have more than an earnings and dividend stream to point to if it came under predatory attack. And external shareholders would have a much clearer idea of the true worth of a business, and whether a predator was offering a premium for control of assets which are truly more valuable to him than to anyone else, or merely seeking to act as an arbitrageur.

The precise method of brand valuation is not of great concern to the external investor. What is important is that a consistent method is applied to allow comparisons to be drawn between similar companies, and that the method applied should be independently certified, prudent and reasonably visible to the external investor.

Chapter 9

VALUATION AND LICENSING

Raymond Perrier

The licensing of a brand provides an important perspective on the commercial value that is attributed to brands by both brand owners and third parties. It is a key example of a brand being identified as a specific intangible asset and then being traded as an asset in an open market. A look at the license agreements that are actually negotiated and used by brand owning companies sheds further light on the basic issues of the evaluation and commercial valuation of brands and the ways in which companies realize that commercial value. At the same time a robust and accepted approach to brand valuation can contribute significantly towards brand licensing by offering parties involved in license agreements a more secure and objective basis for negotiation.

WHAT IS A LICENSE?

A license from one party to another is a granting of permission to carry out an activity that – crucially – the second party could not have otherwise conducted. Intellectual property is the term used for the protectable products of original creativity and research and comprises essentially trade marks, patents, designs and copyrights. Licensing of intellectual property is the means by which the owner of, for example, a patent for a nuclear-powered bicycle can grant permission to another party to exploit the patent and produce that bicycle for a specified period of time and usually in another country.

The instrument for establishing this relationship is a license agreement. The agreement details not only what intellectual property the licensee can expect to be made available to him to use, but also what benefits and compensation the licensor will receive in return. Typically this return is in the form of a royalty payment that is due to the licensor from the licensee every time use is made of the permission granted by the license. The concept of 'buying permission' lies at the heart of licensing and will be fundamental to our treatment of intellectual property values in licensing.

TRADITIONAL LICENSING

Historically, it is patents that have occupied most of the attention of license agreements. Companies, or often individuals, may have invested heavily in the research and development of an invention. A patent allows the inventor to publish details of the technology while at the same time securing protection against others exploiting the invention.

However, patent protection generally lasts only 20 years (the figure varies from country to country) and so in order to maximize return from the invention the patent owner may grant permission to other manufacturers (in other countries or in other markets) to make use of the patent simultaneously. The need to take fullest advantage of a finite monopoly, coupled with the perhaps prohibitive costs of exploiting the invention in other fields or in other countries, makes licensing of patents especially appealing.

Computer programs are by convention protected by copyright rather than patent and are another common subject of license agreements based on a desire by the author to exploit his creativity to the maximum extent before it might be superseded.

Another area in which there has been much licensing activity has been character merchandizing where the copyright, and perhaps trade marks, covering a character such as Mickey Mouse are licensed to manufacturers of a host of products so that they can use the name and design to add value to a product. The creator of the character (the author) would never be in a position to exploit this commercial potential independently but can still derive benefit from others' exploitation of his creativity.

'BRAND' LICENSING

Our interest, though, is in a far less common form of licensing – the licensing of brands. Brand licensing shares many of the characteristics of the licenses described above – the creators or owners of the brand may not have the resources on their own to develop the brand in a wide number of countries or across a range of product areas – and similar licensing agreements are used.

Such brand licensing is essentially the licensing of a trade mark to a party in another country and/or for another type of goods. An Italian manufacturer of, say, a brand of ground coffee may wish to benefit from an opportunity in the United States but not have the resources or experience to develop that market as fully or as commercially as a local company. The brand owner could instead license an American manufacturer to produce and market coffee under that brand name to the benefit of both parties. Equally the owner of the coffee brand may see an opportunity for the brand as a coffee-flavoured snack in Italy but not have the technology or market experience to be able to develop this. A brand license could be granted to a snack foods company to develop and manufacture the product but using the ground coffee brand name, thus earning profits for both licensee and licensor.

But brand licensing is not just about the use of a name or a trade mark. In equating the licensing of trade marks with the licensing of brands we are not suggesting that a brand is nothing more than the rights in the name. There may be other elements that are also important to the brand and which are covered by other forms of legal protection. Trade mark rights often also cover distinctive designs and product get-ups (such as the Coca-Cola bottle shape or the typography in which Coca-Cola is written). Beyond this, a brand could well include the less distinctive aspects of its packaging; the recipe and associated 'know-how' (sometimes difficult to patent); and even slogans and captions associated with the brand (which might be protected by trade mark law or by copyright law or only by common law). The Coca-Cola brand, for example, is integrally associated in many countries with the catchphrase 'It's the Real Thing' and without it promotion of the brand would be handicapped. All of these items contribute towards the totality of the brand and any party licensed to use the brand name would reasonably expect these other features to be available as well.

For example, the foreign licensee of the Hershey name would want access to the recipe and know-how for manufacturing the product, the logo, design and colours used on the packaging and perhaps even the slogan. Without these the brand license would be inadequate because so much of what the brand stands for is tied to these features. However, it is important to realize that if a license were granted that gave permission to use everything *but* the brand name it could not reasonably be regarded as a brand license. The brand name, though not sufficient in defining the brand, is certainly necessary, for without it the brand has no designation either for the consumer or the trade.

COMPOSITE LICENSES

The question of what is a brand license is further confused in cases where a trade mark license is hidden in a 'licensing package', a bundle of licenses that brings together a trade mark license with licenses for other elements of the production and marketing process. The intention is to hold together all the elements that constitute the brand but in reality it often has the effect of lessening the importance of the intangible elements of the brand.

An American company, for example, licensed its brand of microwaveable snack to a British company and agreed a licensing package. The benefit of the patent and technological know-how of the brand were immediately apparent – the British company would have spent much more if they tried to replicate this themselves. But the benefits of an established and international brand name were less clear as the brand's reputation was mainly confined to the US market; and the licensor and licensee were therefore inclined to believe that the technical rights were more valuable in the agreement than the trade mark rights. This was shown in the license agreement where the royalty rate of five per cent agreed was explicitly divided as 3.5 per cent for the patents and technology and 1.5 per cent for the brand name. In the long run, however, it became clear as other developments in food technology were made that the technical rights were less and less important. At the same time, the brand name had become much more important having established and secured a consumer franchise in the UK that went far beyond the original product or production process.

Sometimes this can be used to the brand owner's advantage as a way of getting a brand name established at relatively little cost to himself. In being licensed to produce something according to a patented invention the licensee may also be licensed and encouraged to use the trade mark associated with that patent. Indeed, he may even be *required* to use the trade mark. JVC for example in licensing its home video recorder technology to other consumer electronics manufacturers encouraged use of the brand name VHS by including it in the licensing package, effectively 'for free'. In this way they quickly established currency not only of their recording system but also of their brand name and this conferred great commercial benefits on them as patent owner/trade mark owner, particularly as the rights in a licensed trade mark always accrue to the licensor.

A GENUINE 'BRAND' LICENSE

A genuine brand license is one in which the trade marks (the intangible elements) do not play second fiddle to the technology. A relatively small American food technology company, for example, developed a revolutionary ingredient with applications for a wide variety of foods. The ingredient was securely covered by patents and no competitor could come close to it. Food manufacturers were falling over each other to produce the ingredient themselves but had no choice other than to seek a license from the patent owner. The food technology company thus quickly secured a high level of production and use of the ingredient, but they realized that these licenses were secure only for as long as the patent lasted.

They therefore developed a proprietary name for the ingredient in addition to the generic name and by advertising this name and encouraging consumers to call the ingredient by this name rather than by the much less attractive generic name, they established a true 'brand'. The patents that covered the ingredient expired some years ago, and even though the ingredient can now be bought from other manufacturers or made by the food companies themselves without a patent license, many companies continue to pay the food technology company a royalty for using the brand name that has become associated with the ingredient. In order to get a good return on their original research and development investment the inventors of the ingredient had to license it to other manufacturers. But they have secured a much longer-term return by turning the patent into a brand and licensing the brand to third parties.

It is, of course, clear in many cases that the patent of an invention or the copyright of a computer program is of much greater interest and commercial value, potentially, than the brand name associated with it. In the JVC example it is use of the technology that licensees were anxious to acquire rather than use of the brand, at least at first. Equally, though, there are cases where the value and importance of a trade mark license are disguised within a license package which deceptively places greater emphasis on some other less distinctive element of the package such as the patent or technical assistance. For example, it is the Carlsberg or Heineken or Fosters brand names which are appealing to potential licensees, and inimitable, but permission to use the names may be packaged up with technical know-how so that the true value of the use of the trade mark is hidden from both licensee and licensor.

The clearest example of brand licenses that only cover trade mark rights and have no element of technology or patent is in luxury goods. The names Dunhill, Yves Saint Laurent and Cartier all began life on a very limited range of goods produced by the brand owner (cigars, haute coûture and jewellery, respectively). Now, however, Dunhill is to be found on clothing, Yves Saint Laurent on perfume and Cartier on cigarettes, all of which products are made under license from the brand owners. The reputation that, for example, Dunhill has in importing cigars is not immediately relevant to the production of men's clothes or aftershave. The image and consumer franchise surrounding these brands has, however, enabled them to extend into new areas. But because the brand owner has no expertise or experience in such manufacture the brand has been licensed to other companies.

Interestingly these licenses rarely cover anything other than use of the brand name and 'get up' since there is no recipe or know-how or technical assistance to lend. Even the product design element in a designer brand may not be part of the property that is being licensed. A Cartier wallet clearly trades on the reputation of the name in jewellery but it is not suggested – nor would the consumer believe – that the Cartier workshop designed or made the wallet. Arguably, the brand name now has such a strong reputation in leatherware that many consumers would not even care if the jewellery workshop still existed. Increasingly in fact there are cases where the brand that is being licensed has no real current reputation at all in any field but just trades on and exploits consumers' memories of a former reputation. In these cases the brand owner has no manufacturing or production expertise and is quite simply the owner and guardian of a trade mark and of the brand that has developed around that trade mark.

A license agreement that recognizes the importance of the trade mark element of the license as the most distinctive part of most brands is a genuine *brand* license and a shining example of brand recognition. It acknowledges the existence of the brand as a separable and definable asset that can be valued and traded. However, as explained above, in third party agreements such brand licensing as exists is often disguised behind licenses for patents or technical know-how, which though important features of the brand identity, are not essential to the brand and are often not unique to it either. This means that the licensing agreement – and crucially the royalty payments resulting from it – are related not to the essence of the brand but to its less central features. And though these may be important contributors towards the brand's image and appeal, they are often not its distinguishing features and can never be as important as the brand name itself. A license agreement that demands four times more royalty for the use of a chocolate biscuit recipe than for the use of the chocolate biscuit trade mark may not properly reflect the relative importance of these two elements of the brand.

'Internal licenses' ie licenses between companies within the same parent group also provide an example of genuine brand licensing but before looking at that area in detail it is worth examining how brand valuation could be of assistance in determining royalty rates in third-party license agreements.

ROYALTY RATES

It is when the royalty arrangements of a license agreement are examined that the brand is most clearly seen as having a definable value, however underestimated that may be in many cases. The question of royalty payments and compensation is fundamental to the workings of license agreements since without such a return the owner of the intellectual property would gain no reward from the licensee's use of the property.

If, as suggested earlier, a genuine brand license attempts to treat a brand as a separable definable asset, then the establishing of a royalty payment for use of that brand would reflect the value of that brand as an asset. What is interesting in the context of the brand valuation debate is not only that such ascribing of value takes place but the way in which it happens.

By far the most common method of expressing a royalty payment is as a percentage of the value of sales of the brand with, perhaps, a guaranteed minimum payment. This guarantees the licensor a return on the license regardless of the profitability of the licensed operating company. The thorny issue, however, is what percentage of sales should be paid in royalties.

Brand-owning companies describe their method for establishing the rate of return demanded from a licensee as an 'open market negotiation'. It is as though the brand were being offered for sale – or rather for loan – and the licensee asked to bid a price for the license agreement on offer.

The clearest evidence of this approach to royalty agreements is in the area of luxury goods described above. In agreeing these licenses the most important consideration is, or at least should be, how appropriate it would be for the brand to be extended into this new market or that new product. Having determined that the extension is a good 'fit' and that the licensee will develop a product that respects the established brand equity, an agreement must be reached on the royalty return to the brand owner. Companies in this area are necessarily highly secretive about the licenses they have agreed and the royalty rates negotiated. However, it is known that the royalty paid in return for the license is a percentage of the value of sales and is usually between five and 16 per cent. The licenses also contain stipulated minimum returns as well as ensuring that the brand owner has a say in how the brand is applied.

Owners of brands like these are clear in their understanding that what they are selling is a lease on a piece of property, and that that property is a brand that can and does demand a premium price in the marketplace because it adds value to goods thus branded. The 'open market negotiation' is what determines whether the rate of royalty agreed is five per cent or 16 per cent or anything in between. In negotiating this rate the prospective licensees are making an assessment of the amount of value that the brand might add compared to using a new brand or no brand or compared to using somebody else's brand. This is brand valuation – or at least evaluation – *in germe*.

A more objective approach to the assessment of value would of course take the guesswork out of the negotiation process and would provide a more reliable and consistent way of establishing a royalty rate. A method of valuation such as the one pioneered by Interbrand that involves distinguishing between the marketing strength and the financial strength of a brand is particularly appropriate. This approach assesses the strength of a brand in adding value to the product and, separately, the profitability which is derived from trading in that brand. This same distinction is reflected in license agreements that treat the royalty rate a brand can demand separately from the actual sales or profits the licensee will effect.

The brand strength score which describes the marketing strength of the brand is effectively an assessment of the security of future cash flow from that brand. In Interbrand's 'existing use valuation method' this is interpreted as a multiple that is applied to historic profits or a discount applied to forecast cash flows. The royalty rate agreed in a licensing deal is also a statement of the security of the brand proposition, and so an assessment of brand strength could also be used to decide the royalty rate for the brand by drawing a mathematical relationship between the two.

A brand analysis might show, for example, beer brand X as having a strength of 65 per cent (100 per cent is the mythical 'perfect' brand) and beer brand Y a strength of only 37 per cent. Such an assessment could then be used to determine the percentage rate that the brand could demand in royalty payments. A model of brand return could be constructed according to principles of a price-earnings ratio or a discount rate and royalty rates could then be read off the graph. However, before getting carried away with the attractive simplicity of such a model we should return to the reality of license agreements and negotiations. The way in which royalty rates are negotiated is actually much less like the valuing of a brand on a scientific model and more like the image of a brand trading house.

In license agreements there are factors that determine the value of the license to the licensee other than the strength of the brand *per se*. For example, the duration of the license and the conditions of termination will affect the amount of investment that a licensee can and will commit to the brand and therefore the return that might be possible. The competitive nature of the market will impact on negotiations since the potential licensee may be able to build a more profitable business by manufacturing similar products but under a different brand license.

Equally a licensor will be able to negotiate from a position of greater strength if there are a number of manufacturers who are all in a position to benefit from the brand license being offered. This is more likely to be a factor of technology availability and ease of entry into a market than of the independent strength of the brand in question. The synergy that such a license can have with the prospective licensee's existing products will also affect the royalty rate that he is prepared to offer and if, as is usual, the rate is based on sales rather than profit, the inherent profitability of the market will cause a higher or lower royalty rate.

It might also be the case that a non-exclusive license is granted that allows a manufacturer of similar or even the same goods to use the brand name in the same territory. Though not affecting the strength of the brand itself this would obviously influence the royalty that a licensor could expect and that a licensee would be prepared to pay.

Many of these factors are the same as those which determine how much an acquirer of a brand would be prepared to pay. It is not only the inherent strength of the brand but also wider factors that determine the 'market price' put on a brand. These factors reinforce the view that, although in negotiating a royalty rate for a license a form of brand evaluation is taking place, it is far from being divorced from non brand-related factors and would not work if it were. The two parties are indeed haggling in a market place and, even if a brand does have an independent and assessable value, the license for that brand commands a price that is best determined by supply and demand. If the licensee is 'buying permission' to use the brand then the licensor is clearly 'selling' that permission and, as in any market, the price of what is being sold and its value are not necessarily the same.

The problem is exacerbated by the fact that very many licenses are for brands that are being launched in a new territory or for a product that is new to the brand. In recent years in the UK this has been especially true in the alcoholic drinks market where product bulk and the problems of excise duty coupled with the continuing appeal of foreign drinks brands has seen more and more licenses to produce or to distribute being granted to UK companies. However, very many of these are introducing new brands to the market and so any assessment of the brand's strength would necessarily have to be a judgment based on the success of that brand in other markets and the success of other brands in the home market. Thus it would be difficult to assert with full confidence that one new brand of lager should demand a higher royalty rate than another when the two are both untried.

ROYALTY RELIEF

In saying that the brand valuation technique does not offer a magic solution to the problems of royalty negotiations I do not, however, wish to dismiss it entirely from the picture. Though the *price* of a license may be different from the *value* of the brand there must still be a correlation between the two. In fact one method of valuing a brand does so by calculating a hypothetical royalty rate for the brand.

This model is based on the premise that if the brand manufacturer did not own the brand he would have to have paid someone a royalty for using the brand. If Whyte & Mackay had not bought the Vladivar trade mark but were simply the producers and distributors of the brand they would have to pay Greenall Whitley a royalty for using the brand. That royalty would be similar to the royalties being paid by other drinks companies for other spirits brands that are distilled under license. The amount by which Whyte & Mackay are 'relieved' by virtue of owning the Vladivar brand (the royalty relief) is an indication of the value of the brand. However, such a model only works in industries where a number of comparable licensing agreements have been negotiated and a 'going rate' for such licenses is established. It also does not allow one to distinguish clearly enough between weak and strong brands in the same market or between brands that have successfully extended into other areas.

Turning this model on its head, though, can be a way of finding a practical relationship between brand value and royalty rates. A very well established and highly-prized brand in the stationery market has never been licensed. Nor have any of its comparable competitors been licensed, such is the nature of the market and the industry. However, the owners of the brand recently decided that to extend the brand commercially and successfully into a new but related area could only be done under license. There was no 'going rate' in the market and so the brand owners had to determine for themselves the rate they could demand as the first step in negotiations. They were able to establish an 'existing use' value of over £30 million for the brand by discounting back forecast cash flows. Applying the same discount rate to the cash flows they would have got from royalty payments gave them the basis for a 'royalty relief' model and as a result an indication of what royalty rate they would have had to pay themselves for their own brand (around 10 per cent). This they then used successfully as an argument in negotiating the royalty rate a third party should pay.

Clearly this is only a starting point for negotiations. But what licensors have lacked in the past is an awareness of the value of their brands assessed in an objective and consistent way. Armed with this in negotiations with potential licensees they are better placed to assert the strength of their brand and so demand a higher return on their investment. Too often in the past licensors have been content to accept a payment for use of a brand that seriously undervalued the brand because of a lack of appreciation of what the brand might be worth or the lack of any objective valuation to assist them at the negotiating table.

In licensing negotiations with third parties such a weapon in the brand owner's armoury would certainly be a useful ally. In the area of internal licensing it would be invaluable.

INTERNAL LICENSING

Internal licensing occurs when a multinational company or group of companies holds all intellectual property (including trade marks) in the name of the parent company and at the location of the parent company (though occasionally these rights may be held 'off shore'). It should be explained that in registering a trade mark, a company name (or an individual's name) and an address is included in the registration and the property is deemed to be held at that address.

The parent then licenses its subsidiary companies around the world to produce and market the company's brands, in the same way as in a third party license agreement. Indeed, it is a principle of such internal licensing that it should be conducted 'at arm's length'.

This organization of trade marks is increasingly common among international branded goods companies. A French food company, for example, though developing its international brand in the Middle East and Far East through subsidiary companies, still holds all trade marks in its own name and then licenses them back to the subsidiary companies. The most obvious reason for this is the opportunity it gives to control all intellectual property centrally, to maintain vigilance over use of trade marks, and to guard against possible loss of trade mark rights by neglect, misuse or sequestration.

However, from a financial point of view a much more important but still relatively unknown role for such internal licensing is the opportunity it presents for legitimate transfer pricing. Since a royalty payment can be required for the use of the trade mark under license, the parent company could structure this so that it reduces the amount of tax payable on the profits of the overseas subsidiary.

One of the best examples of this might be an international conglomerate that has its headquarters in a low tax regime. When the group buys any new company it transfers all the intellectual property rights to the parent company and licenses them back to the English or French or American subsidiary that once owned the rights. There is a capital transfer tax involved at this stage but thereafter the parent company legitimately charges the subsidiary companies for the use of the trade marks and other related rights. The charge is not insignificant ranging from perhaps three to six per cent. The lower corporation tax payable on profits in the parent company's home country has made it advantageous to the group in the long run to reduce the profits of the subsidiary companies with a royalty charge and effectively transfer these profits to the parent company.

On a smaller scale a similar policy is operated by a British office equipment company. Its brand is well-known in the UK but because it is trading in a highly competitive market and is less efficient than other manufacturers, the brand is consistently loss-making. However, in the brand's other main market, on the other side of the world, the strength of the brand has made it highly profitable. The Australian subsidiary has always used the brand under license but until recently was only charged a tiny administration fee for doing so. But by charging a legitimate royalty to the Australian company the group has been able to use its tax losses to greatest benefit.

Of course the difference between this form of licensing and the third party licensing described above is the absence of an 'open market'. When licensing negotiations take place between a subsidiary company and its parent (to whom all profits would ultimately be due anyway) they take on an air of unreality. It then becomes difficult to persuade either the subsidiary company or the tax authorities that there is a real transfer of property taking place.

In many companies the trade marks are held centrally but no real royalty is demanded of the licensed users. Very often this may be because there are fiscal or commercial advantages to minimizing the costs of an overseas operation. But it may also be the result of a lack of appreciation on the part of either parent or subsidiary that property of any real value is being exchanged between the two parties. And even when the parent company does admit the value of the brand being licensed it may then prove difficult to persuade the overseas subsidiary that the use of the brand should be accounted as a cost along with all others. It may then be particularly difficult to agree that one brand may accrue a higher royalty rate than another.

Since the two parties are not operating in an open market (there is, after all, an understanding that the subsidiary will be the exclusive and indefinite licensee of the brand) market forces are not able to determine a 'price' for the license. Because of the potentially huge tax advantages to the company this policy of internal licensing is one that has become more common in recent years but also one which is examined increasingly closely by tax officials.

A major problem with internal licensing and the payment of royalties is that the prejudice that such a transaction is not a genuine leasing of property has been shared by local tax authorities. In some countries royalty payments in respect of license agreements are *de jure* unacceptable. But even in countries where such royalty payments are allowed tax authorities then require evidence of why, for example, a royalty of six per cent should be paid instead of three per cent.

There is a fear that such payments could be simply a means of local tax avoidance rather than royalties due because of use of a real piece of property. It is usually easier to demand specific payments for technical or legal services or contributions towards brand advertising than to try and convince sceptical tax authorities of the value of a brand.

THE RÔLE OF BRAND VALUATION

In such an argument an objective valuation of the brand as a separable and potentially saleable asset provides substantiation for the claim that use of the brand should be charged as a cost to the subsidiary. It is clearer what is being given in return for the payment and why some of the properties being licensed are more valuable than others. An existing use value for the brand would in practice be close to the royalty relief value if a royalty rate were calculable and would certainly provide a basis for deciding the return that could reasonably be expected by the parent from the subsidiary for use of each brand.

Moreover, the appearance of such a production cost in the books of the subsidiary would serve to reinforce the understanding of brands as assets that have been developed by the company, invested in by the company and to be managed not only profitably but sensitively by the company. It is often true that things that come free are not truly appreciated and the same is true of brand names that are licensed without payment from one part of a group to another. Companies in which the subsidiaries have had to pay for the use of brand names are usually examples of companies in which brands are treated as valuable long-term assets of the company and not simply as free gifts. Not only do the subsidiary companies recognize what the true earnings of the brand are – by taking into account the value of all assets used in production – but they are also more strategic in their use of brands and brand extensions.

CONCLUSION

The approach to brand licensing, and especially internal licensing, set out above may seem to be severe and purist. In reality there are often very good reasons – commercial, fiscal or political – why such an approach to brand management and licensing is inappropriate for a branded goods company. But more and more companies are realizing that if they are to protect brands as long-term assets and not allow their use by subsidiary companies or by third parties to be taken for granted they must be more rigorous in the way in which they loan out and charge rent on their property. The tax implications of internal licensing are very attractive to some companies but from a general perspective they are most interesting and relevant in so far as they show how an initially sceptical audience can be persuaded that brands are genuine property and can legitimately be treated as such.

Valuing a brand is a way of establishing what that property is really worth. For both internal and external licenses it can provide a context in which royalty rates can be judged and differing rates justified. It is, moreover, a way of making clear to the licensee – and also to the licensor, and this is sometimes necessary – the fact that the intangible property being lent is true property and should be treated with respect. After all, developing a new brand would be a much more costly and high-risk venture.

Chapter 10

VALUING PUBLISHING TITLES

David Andrew

In the media and communications sector the intangible asset at the heart of a business is not described as a 'brand', but as a 'copyright', as 'publishing rights', or, in the case of newspaper and magazine publishing, as a 'masthead' or 'title'.

These intangibles share a number of characteristics with brands, in particular the relationship which exists between the perceived quality of the asset and its capacity for generating profit. The first media organization to recognize the potential of attributing tangible value to intangible assets was News Corporation, based in Australia, which in 1984 took the unprecedented step of valuing its newspaper mastheads and TV licences and putting those values on its balance sheet.

Although there were no accounting rules in Australia to prevent it doing so, the practice of valuing brands was at that time – and until recently has continued to be – virtually unknown. However, taking their cue from News, many media companies around the world have since valued their intangible properties for balance sheet purposes. In fact, until late 1988 the media sector was very much the pioneer in capitalizing the values of hitherto 'unidentifiable' assets.

TREATMENT OF PUBLISHING RIGHTS

As in the case of brand acquisition, the difference between the amount paid for a media property and the net tangible assets acquired was traditionally treated as an intangible asset and capitalized as goodwill. Since accounting standards – and here we speak specifically of Great Britain and Australia – required that purchased goodwill will be amortized to the profit and loss account over a maximum of 20 years, there was an understandable reluctance on the part of the acquiring companies to comply with the standards and suffer sometimes substantial erosion of their annual profits.

However, once it was recognized that publishing rights and titles were capable of being separately identified and transferred to other parties independently of the business, such rights and titles by definition ceased to be 'unidentifiable'. They thus no longer needed to be treated as goodwill – defined as 'future benefits from unidentifiable assets' – which meant that the goodwill component of any media acquisition was minimized and the annual write-off against profits substantially reduced.

Table 1 compares the treatment of publishing rights, titles, etc. by a range of publishers and media organizations in Great Britain, the United States and Australia, and illustrates the broad acceptance of the concept of value attributable to these properties.

A major point to be noted from Figure 10.1 is that while publishing groups such as News Corporation, United Newspapers and, more recently, Lonrho have valued *existing* titles and mastheads, others include values on the balance sheet only when *acquiring* such properties.

Figure 10.1   Comparison of Treatment of Publishing Rights, Titles etc.

Company	Value of publishing rights etc. £000	Net assets £000	Accounting policy
The Adscene Group plc	2,716	4,517	Publishing titles are stated at cost. Having no finite economic life, no amortization is provided. Any permanent impairment of values is written off against profits.
Emap plc	56,831	74,106	Acquired publishing rights, titles etc. which have no finite life are stated at cost less provision for permanent diminution in value.
Home Counties Newspapers Holdings plc	391	7,130	Purchased goodwill is stated at cost to the group and is written off over a period of 40 years. Note: goodwill includes premium on acquisition of shares and subsidiaries.

Company	Value of publishing rights etc. £000	Net assets £000	Accounting policy
Lonrho plc	117,000		Titles, existing or acquired, deemed to have infinite life, therefore no depreciation.
Maxwell Communications Corporation plc	340,600	1,014,300	Publishing rights, titles and benefits are carried forward and amortized over the period expected to benefit therefrom. Where, in the opinion of the directors, these assets have an infinite life, no amortization charge is made, unless there is a permanent diminution in value.
News Corporation Ltd	6,017,385	5,113,575	Publishing rights, titles and television licences are stated at cost or valuation. No amortization is provided on publishing rights and titles since, in the opinion of the directors, they do not have a finite useful economic life. Although television licences in the United States are renewable every five years, the directors have no reason to believe that they will not be renewed and, accordingly, no amortization is provided. The publishing rights, titles and television licences at valuation June 1990 include the original cost and the revaluation increment.
Reed International plc	612,200	1,156,300	Publishing rights and titles and exhibition rights are stated at fair value on acquisition. Having no finite economic life,

Company	Value of publishing rights etc. £000	Net assets £000	Accounting policy
			amortization is not provided. Subject to annual review, any permanent impairment of value is written off against profit. On the acquisition of a subsidiary or related company the purchase consideration is allocated between the underlying net tangible and intangible assets on a fair value basis. Any excess cost or goodwill is written off against consolidated reserves. Other acquired intangible assets are amortized over their useful economic life.
United Newspapers plc	133,000	177,973	Publishing rights and titles which have no finite life are stated at valuation. Provision is made for any permanent diminution in value.

Source: *Hill Samuel*

VALUING NEWSPAPER MASTHEADS

In accounting terms, a masthead is regarded as an intangible fixed asset which, by virtue of the identity established and protected by its trade mark and/or copyright and reinforced by the aggregate components of its posture in the market, can legitimately be considered identifiable and thus treated as a stand-alone asset. As such it can be freely bought and sold, and accordingly is a candidate for valuation.

Valuation of acquired mastheads is usually simply a matter of establishing, at acquisition, the sustainable annual revenues/post-tax earnings/cash flows, and applying a multiple to that figure (see the Reed International example). In such a case the multiple is one commonly used by the company or selected so as to stay on the conservative side of recent sector transactions.

However, valuing a publisher's existing titles, where there is no acquisition price to provide a ready bench-mark, usually involves the calculation of a multiple based on a rigorous assessment of the publication's characteristics (see the News Corporation example). Again, depending upon the company concerned, the multiple is then applied to an average of two or more years' revenue, cash flow or after-tax earnings.

Literally, of course, a masthead of a newspaper or magazine is simply its name as graphically represented on the front page or cover of the publication. For valuation purposes, however – particularly in the case of an existing masthead – it is the sum total of its editorial and advertising content; its distribution; its history and reputation in the market which it serves – and particularly its positioning in that market; the dimensions and calibre of its readership; the influence it exerts plus its format and graphic identity.

These characteristics give a masthead value, because they not only determine the publication's appeal to its market – and hence the revenue it generates from sales to readers – but its appeal to advertisers – and hence the revenue it generates from advertising. (Obviously the two sources of revenue are related, because the scale and quality of readership the publication enjoys impacts directly on both the demand for its advertising space and the advertising rates it can command.)

But the value of a masthead does not begin and end with the revenue it attracts or even its profitability – because the true value to its owner cannot be judged without examining the operating context of the publication itself.

Market size

The size of the market in which it competes, and its market share, are the critical factors in assessing true value: *market (or sector)* size because it establishes the potential revenues to which the publication has access; *share* because it not only quantifies the proportion of that potential the publication is demonstrably capable of delivering, but because it is the measure of the masthead's dominance – and dominance by a publication makes the market that much more difficult for newcomers to penetrate, and hence the masthead is a more stable and reliable revenue source over time.

Obviously there are many other factors that warrant examination in the process of determining a masthead's worth, including advertising and circulation trends; the publication's positioning relative to competition; the strength and dynamics of the competition; and the existence of barriers to market entry.

For a better focus on the methodology of valuation and its effects on the balance sheet we should look at two specific cases:

News Corporation

News Corporation is a multi-faceted international media group operating principally in the United States, the United Kingdom, and Australia. Turnover in 1990 exceeded £4.1 billion.

In the United States the company operates the Fox television and broadcasting networks and Twentieth-Century Fox Corporation, and is the largest publisher of consumer magazines in the country. In the UK it is engaged principally in the publishing of major newspapers, magazines and books and in the Sky Channel satellite television system, now merged with BSB. And in Australia and the Pacific Basin, it publishes a wide range of national and regional newspapers and magazines, is engaged in book publishing and commercial printing, and has interests in transportation and other industries.

As noted above, News Corporation's decision to put values on its mastheads and television licenses and to include them in the company's aggregate of assets was the first time that such assets had been recorded on a media organization's balance sheet at a valuation other than purchase cost.

Prior to that time, media groups worldwide had hesitated to value media assets for balance sheet purposes, principally because they would have been classified as unidentifiable intangible assets like goodwill, and thus been subject to amortization.

However, News Corporation took the position that, unlike other intangibles, newspaper mastheads and television licenses were *identifiable* assets capable of producing revenue in their own right and of being transferred to other parties independently of the other assets of the business. They also were deemed not to have a finite life, nor to be otherwise classified as wasting assets.

This approach was endorsed by News Corporation's auditors, who declared themselves willing to treat the mastheads and television licenses as fixed assets. Accordingly, said the directors in the annual report, 'the directors obtained professional valuations of the Group's readily identifiable assets, being mastheads, titles and licenses, all of which were previously recorded in the financial statements at cost. As at 30 June 1984 they have adopted revaluations to more closely reflect market value, thus substantially increasing shareholders' funds and providing a more accurate representation of the total assets of the company.'

News Corporation undertook to value more than 40 mastheads in Australia, Britain, and the United States. They described the process thus: 'The primary valuation technique used was a methodology based on the maintable revenues of the publishing rights, titles and television licenses. This incorporates multiples which take account of the market factors relating to the rights, titles and licenses and which reflect the composition of the revenues and the profitability, the loyalty of the readership, the risk attaching to the advertising revenue and the potential future growth. The results derived using the primary methodology were supported by an extensive review of market transactions in the United States of America, the United Kingdom and Hong Kong.'

It is interesting to note that the 1987 annual report for News Corporation revealed that a revaluation carried out that year more than doubled the initial values recorded three years earlier. A further revaluation of the Group's publishing titles and television licenses effected in June 1990 yielded a value two and a half times that awarded to these assets in 1987.

Reed International

Once heavily involved in manufacturing, Reed International is today an organization devoted solely to publishing and information. In fact, with an annual turnover in excess of £1b it is the UK's largest publishing company.

Reed's publishing interests include business and consumer magazines; professional and general interest books, journals and educational books; regional newspapers; electronic databases for travel and other industries; and exhibitions.

Reed treats its mastheads, magazine titles and book imprints as valuable brand franchises. In its view, unlike the products of many other services and industries, these brand franchises can not only survive when key people leave the business but can continue to be viable properties even if acquired by other companies.

Since 1984 Reed has employed an accounting policy which involves carrying acquired publishing rights – but not existing ones – on the balance sheet. The actual wording of Reed's policy is detailed in Figure 10.1.

The two major issues posed by the policy are:

- The identification and separability of publishing rights and the distinction from goodwill.

- The substantiation that such rights have no finite life and thus do not require systematic amortization.

As reported by Reed: 'two UK accounting standards are relevant to the policy which the company has adopted in attributing part of the purchase price on an acquisition to publishing rights acquired. SSAP14 (Group Accounts) requires allocation of purchase consideration to the assets acquired "on the basis of the fair value to the acquiring company". SSAP22 (Accounting for Goodwill) defines fair value as the amount for which an asset (or liability) could be exchanged in an arm's length transaction. This standard defines separable assets as "those assets which can be identified and sold separately without necessarily disposing of the business as a whole. They include identifiable tangibles". Goodwill could not be (sold separately). It could only be either acquired or sold as part of the process of acquiring or selling the business as a whole.

'On any transaction, the excess of purchase price over the value of acquired net tangible assets gives the combined value of goodwill and intangible assets. Apportioning the value between the two is a matter of informed judgment; it may be controversial but it is not an unreasonable or impractical task. For some acquisitions, Reed has had help from professional valuers but in most instances the apportionment is decided by the directors, in close consultation with the external auditors. No upward revaluations of acquired publishing rights are undertaken but a close watch is maintained for potential permanent impairment.

'The basic guideline for valuing acquired publishing rights is the sustainable annual post-tax cash flow of the acquired properties qualifying for retention. Sustainable cash flow excludes non-recurring costs incurred in integrating the acquired property into the mainstream business. It normally represents the cash flow in the first full year after acquisition.

'Normal levels of overhead recovery and maintenance capital spending are included in the calculation of cash flow. Synergistic cash flows generated elsewhere in the business can be included in the valuation if they are identifiable and material (ie, over 20 per cent) in the context of total cash flow.

'Cash flow of the acquired property has been chosen in preference to any other financial performance yardstick because it is considered to be the most meaningful measure of the fair value of that particular publishing right to the business. Cash flow is least affected by the particular accounting conventions used to measure financial performance, and it is from the cash flow that the company will be servicing its debt and equity.

'Publishing rights are identified [ascribed] to either specific individual titles or logical groups of titles (or journals) or to house brand names for books. The grouping which is chosen accords with the normal format for management reporting to enable the permanent impairment tests to be performed.

'Multiples of sustainable cash flow used for the valuation can vary if there are special circumstances, but normally the same multiple is applied consistently. It is conservatively set at a level quite significantly below the multiples commanded by publishing companies in recent public transactions.'

Reed undertakes periodic reviews of retained intangibles to determine if any permanent impairment of their value has occurred.

If so, the impairment is written off to the profit and loss account, probably as an exceptional item. The multiple of sustainable cash flow used in this test is normally the same as that being applied for valuing new acquisitions.

In describing the execution of the review, Reed states that: 'publishing rights are grouped into definable related categories. The review takes into account not only the current performance of each grouping but also the prospective capacity to generate earnings and cash flow as against the expectations at the time of the initial investment and cost/value assessment. Where performance is below expectations without a near-term prospect of recovery there is *prima facie* evidence of impairment. However, a thorough assessment of the recoverable value of the asset is made before impairment is identified.

'Even when performance is up to expectation, impairment can nevertheless occur when the carrying value is not supported by current market valuations of similar assets and there is no prospect of a recovery in market valuations.

'Since acquired publishing rights may not be distinguishable from created titles in terms of publishing or management practice, the permanent impairment test can take into account the cash flow contribution from created titles which are in the same market sector. The latter can, however, only be included if insufficient time has elapsed for the acquired titles to be considered as grouped with the created titles.'

CONCLUSION

Newspaper mastheads and publishing titles are now widely accepted as valuable media assets in their own right which provide their owners with an earning stream independently of the other assets employed in the business. Their valuation is a function of the scarcity of these assets, volume of advertising generated, market share and the profit which they contribute.

As is the case with brands, incorporating mastheads and titles into a media group's aggregate assets strengthens the general presentation of the balance sheet; reveals hitherto 'hidden' assets and thus gives shareholders a more accurate picture of the financial position of their company; reduces the amount of goodwill on acquisitions and enables the company to comply with accounting standards on goodwill without sacrificing commercial reality; and by enhancing shareholders' funds increases the size of commercial transactions the company can undertake without referring to shareholders for approval.

Chapter 11

EVALUATING BRANDS – US EXPERIENCE AND PRACTICE

Noel Penrose and Alfred King

The tremendous interest in brand valuation seen in the United Kingdom, Australasia and Continental Europe has not hitherto been matched in the United States, but it would be wrong to assume that brand valuation does not have a role to play in corporate America. Indeed, many of the world's most powerful and valuable brands are American-owned and their owners are acutely aware of their power, rarity and underlying worth. However, little has been done in the US, to date, to quantify such values or to communicate this worth to key audiences such as shareholders, employees or financial institutions.

Why is there such a disparity between practice in the US and in much of the rest of the world? Why does US business appear to recognize the worth and value of its brands and other intangible assets but to be, at the same time, so reluctant to translate this general recognition into hard numbers? Why, despite a reputation for being at the forefront of developments in the marketing and financial areas, does the US seem to lag in this field?

THE ISSUES

Brand names quite clearly can have a value and this value is often considerable. The unanswered questions, however, in the minds of many US observers are:

- Can such values be quantified?

- If they can be quantified, should they be disclosed to shareholders, employees, creditors and others?

- If they are disclosed, should they appear in a company's accounts, either on the face of the financial statements or by way of note to the accounts?

Elsewhere in this book various methodologies for valuing brands are explored in detail and we have no doubt that, properly applied, they result in valuations which are fair, sensible and verifiable. Certainly, such methodologies compare extremely favourably with other types of asset valuations which have been in use for generations and which are now accepted without question by accountants, business managers, tax authorities and others. Methodologies for brand valuation should not therefore prove a problem, though they are relatively little known, as yet, in the US. Perhaps, however, another factor is that the US does not have a history of receiving its business ideas from abroad, but rather is much more comfortable in the rôle of the originator of new ideas.

But the most important reason for the apparent lack of acceptance of brand valuation in the United States, at least for the time being, has much more to do with disclosure than with technical arguments as to the appropriateness or otherwise of brand valuation techniques, and at the heart of the disclosure issue lies the disparity in accounting regulations between the US and many other countries.

ACCOUNTING REGULATIONS

Brand-owning companies in the United Kingdom, Australasia, France, and elsewhere are able to capitalize the value of brands on their balance sheets and such capitalization may be made without the need for any subsequent amortization (ie periodic write-down over an arbitrary number of years) provided the brand asset can be shown to have no pre-determined finite life and provided the intention of management is to maintain or increase the value of the brand through continued support and investment, generally in the form of research and development expenditure, advertising and promotional activities.

Such brands can, therefore, remain in the balance sheet as separately identified intangible assets and often represent one of the key components of the value of the business as a whole. Moreover, trends in brand value can be a useful measure of management skills.

In fact, brands sometimes appear in the balance sheets of American companies, although they are rarely identified as such. American accounting regulations require that intangible assets of any description are written off to the profit and loss account annually over a period not exceeding 40 years. Most companies, where there has been an acquisition which has given rise to goodwill (the difference between the price paid and the fair value of the tangible assets, equipment, inventories, receivables, etc.) choose not to identify separately the component elements of that goodwill in the balance sheet, preferring instead to include the patents, trademarks, etc. under the generalized 'goodwill' heading. Thus specific, identifiable intangible assets are lumped together with less identifiable assets and with the 'premium' element in the acquisition paid to secure control. Therefore, the separate identification of acquired brands is rare and the inclusion of own-developed brands is unheard of.

Goodwill

This disparity in the recognition and treatment of 'goodwill' between the United States and the United Kingdom is further highlighted by the fact that accounting regulations in the United Kingdom (and, indeed, in some other countries such as Australia) permit companies to write off goodwill immediately and directly to retained earnings, thereby avoiding an adverse annual profit and loss impact. For some acquisitive companies this has been used as a highly effective tool in corporate takeovers. The acquisition of Pillsbury by Britain's Grand Metropolitan is a case in point; Grand Met paid some $5 billion dollars for Pillsbury in 1989 of which approximately $4 billion represented goodwill. After a detailed study of the value of the brands acquired, among them Burger King, Green Giant and Hägen-Dazs, some $3.1 billion of this sum was attributed to the value of the brands acquired and the remainder written off to reserves.

US accounting regulations would have seriously handicapped a US corporation in bidding for Pillsbury as the goodwill value of Pillsbury would have been too rich for the blood of most American companies requiring an annual amortization charge against profits of around $100 million – current Generally Accepted Accounting Principles (GAAP) in the US call for a maximum period of 40 years for the write-off of intangibles and most companies prefer the maximum. But GAAP also requires this amortization to take place even if the asset appreciates in value and it does not permit periodic revaluation of appreciating assets, even of land. The basic accounting model in the US is historical cost, written down by depreciation or amortization on a periodic basis. Thus only transactions between unrelated parties provide a basis for putting intangible assets on the books and, once there, a company must start at once to write them off through the profit and loss account no matter what periodic revaluations might reveal. Thus the presence of what has been termed, at least by Americans, an 'uneven playing field' enabled a British multinational to acquire a powerful American food giant and has resulted in a renewed cry for common international accounting standards.

Revaluation

The principal area of difference, however, between the separate bases for accounting treatment relates to the revaluation of assets. UK companies are able to incorporate revalued assets (both tangible and intangible) in their balance sheets whereas such a practice is prohibited in the US under GAAP. Thus UK companies can revalue land, stocks, copyrights and brands while US practice requires the sole application of the historical cost convention whereby value can only be ascribed for balance sheet purposes where a transaction has taken place.

Figure 11.1 shows the accounting treatment of goodwill in the US, UK and in six member countries of the European Economic Community. Although the UK is the only EEC country where revaluation of intangible assets such as brands is reasonably widespread there is an increasing interest on the part of companies in other EEC countries to follow suit. French food giant BSN, for example, incorporated a value of some 4.8 billion french francs (£500 million approximately) for acquired brand names in its 1989 financial statements. Such a policy is possible due to the absence of any requirement to the contrary within EC directives; indeed, under current harmonization proposals it seems likely that specific encouragement may be given to the disclosure and periodic revaluation of major corporate assets, both tangible and intangible. It is also interesting to note that the International Accounting Standards Committee (IASC) is also trying to develop a standard-ized approach to acquisition accounting and the treatment of goodwill, though wide divisions currently exist.

De facto GAAP

At least one major corporation, largely based in the US, has found the use of foreign accounting regulations preferable to those in the US. News Corporation is incorporated in Australia and prepares its financial statements in accordance with Australian GAAP (see also Chapter 10). A report on the company, written by Gary Scheineman, a Vice President at Smith New Court in New York, argues that News Corporation is *de facto* a US company as top management is based in New York and 60 per cent of operating income came from the US in 1990. Mr Scheineman restated News Corporation's figures according to US GAAP, and found that 'Australian GAAP accounting has permitted News Corporation to inflate its balance sheet and report higher profits than it would under a US GAAP basis of reporting. This is due in large part to differences in accounting for intangibles and the treatment of extraordinary items'. Restating the figures in accordance with US GAAP, Scheineman found that gearing trebled and profit before tax fell in absolute terms. Clearly, in this instance it could be argued that US GAAP is a more prudent and conservative approach than Australian GAAP, an argument which is reinforced by the difficulties encountered by News Corpora-tion in the recession of 1990/91. Those opposing this view would argue, on the other hand, that it should not be the purpose of Generally Accepted Accounting Principles to 'mute' corporate performance and present weakened corporate balance sheets for the

Figure 11.1 Comparison of Accounting Treatment of Goodwill between United States and key member countries of EEC

	United States	United Kingdom	France	Belgium	Italy	Spain	Germany	Nether-lands
Option to show purchased Goodwill as an asset	Mandatory	Yes	Yes	Yes	Yes	Yes	Yes	Yes
Option to eliminate Goodwill against reserves	No	Yes	Yes	Yes	Yes	Yes	Yes	Yes
Most common accounting treatment	Asset	Eliminate	Asset	Asset	Asset	Asset	Asset	Either
Typical amortization life for Goodwill write-off (years)	40	*	20	5	10	**	15	15

*Insufficient data available since write-off option rarely used.
**Goodwill is generally not depreciated since it is not tax deductible.

Source: *Accounting for Europe, Touche Ross, 1989*

sake of prudence; their job is to present a true and fair picture and it is neither true nor fair to write out of the balance sheet valuable assets, both tangible and intangible, and thus seriously to understate the worth of businesses.

TAX ISSUES

Tax allowances

Though the balance sheet debate has largely passed corporate America by, there is evidence of extensive valuation activity of intangible assets consequent to an acquisition for taxation purposes. The US Tax Code requires that the full amount of the purchase consideration be allocated to all of the assets acquired, both tangible and intangible, such that fair values are attributed. Intangible assets here may include patents, 'non-compete' agreements, copyrights, designs and client lists as well as brand names and trademarks.

The Tax Code requires, in effect, that determinable assets be specifically identified, values be ascribed and a specific life be assigned to each. For assets with specific wasting lives, for example non-compete agreements with a fixed term, or patent rights, tax allowances are available for the whole of the ascribed value over the agreed period of the life of the asset. The position of the tax authorities as to the life to be assigned to brand names and trade marks appears to be that a write off for tax purposes may only be available where the brand is either disposed of or abandoned; thus no periodic tax write down is available.

The consequence of this is that brands are rarely separately identified, but merely lumped together under the general heading of intangible goodwill and attempts separately to attribute value are often only made later if abandonment or disposal takes place. Furthermore, the general basis for valuing the goodwill balance tends to be the 'residual value' approach whereby brand names and trademarks merely form part of the 'rump' and are not separately identified or valued.

It is interesting to note, however, that the Revenue Reconciliation Act of 1989 provides that amounts paid for the licensing or franchising of trade names and trademarks can be tax deductible. A restriction is set in the form of a monetary limit, $100,000, and this is deductible only if paid in a fixed sum amount or if made in annual payments that are substantially equal in amount. The Act further provides that non-deductible amounts (those sums in excess of $100,000) may be amortized over 25 years. Thus, from a tax standpoint, whilst there is little incentive to brand owners who use their trade marks themselves to value these trade marks, tax considerations could lead to an increase in brand franchising.

Transfer pricing issues

Another highly controversial issue arises in the form of transfer pricing. Section 482 of the Internal Revenue Code attempts to prevent the transfer of income from high-tax to low-tax jurisdictions and is aimed specifically at overseas transfer pricing. It therefore particularly relates to federal tax. However, there are a number of states within the US which levy no local state tax on corporate profits (these include Delaware, Connecticut, etc) and these contrast sharply with states where state income taxes of seven or eight per cent are commonplace. Thus there are considerable incentives for ensuring that profits are generated in the appropriate state and that taxable deductions are properly handled.

In recent years the preferred means to achieve this became known as the 'Delaware Dodge' – a brand-owning company would establish a properly staffed investment holding company in, say, Delaware, and the operating company would then transfer its trademarks to the investment company at fair value (an internal transaction exempt from capital gains tax liability) but would continue to use the trademarks in its operations. The investment company would then charge a royalty to the operating company for use of the trademark, perhaps based on sales, and this charge would represent a taxable deduction against the profits of the operating company. The investment company would thus show royalty income free of state taxes and, without affecting its overall federal tax liability, the company would in effect have shifted income to a state where it would incur little or no state tax liability. Not surprisingly, states which charge local profit taxes are becoming increasingly hostile to such transactions and are now erecting strong barriers. However, such arrangements clearly suggest that the principle of valuation of brand names and trademarks can have significant long-term tax consequences.

RECENT DEVELOPMENTS

Audit

Present accounting systems in the United States are undoubtedly archaic and anachronistic. They are based on nineteenth century concepts of value creation and pay little regard, at times, to the ways in which 'worth' is created by modern businesses. Nonetheless they have one striking advantage, though seemingly only for auditors. The requirement that, for inclusion of a valuation in the financial statements, a transaction must first have taken place means that auditors (who in any case are only really comfortable with things they can kick or touch) are spared the need to have to assess value or worth or pass any judgment on valuations performed by others.

Additionally, by the establishment of a fixed period for write-off of the cost, auditors do not need to expose themselves to the challenges of reviewing or approving a useful life for the intangible asset. By categorizing brands as goodwill US GAAP makes life easy for the auditor though at the expense of management. Thus US accounting treatment may not reflect reality, but it does provide easy answers for auditors. (Though, in partial defence, auditors would argue that the same rules apply to everyone, and at least 'unreal' US corporate accounts are comparable one to another, something which, they would argue, is not necessarily the case in other countries). But should audit convenience govern crucial corporate decision-making? Is anything being done to address the issue? Some interesting insights are provided by opinions on valuations rendered in related areas.

Financial Accounting Standards Board

Accounting issues relating to foreign exchange, pensions, and income tax are often far more complex than those relating to the valuation of brand names yet the financial community has wrestled with these and other similar issues and arrived at acceptable compromises. It would be perfectly reasonable, therefore, to assume that some accommodation could be reached on valuing and accounting for brand names and other valuable intangible assets.

A December 1988 Financial Accounting Standards Board report which considered 'Post Retirement Benefits Other Than Pensions' commented as follows:

> The Board realizes that [these] estimates may have a larger margin of error than some other estimates used in financial reporting. Few would argue, though, that no asset exists or that non-recognition is a better measure of the asset. A 'best efforts' measure of the asset based on the application of the principles outlined in this report is better than implying [by making no accrual] that no asset exists.

The report then went on:

> Almost all accounting measurements involve estimates of the future. Estimates of the useful life of a machine...have become well accepted even though those estimates are sometimes wide of the mark and need to be subsequently adjusted.

Exactly the same arguments could be applied to brands, for the same logic applies to the valuation of brand names and the disclosure of these values to shareholders. There may of course be imprecision but shareholders would be better off with such information, whether as part of the balance sheet or by way of note to the accounts, than with no information at all.

It is also clear that the US Financial Accounting Standards Board has yet to come to grips with the international changes underway in accounting for goodwill and intangibles. Although a re-examination of the issues has been promised, whether the Standards resulting from this re-examination will contain any changes in accounting rules remains to be seen. If the past is a good indicator of the future, the capitalization of goodwill will be at the centre of intense discussions since major revisions of the Accounting Rules for Business cannot occur without a change in the profession's concept and understanding of goodwill and other intangibles.

The Securities and Exchange Commission (SEC), which has significant influence on both the Financial Accounting Standards Board (FASB) and the American Institute of Certified Public Accountants, will no doubt support the traditional historical cost accounting methods currently in place. Based on recent rulings, the FASB is leaning towards issuing authoritative guidance on the impairment of assets, and the need for possible write downs, rather than on the inclusion of assets such as brands on the balance sheet.

However, the prospects for brand valuation as a financial and management instrument go far beyond the rather narrow, technical balance sheet issue and brand evaluation and audit techniques are proving of major interest to US companies who never before have had such a powerful tool to understand and manage the valuable assets which are in their possession.

MANAGEMENT INFORMATION

Before any business asset can be properly valued, the valuer needs fully to understand and appreciate the nature of the asset, its prospects and the market it serves. Thus in the case of brand valuation, a brand must be viewed as a marketing as well as a financial asset, and must be evaluated as such if its worth is to be accurately measured. Thus the brand valuation process (effectively a brand audit) can be of enormous value to management in identifying strengths and weaknesses, threats and opportunities as well as in providing a solid base for brand tracking and performance measurement. Indeed, the benefits of brand valuation as a management tool arguably outstrip the benefits of this technique as a balance sheet or financial tool and it is in this area that US businesses are starting to show the most interest, arguably somewhat later than businesses in certain other countries.

CONCLUSION

US businesses are prevented at present from putting brands on their balance sheets by the failure of current regulations to recognize these valuable intangible assets, by a prohibition on the revaluation of such assets and by the need for amortization. There is no solid reason, however, why companies should not conduct valuations for separate disclosure by way of note and, indeed, there are some very good reasons to do so. The information generated is, for example, of proven benefit to forward-thinking marketeers. There may be tax advantages in the medium term, and shareholders surely deserve to be advised of the value of the principal assets owned and used by a company in which they choose to invest.

For too long US management, prompted by accounting regulations, has tended to view its brand assets in rather 'soft', non-specific ways. US management literature is full of references to 'brand equity' but virtually no attempt has been made to translate this concept into hard methodologies or principles. The new techniques which are creating so much interest in, mainly, the UK, Continental Europe and Australasia provide American management with the chance to translate rhetoric into initiatives leading to better brand management.

The purpose of accounting is to make those responsible for the management of businesses accountable for them but present US regulations for intangible assets do little to help in this regard. Brands are assets of significant importance and their value should be known and appreciated by all those who manage them, own them and have an interest in their worth.

Chapter 12

BRANDS AS LEGAL PROPERTY

Janet Fogg

BRANDS AND TRADE MARKS

A brand is, in one sense, simply a trade mark which is in use and which has gathered to itself appeals and values. Nonetheless, in legal terms the trade mark is at the heart of a brand, and it is this which enjoys the strongest legal protection. Indeed, trade marks, as pieces of property, are every bit as 'crisp' in legal terms as tangible assets such as freehold property and plant.

Many leading companies realize the value of their trade marks and protect them carefully. But this attitude is by no means universal and it is still quite common to hear of companies losing their trade marks in one country or another because they have failed to register them or guard them sufficiently carefully. This chapter explains what a trade mark is, its function, the registration process, advantages of registration and how trade marks can be bought, sold or licensed. It also briefly compares trade marks with other types of intellectual property such as patents, copyright and designs. To avoid unnecessary complexity we will focus mainly on British trade mark law. The broad principles of trade mark law are, however, similar around the world, though practice can vary widely.

WHAT IS A TRADE MARK?

A trade mark can be a word or words, letters, numbers, symbols, emblems, drawings, pictures, monograms, signatures, colours or combinations of colours, or any combination of these individual elements. In some cases a trade mark can be a phrase, a slogan, the shape of a container or even a smell or sound. The term also includes what are often referred to as brand names and trade names. In some cases a company name can also function as a trade mark.

A trade mark has three main functions:

- To distinguish the goods or services of an enterprise from those of others

134

- To indicate the source or origin of the goods or services

- To represent the goodwill of the trade mark owner and to serve as an indication of the qualtiy of his goods or services

As the use of trade marks to perform these functions results in the trade marks acquiring value, the law specifically recognizes the rights and values accruing to trade marks and affords them powerful protection.

WHY REGISTER?

In the UK and other common law countries, rights in a trade mark are acquired primarily through use rather than registration and the owner of a mark, whether it is registered or not, can object to the use of the same or similar mark on the grounds that such use amounts to 'passing off'. In an early case it was stated in the English courts that 'nobody has the right to represent his goods as the goods of somebody else' and this is still valid today.

The first formal registration system for trade marks began in the sixteenth century and was set up by the Sheffield cutlery manufacturers to control the use of marks by makers of knives and other cutlery in the Sheffield area. The first Act of Parliament in the UK to provide for trade mark registration for all kinds of goods was in 1875 and this has since been replaced by successive new Acts. The current Act is the Trade Marks Act 1938, which was amended by the 1984 Act to cover service mark registration (until 1984 registered trade marks in the UK covered only goods and not services). However to comply with an EC directive aimed at harmonizing the trade mark laws of member countries, and to enable the UK to join the International Registration system, a new Act is planned which should come into force by the end of 1992. The first trade mark registered under the 1875 Act was the famous red triangle beer label belonging to Bass the brewers, and this registration is still in force today.

The purpose of registration is to provide the owner of a trade mark with a statutory monopoloy in the mark for the goods or services covered by the registration and, in the case of the proposed new Act, for similar goods or services. Through an action in the High Court for trade mark infringement the owner has the right to prevent the unauthorized use of the same or a confusingly similar mark on any of the goods or services covered by his registration. If the infringement action is successful the trade mark owner will be entitled to an injunction preventing the infringer from continuing to use the mark as well as an award for damages and the legal costs of bringing the action.

Registration of trade marks is not, however, compulsory and, as already mentioned, in the UK and other common law countries a trader can rely on the common law action of 'passing off' to protect his mark. However, registering a trade mark has the following advantages:

- To succeed in an action for passing off, the plaintiff has to establish to the court's satisfaction that he has a reputation and goodwill in the trade mark and that what the defendant is doing amounts to a misrepresentation, which is confusing, or likely to confuse, a substantial number of people into thinking that the defendant's goods or services come from the plaintiff, thereby causing damage to the plaintiff's business. Common law rights are therefore difficult, time-consuming and expensive to establish and to enforce and the outcome of legal actions involving common law rights is frequently unpredictable. By contrast, to succeed in an action for trade mark infringement, the trade mark owner merely has to establish that his registration is valid and that the defendant is using the same or a confusingly similar mark on goods or services covered by his registration. The rights acquired through registration are therefore relatively simple and inexpensive to enforce and the outcome of trade mark infringement actions is generally more certain

- It is not necessary for a trade mark owner to be using his mark before applying for registration. An application can instead be based on a genuine intention to use the mark in the future. This means that the mark can be protected before the product or service on which it is to be used has been launched. Common law rights in an unregistered mark on the other hand only arise through use over a period of time and the owner of the unregistered mark clearly runs the risk of a third party entering the fray before sufficient use has been made of the mark for that mark to enjoy any protection

- The owner or registered user of a trade mark registration can prevent the importation of infringing goods by lodging a notice with the Customs and Excise authorities specifying the time and place where the consignment is expected to arrive

- In countries where there is no common law system (and this includes much of Europe apart from the UK) rights in a trade mark are acquired by registration rather than through use. Although unfair competition law exists in some countries, unregistered trade marks are very difficult to protect

- A trade mark registration acts as a powerful deterrent to competitors considering the adoption of the same or similar mark because most manufacturers and traders carry out availability searches of the relevant trade mark registers before adopting a new mark so as to ensure that it does not conflict with existing third party rights. Moreover, any infringer is more likely to be persuaded to back down when faced with an existing trade mark registration than with claimed common law rights

In contrast with copyright (which is discussed later in this chapter), in order to succeed in an action for passing off or trade mark infringement it is not necessary to show that there has been intentional copying by the defendant. Indeed, in many cases there will have been no intentional copying at all and the defendant will have selected the conflicting mark quite independently.

WHAT CAN BE REGISTERED AS A TRADE MARK?

The criteria for registrability of a trade mark differ substantially from country to country. The UK has a fairly stringent system which includes examination of a mark for inherent registrability, and for conflict with prior registered and pending marks, before registration is granted. To qualify for registration a new trade mark should not be deceptive or scandalous and should consist of or contain one or more of the following elements:

- An invented word or words

- A word or words having no directly descriptive meaning in relation to the goods or services applied for, and not consisting of surnames or geographical names

- The name of a company or individual represented in a distinctive way

- The signature of the applicant or one of his predecessors in the business

- Any other distinctive mark such as a device or logo

Generally, the most important factor in selecting a trade mark is *distinctiveness* – the trade mark should stand out from the crowd and unequivocally distinguish your goods or services and no one else's.

It is, however, sometimes possible to obtain registration of a mark which would not otherwise qualify by providing evidence to show that the mark has been used for the goods or services covered by the application over a number of years prior to the date of application. The rationale for this is that the mark may have become distinctive through use and should therefore qualify for registration on these grounds.

Although from the trade mark owner's point of view the most attractive mark is often the one which best describes his goods or services, from a legal viewpoint the strongest type of trade mark is normally one which consists of an invented word because such a mark will be much easier to register and protect on an international basis. Examples of well-known invented trade marks are Kodak, Oxo and Xerox.

REGISTRATION PROCEDURE AND COSTS

Before adopting a new mark it is advisable to carry out searches of the trade mark registers of the relevant countries to ensure that the mark does not conflict with existing third party rights. Although a search in one country is usually quick and inexpensive, it is far more difficult, time-consuming and costly to clear a mark for international use, especially for such goods as pharmaceuticals and computers where the registers are already very crowded. Also, searches need to be carried out on a country-by-country basis, though once the proposed Community Trade Mark system is properly in place the process will be easier, at least for Western Europe. Searching is, however, essential to ensure that the launch of a new product or service will not give rise to third party objections, or even infringement proceedings.

In the UK and other common law countries it is also a good idea to carry out additional searches of the index of company names, and of relevant trade and telephone directories, to ensure as far as possible that there are no potential problems from unregistered marks.

Once a mark has been cleared in the applicant's home country it is sensible to apply immediately for registration in order to lay claim to the mark pending completion of the international searches. It is possible to do this because many countries belong to a convention whereby once an application has been filed in one's home country, the applicant then has six months within which to file corresponding applications in other countries, claiming the filing date of the first country, thus giving him priority over any conflicting applications filed in the intervening period. Of course, if you decide as a result of the international searches not to proceed with the mark you simply withdraw your home country application.

This initial six-month period can be extremely useful because it 'freezes' the position internationally and gives the applicant time to complete the further searches, negotiate with the owners of any potentially conflicting prior marks and check whether apparently conflicting marks have in fact been used. (In many countries registrations can be cancelled on the ground of five years' non-use.)

It is most unusual for international availability searches not to locate potential problems, at least in one or two countries. This is especially true of searches in more crowded product or service categories. However, it is often possible to overcome such problems by negotiating with the owner of the conflicting mark, who may agree to restrict use of his mark to particular goods or services. Alternatively, it may be that the owner of the prior mark has lost interest and is prepared to assign his registration for a cash payment.

The actual registration procedure differs quite considerably from country to country and ranges from a simple deposit system, such as in France and Italy, to a system involving thorough examination, both as to inherent registrability and conflict with prior marks, as in the UK and USA.

For the purposes of trade mark registration, goods and services are divided into 42 classes known as the International Classification of Goods and Services. In the UK a separate application must be filed in each class for which protection is required, specifying the goods or services in that class for which the mark is to be used, though under the proposed new Act multi-class applications will be possible. Once the application has been filed, a filing receipt is issued by the Trade Marks Registry confirming the application date and number. This date is important because any rights eventually granted by registration are backdated to the original application date.

In the UK, approximately six months to a year after the application is filed it will be examined by the Registrar of Trade Marks to see whether the mark qualifies for registration (ie the Registrar checks that it is distinctive, that it is not merely descriptive and also that it is not deceptive etc.). The Registrar also checks that it does not conflict with existing registrations or applications. If objections are raised on any of these grounds it is often possible to overcome them by arguing the case with the Registry, or by submitting evidence to show that the mark has been used in the UK over a number of years prior to the date of application. Objections can sometimes also be overcome by amending details of the goods or services covered by the application or by negotiating with the owners of conflicting prior marks.

Once the application has been accepted for registration in the UK it is advertised in the Trade Marks Journal so that any interested third parties can oppose it. Provided no oppositions are filed, the application then proceeds to registration. For a reasonably straight-forward application in the UK, the registration procedure is likely to take approximately a year and a half to complete. Elsewhere, registration can take from six months to three years, or even longer in exceptional cases.

The cost of obtaining a trade mark registration in the UK averages about £500 to £600 provided no serious problems are encountered, and this sum covers official fees as well as the charges of a trade mark agent. The cost in other countries ranges from £300 to £2,000 or even more. Trade mark protection is therefore relatively inexpensive to obtain and the rights conferred are powerful and extensive. However, when a mark is protected in two or three classes; when a series of marks needs to be protected to cover a brand (eg. the name itself plus a distinctive logo or device); and when a number of countries are involved, the costs of securing strong international protection for a brand can be substantial. An important international brand may well be protected by dozens or even hundreds of individual trade mark registrations.

THE LIFE OF A TRADE MARK

In the UK a trade mark registration lasts for seven years from the date of the original application and can then be renewed for further periods of 14 years. The duration of overseas registrations varies from country to country but in many cases it is ten years, the same as under the proposed UK Act. However, even if a registration has been renewed, in most countries it can be cancelled on the grounds of non-use – at the instigation of an interested third party – usually after five years. In some countries it is necessary to prove that a mark is being used before the registration will be renewed. In every country, a registration may be renewed indefinitely – unlike other forms of intellectual property such as patents and copyright, trade marks have potentially an unlimited life provided they are properly used, properly renewed and otherwise cared for – eg, guarded against infringement and counterfeiting.

LICENSING A TRADE MARK

Licensing of trade marks occurs where the trade mark owner allows others to use his marks, often in return for a royalty payment or for other consideration. UK trade mark law permits licensing, subject to certain conditions, and the licensee can be recorded in the register of trade marks as a 'registered user'. Use of a mark by a registered user is deemed to be use of the mark by the owner. However, the Registrar of Trade Marks will not allow a licensee to be registered as a registered user unless he is satisfied that the licensee's use of the trade mark is controlled by the registered proprietor, either through being a subsidiary company or by a licence agreement. In particular, the registered proprietor is required to be able to control the quality of the goods sold under the trade mark so that the function of the mark as providing an indication of origin is not destroyed. (Under the proposed new Act the Registrar of Trade Marks will take a less active rôle in ensuring that the principles of ownership and control are maintained; the onus will then be on the trade mark owner to ensure that his licensing arrangements protect his proprietorship of the trade mark.)

Trade mark licensing is of particular importance to the fast-growing franchising industry. Trade mark licenses are at the heart of most franchise systems as it is the right to use the franchisor's mark which is perhaps the most important element in the total package which the franchisee acquires.

Although the concept of licensing of trade marks is recognized in many countries, it is important for a trade mark owner to comply with any local requirements to ensure that his registration is not invalidated. In particular, it is common for licensees to come to regard the mark as really 'theirs' and not the licensor's and it may be particularly important to ensure that this does not in fact come to be the case.

TRADE MARK ASSIGNMENTS

In the UK the transfer of ownership of a trade mark registration can take place with or without the goodwill of the business in the goods or services for which the mark is registered. An assignment has to be executed by the assignor and an application filed at the Trade Marks Registry in order to have the transfer of ownership recorded on the register. An unregistered trade mark may also be assigned but usually only with the goodwill of the business.

Failure to record an assignment on the Trade Marks Register can lead to problems and delays if the new owner wishes to sue for trade mark infringement. It is therefore important to take appropriate steps to have assignments recorded as soon as possible.

OTHER TYPES OF INTELLECTUAL PROPERTY

Intellectual property is the collective term for trade marks, patents, copyright and designs. Each of these rights is quite different even though the terms may sometimes, mistakenly, be used interchangeably.

Patents

Patents protect new inventions by providing the inventor with a statutory monopoly in his invention for a set period of time. In the UK this is 20 years. Patents are designed to promote innovation by giving the inventor an opportunity of exploiting his invention before it is made available for general use.

To qualify for patent protection an invention must be novel; it must also involve a new inventive step and *it must not be obvious.*

The monopoly granted can relate either to the product itself or to the process by which it has been made. Because patents only last for a specific term, manufacturers often attempt to use the trade mark under which the patented product is marketed as a means of securing market share and preventing the onslaught of competitive products once the patent expires.

A patent is infringed by the unauthorized making, selling, importing or use of the patented product or by unauthorized use of the patented process; it is not necessary to prove that there has been deliberate copying.

Copyright

Copyright, which in the UK is governed by the Copyright, Designs and Patents Act 1988, is a property right which arises automatically in new literary, dramatic, musical or artistic works, sound recordings, films, broadcasts and computer programs, and in the typographical arrangement of published editions. Copyright is usually owned by the author of the work and, depending on its nature, lasts either for 50 years after the author's death or 50 years from when it was made.

There are no registration requirements – in other words, copyright exists once a new work is created, though the owner of copyright needs to retain all original drawings, proofs and roughs so as to be able to prove title. It is also sensible to keep such material where multi-authored works are involved or when an agent, sub-contractor or someone in employment produces copyright material; it may be necessary to define who owns the copyright – it may by no means be clear.

The copyright owner has the exclusive right to reproduce the work and this is infringed by the unauthorized reproduction of the work by others. However, the defendant must have actually copied the work – if he came up with it independently then there is no infringement. Labels, logos and a product's general 'get-up' can be the subject of copyright in addition to any trade mark or common law rights which may exist.

Designs

A design, which relates to the physical appearance of an article, is protected in the UK by the Registered Designs Act 1949, as amended by the Copyright, Designs and Patents Act 1988, for periods of 15 or 25 years depending on the nature of the product and its function. Designs will seldom have any significant bearing on the protection of brands except in the case of particular container shapes such as the Coca-Cola bottle.

CONCLUSION

Brand and trade marks are frequently seen as being hazy and insubstantial pieces of property. In fact, the rights attaching to them can be very powerful indeed and every major country in the world has well-developed systems for the protection of these rights.

The cost of establishing these rights is also comparatively modest, particularly when compared with the cost of establishing and maintaining brands and even with the cost of patenting.

Perhaps most importantly, trade marks do not have a finite life. Provided the trade mark owner maintains and renews his trade marks they can go on indefinitely and gain in value and power with investment and exposure in the market place. They are therefore fundamentally different from patents and other forms of intellectual property.

But trade marks are also relatively complex, and care must be taken in their creation and management. It is all too easy, for example, to adopt a new mark with only very narrow protection, or with other legal defects, or which is strictly limited in its geographical scope. Alternatively, it is easy for a mark to be damaged by poor brand or trade mark management or by adopting a too *laissez-faire* attitude towards, for example, the precise way in which the mark is used, or towards the combating of counterfeiting.

Chapter 13

BRAND ACCOUNTING

Martin Moorhouse

'Brand valuation . . . is a unique management tool . . . [aiding] brand planning and the determination of advertising and marketing strategies.'

'This statement from Ranks Hovis McDougall's "defence document" on brand valuation (issued 16 January, 1989) is of far greater significance than any other utterance or action concerned with the large but fundamentally misguided debate around brand accounting over the past 12 months.'

Marketing Accounting Research Centre, Cranfield School of Management, May 1989.

Traditionally, management accounting has been separated from financial accounting. One system has been concerned with providing the base data for decision-making and for reviewing the results of these decisions, the other with reporting those results to the world at large. While each system must to some degree reflect the other (for it is in nobody's interest for the figures to tell different stories) it is management information that must lead the way. Brand accounting therefore does not exist in its own right but is the method by which management assesses the financial implications of brand management.

WHY ACCOUNT FOR BRANDS?

Long-term versus short-term

Marketing decisions do not have merely a short-term influence. The implications of today's decisions may stay with a company or a brand for many years as marketing decisions are not susceptible to frequent review and once made may be difficult and expensive to change. They are therefore constantly reinforced through advertising or pack designs and brands in particular, once built, need continual support as users need to be reminded of their special nature and discouraged from trying the competition. This year's marketing initiatives affect not only this year's sales but next year's and the year after's. Market share, once lost, is particularly difficult to claw back.

Yet no company can base all its decisions on the long term: marketeers may promise jam tomorrow but what about this year's profit? Reducing advertising is an easy way to make short-term profits but unless we understand how this affects the future how can we make a decision about whether to advertise this year and to what extent? Many brands can survive lean years of support and still maintain their position, others cannot. How can we make such decisions correctly if our management systems do not help by providing us with the information we need?

Capital versus revenue

Most companies have procedures for evaluating capital expenditure proposals, criteria as to minimum acceptable rates of return and yet more criteria for judging the ultimate success or otherwise of this expenditure. The traditional view of what constitutes capital (something you can kick) makes it easy for everyone to understand what it is. When times are hard capital budgets can be cut, just like anything else, or the criteria can be changed so that only fast-payback or high-yielding projects are approved. But as capital expenditure does not directly hit the profit and loss account the problems of short- and long-term thinking are less acute.

Established guidelines and well-practised systems ensure that most projects are accurately costed and benefits quantified. Discounted cash flow (DCF) techniques are relatively easy to apply and the results readily understood. Why should marketing expenditure be any different, particularly when the implications of such expenditure are by no means less profound?

Advertising expenditure is often split between *theme* and *scheme* advertising. Theme advertising is designed to build a brand over time, to place the brand at the forefront of customers' minds and keep it there. Thus it has many attributes of capital expenditure where the benefits flow through in years to come. Scheme advertising is designed to boost short-term sales, to sell the product today and, as such, can clearly be considered as revenue. Life is, however, never simple, and although scheme advertising may have a primary aim it also has some impact on the longer term and hence some capital attributes. Moreover, theme advertising might equally be expected to help boost sales in the short term.

A similar split can be identified between 'brand *maintenance* expenditure' (which can be defined as the ongoing level of support needed to maintain the brand's position in the market) and 'brand *development* expenditure' (expenditure to improve the brand's position in the market or to establish it in new markets).

Financial accounting prudence sensibly requires us to write off all marketing expenditure as incurred. Thus our capital expenditure on brand-building becomes revenue and directly impacts on our results in the year we incur it, whenever the benefit might be expected to arise. Thus, unless we use brand accounting techniques to evaluate the capital element, there is a danger that short-term requirements may impact adversely on the brand strategy needed for the future.

Capital appraisal

By its very nature marketing is a less exact science than production. Yet, as we have seen, the impact of marketing decisions of a capital nature is greater on current profitability than those concerned with investment in tangible assets. It is therefore critically important that we have accounting systems that enable us to identify where to direct expenditure, evaluate where the highest return can be achieved for a given cost and identify the level of expenditure that will produce the greatest return both now and in the future.

Marketeers have long boasted of the quality of their modelling and analysis techniques yet accountants have found it difficult, often impossible, to translate 'marketspeak' into hard financial data. The accountants have, to date, therefore largely failed in their duty to present usable financial management information in the marketing and branding area. (It should, however, be said in our defence that marketeers have often gone out of their way to shield the marketing process from our prying eyes.)

BRAND ACCOUNTING – THE PROBLEM

Let us take as a simple example an imaginary company that produces three different types of products at two factories and operates a single distribution network. All three product types are sold to the same customers. Management accounts might be organized on a factory basis as shown in the table on page 148. Once it is explained that Factory 1 is altogether newer, more capital-intensive and more efficient all is clear. However, though this analysis may help us run and control our factories better (which should by no means be decried) it will not provide much help with product profitability profiles.

If we now turn to the three product categories we can produce the same information but in a very different way. In this example Product A comprises two different but very similar versions of the same product – one a brand, the second a retailer's own brand equivalent. Product B is purely branded, while Product C is exclusively an own-label product for a retailer. Our new simplified management accounts might show:

	Product	Factory 1 (£000)	Factory 2 (£000)	Total (£000)
Sales	A	2000	1500	3500
	B	1800	–	1800
	C	–	2200	2200
		3800	3700	7500
Contribution	A	700	300	1000
	B	600	–	600
	C	–	400	400
		1300	700	2000
Factory fixed overheads		(400)	(200)	(600)
Factory contribution		900	500	1400
Distribution				(200)
Selling and admin.				(200)
Marketing				(600)
Net profit				400
Capital employed		3000	1000	4000
Factory return on capital employed		30%	50%	35%
Factory return on sales		24%	14%	19%

	Product A	Product B	Product C	Total (£000)
Sales Branded	3000	1800	–	4800
Non-branded	500	–	2200	2700
	3500	1800	2200	7500
Contribution	1000	600	400	2000
Marketing	(100)	(500)	–	(600)
	900	100	400	1400
Factory fixed overheads	(280)	(180)	(140)	(600)
Product contribution	620	(80)	260	800
Distribution				(200)
Selling and admin.				(200)
Net profit				400
Capital employed	2100	1400	500	4000

Suddenly we find that Product B is making a loss and the marketing department will of course be called to account for its actions, and an emergency rectification plan will be demanded. Yet this analysis does not even begin to ask the right questions, let alone provide the answers.

Let us look more closely at what is happening with Product A. Closer examination reveals the following:

	Branded (£000)	Non-branded (£000)	Total (£000)
Gross sales	4150	850	5000
Discounts	(1150)	(350)	(1500)
Net sales	3000	500	3500
Direct costs	(2075)	(425)	(2500)
Contribution	925	75	1000
Marketing	(100)	–	–
Factory fixed overheads	(230)	(50)	(280)
	595	25	620

There is, of course, nothing new in this analysis; indeed, the production of non-branded goods, usually at lower margins, to help absorb overheads is commonplace. One might question the allocation of direct costs and fixed overheads between branded and non-branded products (we will discuss this later). What is clear is that any increase in branded volume would produce substantial rewards if margins could be maintained. The question is therefore one of the marginal impact of additional marketing expenditure.

Let us now turn to Product B, where the situation becomes more complicated:

Historic Year before last (£000)	Last year (£000)		Current year (Actual) (£000)	Next year (Budget) (£000)	Following year (Plan) (£000)
2040	1950	Sales	1800	2400	3200
(1360)	(1300)	Direct costs	(1200)	(1600)	(2100)
680	650	Contribution	600	800	1100
(180)	(180)	Factory fixed overheads	(180)	(190)	(200)
500	470		420	610	900
(100)	(50)	Scheme advertising	(100)	(100)	(100)
400	420		320	510	800
–	–	Theme advertising	(400)	(50)	(50)
400	420	Brand contribution	(80)	460	750

This is a familiar scenario: over the past few years sales have fallen slowly but steadily; profits, however, have been maintained by reductions in marketing expenditure. But this cannot go on for long – this year a considerable investment in marketing is needed to boost sales and future profitability and the result is a substantial loss in the current year. This situation is surely a much more common problem than most companies would care to admit. It is also the area where traditional accounting fails us. This failure manifests itself in at least three ways:

- It fails to identify the impact (on the capital value of our brand) of savings made through advertising cuts

- It records a loss in one year when the funds expended in that year are forecast to benefit at least the two following years, ie it fails to distinguish between brand maintenance and brand development expenditure

- It does not provide a means of monitoring the impact of our marketing expenditure over the coming years either on profits or capital values, ie it does not provide financial criteria with which to judge the marketing function

THE BRANDS RE-EXAMINED

The object of brand accounting is to provide information for decision-making rather than to pre-empt those decisions. It should provide a financial framework to assess the effects and implications of marketing decisions and hence the performance of the marketing department.

Let us assume that Product B has an ongoing annual requirement of some £150k of marketing expenditure in order to maintain its position in the market and to support a price premium over its competitors. We can then analyse its true profits as follows:

Year before last (£000)	Last year (£000)		Current year (£000)	Next year (£000)	Following year (£000)
350	320	True brand contribution	270	460	750
50	100	Variation of maintenance expenditure	(350)	–	–
400	420	Reported brand contribution	(80)	460	750

While this analysis gives us a different perspective of profit it says little about the performance of the marketing function and the impact of marketing decisions on brand worth – for this we must turn to a capital analysis. This can be done using DCF techniques, but here the analysis is based on the methodology deveoped by Interbrand and Ranks Hovis McDougall and described earlier in this book. This method produces equally valuable results and also provides the key to a non-financial appraisal of the success of marketing policies and decisions.

Year before last (£000)	Last year (£000)		Current year (£000)	Next year (£000)	Following year (£000)
		Reported brand contribution:			
380	400	Last year	420	(80)	460
400	420	This year	(80)	460	750
420	(80)	Next year (expected)	460	750	800
400	245	Average (A)	265	375	670
		Brand score (actual/expected)			
55	45		60	65	70
5.8	4.2	Derived multiplier (B)	6.5	7.3	7.9
2320	1030	Capital value (A×B)	1720	2740	5290

Brand contribution

The period over which the brand contribution should be analysed in order to achieve an average level of profitability is largely a matter of choice. One year is certainly not enough as one-off expenditure or windfall profits can easily distort the picture. Cash flows can of course be substituted for contribution if this is a more appropriate measure within the reporting requirements of the company, or if there are significant variations between cash and contribution.

Brand score

The brand strength score should be measured regularly, probably at the end of each year, and provides an excellent measure of the success or otherwise of the company's marketing. Each brand can be examined independently of the marketing department concerned and achievement targets can be set for each brand during the budget process or as part of the longer-term marketing or overall strategic plan. Thus a performance measurement is introduced for the marketing function and at the same time 'triggers' can be set in place to provoke future management decisions. With careful control this system can be used to identify those brands that should not receive further support as well as those that will benefit most from either one-off or sustained injections of expenditure.

For example, a brand with a strength score of, say, 35–50 is a problem brand as it usually commands only a poor second (or lower) place in its national market. Normally such brands do not command premium prices and are unlikely to generate sufficiently stable volumes to give 'long run' production benefits.

In the longer term, brands normally cannot be allowed to languish in this twilight zone and must either be moved up or moved out – a classic example for the prioritization of expenditure. A good marketing department will already know all this, but brand accounting gives us that extra dimension to judge, on a regular basis, the success or otherwise of the long-term marketing plan using hard financial criteria. (For illustrative purposes, the brand scores used in my example are much more volatile than one would expect in a real situation.)

Derived multiple

The multiplier is derived directly from the brand score using the Interbrand 'S' curve. In our example the top multiplier (ie that applied to a notional perfect brand with a brand score of 100) is taken at 10 for reasons of convenience only. Again for simplicity, a pre-tax pre-central expenses profit figure has been used though this is not ideal and would not normally be acceptable for a true capital value approach.

The principal function of the multiplier is to convert the largely non-financial assessment of the brand (the brand strength score) into a hard financial number.

Capital value

The capital value is a function of two variables: brand strength and brand profitability. Thus while, in the short term, profitability may be reduced by, for example, an international launch, the capital value may be maintained or even increased by the uplift in brand strength resulting from increased internationality. Once the international launch has been successfully achieved, and profits begin to flow, a further increase in value results – the proof of success. Failure too can be recognized as there will be no long-term increase in brand strength and probably, too, no increase in profitability; indeed there may even be a decrease.

PROBLEMS

As with all reporting systems, brand accounting is not without its problems. Three key problem areas are the allocation of direct costs, the allocation of fixed overheads and the impact of external factors.

Direct costs

Our analysis of Product A apportioned direct costs *pro rata* to gross sales (which equates to volume) between branded and non-branded production. Within the generalized area of direct costs there will be, however, some premium costs such as overtime. The allocation of these premium costs can have a significant influence on the resulting analysis – the marginal cost of the last batch off the production line may in fact be close to net sales value. Brand accounting, if it is to be valuable, requires that these costs are identified and allocated but so too does any other serious profit analysis. Most accountants have at some time encountered the situation where one product, always considered to be profitable, was in fact found not to be profitable when the full costs of production or distribution were identified. There is no easy answer to this problem; we can only suggest meticulous analysis.

Allocation of overheads

The question of overhead allocation remains as important in brand accounting as in any other area of management accounting. In order to identify the true level of brand profitability overheads must be allocated fairly between branded and non-branded production. Yet again, this area is one which can lead to serious profit miscalculations. The allocation of overheads is frequently a highly subjective exercise yet one that creates an impression of objectivity. Often, accounting systems tackle the direct cost analysis in enormous detail and then present an apparently highly accurate picture of direct contribution on a product-by-product basis then, in one line, throw all the benefit away with the words 'allocation of fixed overheads *pro rata* to . . .'.

The real value of a brand to its owner may well lie in the level and stability of demand rather than in premium pricing. Thus, for example, shorter non-branded production runs may need to be allocated proportionately higher overheads (due, for example, to increased set-up times) if the true level of brand profitability is to be established and measured. Once again, there is no easy answer to a problem that besets all management accounting systems. Again, we can only suggest meticulous analysis and much hard work.

Perhaps, once the true allocations of overheads and direct costs are made it may be that in Product A our non-branded production does not in fact cover overheads, and that every effort should be made to increase branded output and reduce non-branded. Perhaps by seeking to fill the factory by producing own-label brands, our company is actually reducing its profit, its brand value and even, possibly, its shareholder value.

External factors

A main focus of management accounting is the measurement of internal performance against internally controllable factors. However, many functions, for example sales, do not fall easily into this analysis as competitive actions and general economic trends play their part in determining values and volumes. Brand accounting techniques should help us to identify and, more importantly, quantify the impact of external factors on company sales, as well as to analyse the impact of competitive actions. After all, we can use brand accounting techniques to quantify, analyse and even predict our competitors' performance too.

Perhaps the most frequently voiced criticism of brand valuation (and hence of brand accounting) is its subjectivity. Yet is it any more subjective that the arbitrary allocation of overheads? Brand valuation (like all other valuations) must, by its nature, involve some degree of subjectivity and, while it is important that this is recognized, it does not reduce brand accounting's value as a decision-making tool. Surely brand accounting is a vast improvement on the suggested alternative of doing nothing or, alternatively, of relying on pure guesswork? The London Business School, in its attack on brands on the balance sheet, accepted this fact when it stated: 'it [brand valuation] may aid internal disclosure and visibility and it may help both brand managers and senior management to gain a much deeper understanding of their brands and take a long-term view of the development and exploitation of brand equity'.

IN SUMMARY

My own company, Ranks Hovis McDougall, did not immediately appreciate when undertaking a brand valuation the impact the valuation might have in the areas of brand management, brand strategy and, importantly, brand accounting. Indeed, it was only when we used the brand profitability figures for the purposes of brand valuation that the true power of this type of brand accounting became apparent to us.

Nonetheless, we are confident that this new tool will be of substantial and continued benefit and might in time change beyond recognition the face of brand management.

Chapter 14

MANAGING THE BRAND MANAGER

Gil McWilliam

Many years ago, during an interview for a job as a brand manager, I was asked what I thought were the characteristics of a successful brand manager. Armed only with the knowledge gained from reading two books on marketing, I smartly answered that brand managers, I felt, had to be 'two-faced'. Ignoring the somewhat startled look on the face of the group brand manager interviewing me, I ploughed on, offering by way of explanation that 'like the god Janus – who looked both backwards and forwards and from whom the month of January receives its name – the brand manager is required to look in two directions simultaneously; he has to look both outwards to the buying public, and inwards to the organization, in order to match the needs of the two'. I didn't get the job, but two decades later I still believe that successful brand management is about being two-faced – in the way that Janus understood it.

The problem as I now see it, is *not* that brand managers don't know that this is what the job requires them to do – any brand manager worth his salt will have in his mind some definition of marketing which centres around 'matching' the needs of the customers with the needs and resources of the organization. They therefore understand that the job entails examining the attitudes, behaviour and needs of the buying public, and also the resources of the company. Rather it's just that often they don't appear to do it very well.

The problem seems to be that they don't know how to look properly (in either direction), and they don't know what to do with what they see. And if this is a problem with marketing managers in general, then it is an even greater problem for brand managers, because of the inherent complexity of what they have to manage, and the importance which brands increasingly have for their companies.

It would be a strange (and not very alert) brand manager who has not heard about the financial values which are being placed on brands; their appearance as intangible assets on the balance sheet; and in consequence their financial importance to companies. Since I frequently find myself in the position of teaching brand managers, I can also testify that most of them understand that 'consumers buy brands not products'. They can also give a creditable stab at discriminating between products and brands, and also have some understanding of terms such as 'brand values', 'emotional values', 'beliefs about quality', and 'brand personalities'. In short, brand managers understand that brands are complex entities and that they are important and valuable to both company and consumer. What they are not very clear about is why this is the case. Knowing that brands are important is to see only part of the story – understanding why, and what role they play, both inside and outside the company, is the first vital step in developing a framework in which to see brands, and their role within the organization, more clearly.

THE BIGGER PICTURE – THE ROLE OF BRANDS IN CONSUMER LIFE

There is a good deal of research which indicates that there are four broad reasons why consumers often prefer to buy brands rather than mere products. They are as follows.

An identifying device

At its very simplest, a brand is a means of identifying one product offering from a similar product offering. As with livestock, a brand enables the buyer to spot 'the owner' and exercise choice between competing offerings. Because of what we know about the psychology of names and naming, we know that many buyers find it easier to remember names rather than numbers and, more importantly, will read *meanings* and *form associations* based on the name itself, or indeed on the fact that the product has a name at all.

But branding is more than just a naming device, and consumers place greater value on brand names than just having a name suggests.

A guarantee of consistent quality

One reason consumers buy brands is as a way of guaranteeing that if they buy the same brand from one week or one year to the next, they can be 99.9 per cent sure that what they get this time will be of the same quality as what they got last time.

A shorthand

Brands and brand names often act as a shorthand for a compendium of product attributes and competitive positioning. For the most part, consumers do not agonize over each purchase in the supermarket;

indeed, they barely give it a second's thought. Just as they do not spend hours processing all of a person's features or physical attributes, but instantly recognize that person, not as a unique bundle of attributes, which they are, but as a name, so too do they recognize brands.

A means of self-expression

There is a good deal of evidence to suggest that *some* brands are bought not for what they say about the purchase, but for what they say about the purchaser. This is particularly true for products which are highly conspicuous (clothes, watches, cameras) or which are consumed socially (alcohol, cigarettes). But it also seems to be true for some products which only the owner/user knows about (ingredients in cooking such as Oxo) or which they would be unlikely to show or discuss (eg detergents and washing powder). Consumers may buy a brand, therefore, because that brand will convey something about themselves to others: either how they perceive themselves to be, or how they would like others to think they are.

BRANDS AS RISK-REDUCERS

Whether consumers buy brands for their consistency of product functioning (taste, strength, reliability) or whether they buy them as a means of expressing their own personalities, there is always a sense in which they do so in order to reduce any risk that the product will not perform the roles they wish it to. Buying a brand reduces the risk of failure. If I buy Heinz baked beans I know in advance what the taste will be like, and I am unlikely to be disappointed in my expectation. If I buy a Gucci handbag I know in advance that people will recognize me as someone with expensive and classic tastes. Given a need for certainty (for taste or for a particular expressed self-image) then, the brands I buy must fulfil those needs. If no-one had ever heard of Gucci then there would be little point in spending all that money. If beans varied from one tin to another, there would be little point in always buying Heinz.

The ability of the brand to fulfil my needs of reducing risk in both physical and psycho-social contexts is a function of the brand's *consistency* in both product and image terms over a long period of time – sufficient time for me to develop liking and trust in the consistent delivery of physical or psychological benefits, and sufficient time for the imagery to be developed, shared and understood by my peers. Without this consistency over time there is no risk reduction for me and each purchase would seem as risky as the first.

The idea of brands as risk-reducers is not new, but it is very important. Most consumers are risk-averse. This fact is not only important in terms of the way in which consumers are addressed – through advertising for example – it has significant implications for the way in which brands are managed internally.

CONSISTENCY OR CHANGE?

The actions of many brand managers seem calculated to *increase* the risk in a purchase, not reduce it. In their rush to alter the formulation slightly, or alter the packaging and imagery, they often seem intent on destroying any sense of consistency. It is easy to see why this is the case given the status of the average brand manager within many fast-moving-consumer-goods companies. Brand management (especially single-line brand management) is not a job to aspire to, it is a staging post on the way upwards to other jobs (group brand manager, senior brand manager, marketing director, group marketing director etc.). Indeed it is often one of the jobs given to the younger members of the marketing team. If they are to make their mark within the average two-year period served on any one brand, then they have to do something to signal their presence: 'I was the one who introduced the new flavours,' has a much better ring to it than 'I didn't dare change a thing'.

In fairness, their room for manoeuvre is relatively restricted on an established brand – any major changes would more often than not involve decision-making at senior levels, and many of the traditional marketing decision areas are fixed (eg distribution and pricing policies). But even relatively junior brand managers can and do re-brief promotions, packaging and advertising agencies, and change product formulations.

The problem with using brand management as a system of apprenticeship is that not only may any sense of consistency of decision-making be lost with the ebb and flow of managers, but the consequences which flow from their decisions are never experienced by their initiators. By the time they have evaluated the current packaging, briefed a new agency, received and reviewed the various options, tested several, agreed a winner, informed the sales force, briefed printing and production, staged an announcement in the trade press, and got the product on the shelves, it is time to be moving on to the next brand in the brand seniority hierarchy.

Brand management is not a good training ground as it is currently practised, since managers move before any learning (in the sense of feedback) can take place. Moreover, new brand managers cannot wait for the results of their predecessors' decisions before they too must begin to carve their own initials on the brand.

Consistency over time demands consistency of brand personnel. In Matsushita Electric in Japan, product managers stay in the same job for an average 14 years – a sense of genuine responsibility and ownership is inescapable. The need for consistency also demands managers who are rather calm and mature in their approach to their brands, and their role in the company. It requires someone who does not need to dash down to the advertising agency in London every five minutes for an injection of glamour; who does not feel bored trying to understand the latest set of figures about product or account profitability; who is meticulous in updating the 'Guard Book' which contains details of every promotional activity, every advertising campaign, every packaging change over time, so that a sense of continuity is ensured; and one who will find time to study the macro environment and the greater forces driving his brand and informing his consumers' decision-making.

This is not very exciting work. It is frequently tedious, and it is for those managers who do not feel the need for instant gratification by seeing immediately the results of their labours. It is, however, the stuff of brand management and can only succeed when senior brand managers recognize that this is what is required and set an example. This will only happen when deeper and wider strategic thought and analysis are valued and rewarded in the company. If dashing about and fiddling with the packaging (activities often erroneously described as 'fire fighting', or even 'brand building') is accepted as the norm and moreover seen as useful *training* (for what – more fire fighting?), then so-called 'fire fighting' will always be the norm.

All graduate recruits to Matsushita Electric undergo an initial seven-month training programme. The first three weeks comprise 'general education' courses – a major component of which is understanding the corporate philosophy in its operation and relation to its outside world. The next three *months* are spent with regional retailers who deal mainly with Matsushita goods. The aim here is to allow each employee to experience selling, servicing and actual customer contact. As a side benefit, Matsushita develops a close working relationship with shop managers. The final three months are spent in a factory, on a production line. This experience is expected to 'sensitize the employee to the psychology of workers, cost consciousness, safety, and the mechanics of material handling and purchasing'.

BRANDING FOR BRANDING'S SAKE

What we seem to be witnessing with the current practice of brand management is another form of marketing myopia – where many companies now concentrate so much on the *activity* of marketing, they have forgotten why they are doing it in the first place.

But it is not just negligent brand management or even the brand management structure which is to blame. These are simply symptoms of a much greater failure on the part of many brand owners: a failure to realize why they are branding in the first place; what role it plays in the lives of their consumers, and what role it plays in the life of the company.

Indeed, it may well be because they have forgotten to ask why they are engaging in this costly exercise of branding, that manufacturers in particular have ended up in the threatened position they are in, vis à vis retailer brands. And branding is costly. McKinsey consultant Ian Davis has estimated (in his article *Does Branding Pay?*, Admap, 1986) that 23 per cent of the costs of a large branded foods manufacturer were directly attributable to its branding approach. Much more alarming was his finding that:

> 'In themselves these high costs might not have mattered had they been justified in terms of extra consumer value. In fact, however, consumers could not perceive the quality difference between most of the company's brands and other cheaper products, including retailers' own brands.'

Branding is all too often seen as an end in itself and not, as it was originally intended, a means to an end. It is almost as if the very fact of having brand managers had locked companies into having brands, without questioning what the role of a brand is and whether it is still appropriate to, and robust enough for, the task.

But appreciating the complexity of consumer decision-making, and the role of branding in the lives of consumers, is still only half the story. Indeed it is also the easiest part to get right. Millions of pounds are spent annually in sophisticated market research and analysis to enable brand managers to appreciate the psychological, sociological, even anthropological, needs of their buyers. But Janus The Brand Manager has to look internally as well as externally, and it is the internal understanding which seems to be most elusive.

LOOKING INTERNALLY

In his book *Brand Management: Planning and Control* (Macmillan Press Ltd, 1981), J R Bureau outlined four responsibilities for the brand manager. He should, he said, be a:

- Market analyst
- Planner
- Co-ordinator
- Controller

Of the co-ordinating function, Bureau wrote:

> Once the plan has been agreed, logic dictates that the plan-maker should be given the responsibility for its enactment. Having no direct authority over those individuals or departments who will need to take action in order to meet the plan's requirements, the brand manager will need to work through persuasion and co-ordination if his plan is to be implemented. If his roles as market analyst and marketing planner make the greatest demands on his intellectual and creative abilities, the brand manager's role as co-ordinator will make the greatest demand on his capacity for leadership and motivation. He will be spurred in this capacity by the thought that nobody within the organisation will care more than he does that the marketing goals are achieved, and that no one in the organisation is likely to be as well informed as he is as to the totality of the problems to be overcome before such goals are attained.

There is a sense in which some of this is, of course, true. I would add however, that a 'capacity for leadership and motivation' is not only a rare commodity, within *any* organization, it is also one which comes with age, maturity and experience. It is not one which is readily associated with 25-year-old brand managers. Moreover, if such a brand manager is 'spurred' by the thought that within the organization nobody will 'care more than he does that the marketing goals are achieved' nor be 'as well informed as he is as to the totality of the problems to be overcome before such goals are attained', then we have a recipe for internal disaster and not one for leadership and motivation. Such a belief is more often likely to lead to the 'galloping midget' which Hugh Davidson (in *Offensive Marketing: Or How to Make Your Competitors Followers*, Penguin, 1987)) describes:

> He is almost invariably male, twenty-five years old and with four years' experience in marketing. He defines marketing as the 'total business operation' (hardly acknowledging the existence of industrial relations or financial planning). Marketing is the only part of the business that matters and every department exists just to provide a service to it.

If the brand manager is to co-ordinate the internal resources to provide direction and motivation for others so that they too might understand the role and importance of his brand, then he needs to give as much thought to the company's internal audience as to its consumers. He must understand their motivations, their decision processes, what makes them 'tick' just as with consumers. Moreover, he needs to understand that the concerns and motivations of his colleagues within the organization will in all probability be different from his own (but no less valid).

160

Davidson talks about offensive marketing requiring an 'integrated approach' where all departments see themselves as striving towards the same goal (that of relating their work to the needs of the marketplace and to balancing these against the firm's own profit needs). He sees the marketing function as analogous to the orchestral conductor (with the caveat that this may be overtly flattering to the marketing department!):

> What the marketing person and the conductor have in common is a programme whose execution depends on the combined efforts of a number of specialists. In the case of the conductor these are instrumentalists; for the marketers they are copywriters, engineers, operations people, accountants, salesmen and researchers.
>
> Neither the symphony orchestra nor the marketing plan will succeed unless each specialist clearly understands their own role and how it relates to others. Equally, the failure of one specialist to perform effectively, whether they are oboists who miss an entry or operations managers who miss an agreed deadline, can sabotage the whole programme. It follows that, like the conductor, marketers must know their overall objectives, and brief, motivate and co-ordinate their specialists in order to achieve these in an integrated way.

But however right Davidson is, this is still easier to say than to do. It is not enough to tell brand managers that they must go and motivate the production department and persuade them about the pre-eminence of customer-orientation and the righteousness of the marketing philosophy, so that they will deliver the goods at the right time, in the right sequence, and in the right quantities and at the lowest costs. The production managers will, after all, have heard all this before. The issue still remains as to *how* does this 25-year-old brand manager motivate, persuade, and co-ordinate specialists and exercise leadership?

One way is to make sure that the brand manager has a full understanding of retailer and production realities by experiencing them directly. This is what Matsushita tries to do in its initial seven-month training programme for new recruits (instructively, *all* recruits, not just those destined for marketing positions). Another way is to encourage the exercise within the organization of those skills and techniques which the brand manager needs to bring to the analysis of the marketplace. The brand manager needs to engage in *internal*, as well as external, marketing.

The brand manager knows that if he wants customers to part with their money and buy his company's brands he must provide them with the total package of satisfactions that they require. Similarly, if the brand manager wants the accounting department to spend time providing him with the appropriate figures to calculate brand profitability, or the production department to experiment with a different ingredient, or the salesforce to give extra priority to his latest promotion, then he must understand that they are being asked to give up something (time, effort etc.) and they will require some sort of benefit in return. Those benefits can be as esoteric as feedback of the results (to enhance the learning and satisfaction of their job); the possibility of being associated with success; the promise of more accurate information about other issues; the easing of burdens in

Figure 14.1 Systematic differences between R&D and business market research people

Key dimensions	R&D personnel	Business market research personnel
Work environment		
1. Structure	Well defined: • Existence of research tradition • Clearly defined positions	Ill defined: • No real research tradition • Positions less clearly defined
2. Methods	Scientific and codified	Ad hoc and uncodified
3. Data base	Systematic and objective	Unsystematic and largely subjective
4. Work and time pressures	Mostly internal: how long does it take?	Mostly external: how long do we have?
Professional orientation		
5. Operating assumptions	Serendipity	Planning
6. Goals	'New' ideas: Can it be improved?	'Big' ideas: Does it work?
7. Performance criteria	Quality of investigation	Quantity of results
Quality of personnel		
8. Educational background	Ph.D.	Bachelor's or master's degree
9. Experience	Deep and focused	Broad and dispersed
Personal interests		
10. Career objectives	Become venture manager?	Become venture manager?

other areas; or simply a sense of involvement, sharing and teamwork.

Which benefits are appropriate will depend on an understanding of what motivates the brand managers' customers', an understanding of the pressures and constraints inherent in their work; an understanding that their needs are different from the brand manager's; and an appreciation of the psychological and sociological differences inherent in each function. The difference in basic drive and orientation between the functions are very real, and must be appreciated and valued before they can be managed. For example, Burgleman and Sayles (in *Inside Corporation Innovation: Strategy, Structure, and Managerial Skills*, MacMillan Inc., 1986) have shown that there are inherent differences in the motivations, preferred style and behaviour of R&D and business market research personnel within an organization. These are set out in Figure 14.1.

A research study carried out in 1985 at Wharton Business School by A.M.R. Trompenaars, showed that the different functions of marketing, manufacturing, and R&D have different views about their temporal orientations. As Figure 14.2 illustrates, while marketing and R&D personnel saw themselves as being mostly 'future oriented', those in manufacturing were mostly concerned with the present. It is little wonder that the marketing manager experiences difficulty in getting the production manager to focus on his plans for the future, when the latter is (albeit, understandably) so preoccupied with what's happening today.

Furthermore, the brand manager must realize the value of the currency in which he is dealing internally. If he is asking for information in order to co-ordinate and plan better, then he must realize just how expensive the currency of information is. Information is usually costly to gather, time-consuming to transform into an appropriate and useful format, and may also represent status or security – to give up information is often to give away a piece of power or to invite scrutiny and interference. If the information which the brand manager is seeking is valued by its owner in any of these ways, then the *quid pro quo* must have similar value for the exercise to be repeated.

The exchange of information, help and ideas will not be repeated if the brand manager takes all the glory for himself, or undermines the contribution of colleagues. It will not be repeated if the production department, administration department, finance department or sales force does not trust that brand manager for whatever reason.

NOT BY BRAND MANAGER ALONE

All too often the reality is, however, that the young brand manager

Figure 14.2 Time orientation – different business junctions

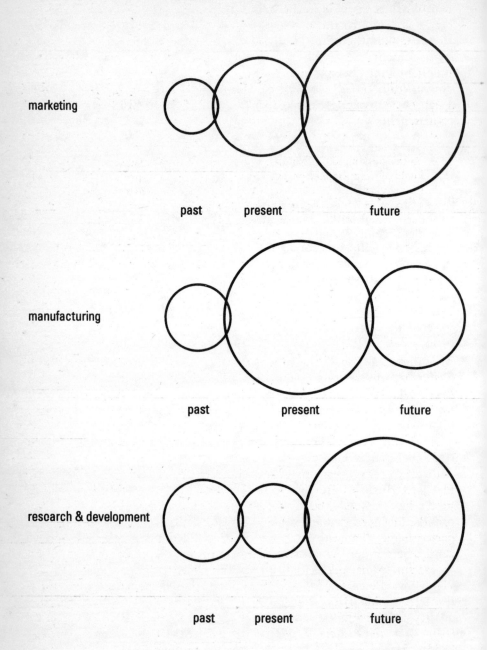

marketing

past   present   future

manufacturing

past   present   future

research & development

past   present   future

erroneously sees himself as single-handedly responsible for the brand's success (although rarely its failure). And the danger is that if we start to place financial values on our brands and show them on the balance sheet, our young brand manager's ego is likely to become even more inflated, not less.

It is therefore vitally important that at the very outset a sense of teamwork is instilled in the branding process. It is also vital that due credit is given to the production, finance and sales departments for the success of the brand. It is too easy to believe that successful brand management is only as a result of clever market analysis and, as Stephen King has pointed out (in *Has Marketing Failed Or Was It Never Really Tried?*, Journal of Marketing Management Vol. 1, No. 1, pp. 1–19), young brand managers are often skilled in contributing to this belief:

> This new breed of bright young men rapidly disguised their lack of experience in the real world, and impressed their managements, with talk of brand switching matrices, multivariate analysis, competitive preference scores, socio-economic segmentation, n-dimensional concept space, day-after-recall and similar gibberish. The Production Manager felt that discussion of the worn bearings on no. 3 machine couldn't really compete; he suffered a considerable loss of prestige and confidence in his own skills and judgments about what sort of products he ought to be making. The R&D Manager went on dreaming of being a Real Scientist and winning a Nobel prize. Departmental barriers were significantly strengthened.

This undervaluing of the other functions' role in successful branding is all the more serious given the plethora of studies which show that time after time brands fail not because the advertising copy was inappropriate, the advertising spend insufficient, or the TV film badly shot/cast/directed, but more often than not because they fail to achieve significant levels of *repeat* purchase – ie the consumers have tried them and found them wanting.

In 1976 Davidson (in *Why Most New Consumer Brands Fail*, Harvard Business Review, 54) confirmed previous Nielsen studies when he analysed 100 new grocery brands in the UK. Of these brands, 50 succeeded and 50 failed. Of the successes, 37 offered better performance than the competition, and 22 of these offered significantly better performance. Of the failures, 40 offered the same or worse functional performance than the competition.

In 1983 Peter Carter and Roz Hatt published findings of their research within Brooke Bond Oxo Ltd into the role which product quality and product functioning play in determining brand loyalty (*How Far Does Advertising Protect The Brand Franchise?*, Admap, 1983). Based on blind and branded monadic in-home testing procedures across three different markets, they convincingly demonstrated that product improvement does improve brand loyalty, and that while advertising affected penetration levels and created positioning expectations, it was actual product functioning which was the ultimate determinant of brand loyalty:

'Unless the branded products are actually superior in a blind product test we should expect any upset in the market equilibrium to cause long-term erosion of the brands.'

The need for the brand manager to be in daily close contact with his production department appears therefore to be vital (although it will certainly be less exciting than a trip to the advertising agency).

There are many reasons why companies will want to value their brands as assets to appear on the balance sheet. But the implications for so doing stretch beyond the obvious ones such as reduced gearing ratios, stock exchange class tests, correcting 'undervaluations' of companies, and improved shareholder communications. While the increase in financial information about the brand will significantly aid the brand manager in his decision-making and sense of accountability, the placing of brands on the balance sheet also places a considerable responsibility on the brand manager's shoulders.

Since brands will be treated as assets, shareholders will increasingly expect to see significant returns on those assets and significant growth in those returns. The brand manager not only will feel pressure from the customers and retailers to 'deliver' the goods, he may also feel it from the shareholders. This is a large burden of responsibility to place on the shoulders of the young manager. But in any event, it is perhaps no longer valid (if it ever were) to persist in encouraging the belief that the brand manager is *singly* responsible for the brand.

If we are seriously to place financial values on our brands, then we must train our brand managers to value those who contribute to the brands. Our brand managers need to see themselves not as supreme and lonely champions doing battle with the production department, the finance department and the distribution department, but first as team members. They need to value and appreciate the differences inherent in the different specializations which they must co-ordinate; and they must earn the trust of the participants in the branding process before they can be granted their leadership spurs. They must learn to market internally as well as externally; to look, Janus-like, in two directions at once; to interpret what is happening outside the organization, so that those inside may *all* participate in the creation of successful and valuable brands.

Chapter 15

THE CORPORATE BRAND

John Murphy and Chuck Brymer

Those brands which are most readily valued are 'freestanding' brands in such areas as foods, drinks and toiletries. Brands in these areas are classic *fmcg* (fast moving consumer goods) brands and are readily transferable assets as companies such as Grand Metropolitan, Unilever and SmithKline Beecham have shown. They therefore have truly independent status and their strength and the cash flows attributable to them can be readily identified.

Branding is, however, used in many ways other than on freestanding, independent brands: an entire company, for example, can be treated as a brand in the sense that a corporate brand can offer to consumers reassurance as to the consistency, quality and value of the products or services provided by the company, or corporate brands can be used in conjunction with product brands. Within companies branding is normally used in three main ways, as follows.

THE MONOLITHIC APPROACH

This approach is used by companies such as Sainsbury, IBM and British Telecom and is characterized by the fact that the corporate name itself is used as the primary communications tool at all levels in the company and at every point of contact which the company has with its various audiences. It may be used therefore in dealings with the stock market, on employee pension plans, in the sponsorship of civic events and on all products and services produced by the company, ranging perhaps (in the case of IBM) from mainframe computers to widgets or (in the case of British Telecom) from communications satellites to novelty telephones.

The 'monolithic' branding approach is most commonly used when the activities of the company and the markets it serves are essentially homogenous. This approach is also often used when the company has developed mainly by organic growth rather than acquisition and when the company has as a result a single internal culture.

Although the use of 'monolithic' to describe such a branding policy is slightly pejorative and perhaps does less than justice to the remarkable successes of companies such as IBM, Hertz, Mercedes-Benz and Sony, it does nonetheless capture one of the features of this branding strategy – its relative inflexibility. Indeed, in order to achieve greater flexibility IBM has recently started to develop sub-brands for important individual products and services – hitherto the exclusive use of the IBM corporate name as the key component in the company's brand communications has prevented the development of separate brand personalities and, it is believed, has left the company open to niche competition from competitors with more targeted brand strategies. Apple, for example, has been remarkably successful in targeting the microcomputer sector of the market and, more recently, the desk-top publishing and computer-aided design sectors. Its more user-friendly brand personality has played a significant role in its success.

THE ENDORSED APPROACH

The endorsed approach is one where the corporate name is used in association with product or divisional brands so that endorsement is provided to the individual product or service yet at the same time each product or service is allowed to develop its own separate personality. For example, Rowntree has, in recent years, increasingly used the Rowntree house brand as a corporate endorsement across its entire range of confectionery products (eg Kit Kat by Rowntree). Many car manufacturers have always boldly endorsed their products so that the corporate name is used in close association with the model name: Model T Ford, Triumph Spitfire and Vauxhall Cavalier are just three examples.

The use of a corporate endorsement as a form of 'umbrella' brand lends security and authority to the individual product brands and, when properly used, this approach can arguably result in the best of all worlds for the brand owner. When United Biscuits, for example, launched their Hob-Nobs brand they did so under the McVitie's umbrella brand. McVitie's is the clear market leader in biscuits in Britain and so this umbrella name lent the product brand enormous credibility with both the consumer and the retail trade. Much of the equity of the McVitie's brand was thus extended to the Hob-Nobs brand yet, over a relatively short period of time, the Hob-Nobs brand has achieved such clear differentiation that the McVitie's umbrella could probably now be withdrawn without any negative effect on the Hob-Nobs brand.

The advantages of the endorsed branding route are that it allows a new brand to develop its own differentiated personality while at the same time permitting positive existing brand equities to be transferred to the new brand. The difficulties of this approach lie primarily in the area of execution. It requires skill and sureness of touch to blend harmoniously two separate brand personalities in a way that allows the development of a new brand personality without confusing or damaging the personality of the house brand.

THE 'SIMPLE' APPROACH

The term 'simple' covers independent, freestanding brands, particularly those described earlier as fmcg brands, and it too probably does less than justice to this branding approach and to the many successful companies that have applied it so skilfully. Under this system the brand is king and is used as the sole means of communicating brand values to the consumer. The corporate brand therefore plays little or no part in communications with the consumer and is used primarily for communications with specialist audiences such as investors.

This branding philosophy is followed by such leading brand owners as Guinness, Mars, Procter and Gamble, and Unilever, all of whom enjoy a formidable reputation for their skills in brand management. Indeed, Mars have refined the strategy further into one of 'power branding', an approach to branding which seeks to create brands which dominate their sectors; set and maintain the benchmarks of quality, price and product specification; and subordinate all other brands to the authority of the market leader.

'Simple', free-standing brands flourish in such markets as confectionery, pet foods, soft drinks and detergents where an individual brand can achieve considerable volume and can thus justify the considerable costs of launch, brand building and brand maintenance. The 'simple' branding approach works less well in more fragmented markets such as mainstream human foods where consumers constantly seek new varieties and flavours and thus where umbrella brands tend to be used. Heinz, Campbell's and Crosse & Blackwell all use endorsed or umbrella brands and there is a wide proliferation of different products sold under each of these brands. In such instances the cost of supporting each flavour variant or group of variants as a separate brand would be prohibitively expensive and endorsed branding is the only realistic strategy.

'Simple', free-standing brands represent in some ways the 'purest' type of brands and such brands (for example Coca-Cola, Mars, Persil and Marmite) are those which are easiest to value, transfer and, in many respects, to manage as they are distinct, unequivocal pieces of property. They are also, however, the most difficult and expensive brands to establish and maintain, particularly in today's markets with escalating media costs and massively increased competition.

PREFERRED BRANDING STRUCTURES

There is no 'correct' way for a company to structure its branding
activities, and even some of those companies cited earlier as
examples of a particular approach in fact adopt in certain instances
a more hybrid approach. McVitie's, for example, is an umbrella
brand within the United Biscuits organization but is not a true
corporate brand which is also used for other audiences – for example
relations with investors – as this is done under the United Biscuits
name. It is also not the only umbrella brand used within United
Biscuits as other brands such as Ross and Youngs are used in other
product areas. Sainsbury is another company which adopts a
'hybrid' approach – though it primarily follows the monolithic
approach it has started to develop closely targeted product brands
under the Sainsbury endorsement; the company is therefore moving
from the monolithic to the endorsed approach. Unilever is yet
another example of a company using a complex branding structure:
even though the detergent brands are primarily free-standing (and
hence 'simple') brands, the Lever house brand is now used, albeit in
a somewhat low-key fashion, as a form of umbrella endorsement.
Thus, in this sector of its business, Unilever is also starting to move
from a simple to an endorsed approach.

Indeed, there is evidence of an increasing trend towards endorsed
branding by companies which previously relied upon either the
monolithic or the simple approach. On the one hand, companies that
have traditionally used a single corporate brand on all their products
and services are finding that this approach affords little opportunity
for the development of closely targeted brand personalities; they are
therefore increasingly seeking to develop product brands or sub-
brands in close association with the main corporate brand in order
to provide differentiation for their products. On the other hand,
companies such as Mars and Unilever, which traditionally have used
a simple branding structure whereby each brand has acted as a
separate profit centre with its own advertising budget and brand
management structure, are finding that the costs of continuing this
policy are becoming so great that there are benefits in 'stretching'
each brand a little and thus using more effectively the equity inherent
in their brands. They are therefore looking at line extensions as well
as at introducing a more generalized corporate endorsement into the
branding structure so that each brand will receive some corporate
support even if, on a year-on-year basis, it does not always receive
its own substantial promotional budget. (Mars, for example, has
recently introduced ice cream and a chocolate drink which bear the
Mars brand name.)

The benefits of a corporate endorsement can also be exploited
through licensing. Porsche, for example, gain a considerable income
from licensing their name for use on products such as sunglasses and

watches. Jaguar has now started to license the Jaguar name in respect of men's fragrances; and both Martini and Cinzano use their corporate names to endorse ranges of clothing.

As the value and importance of brands becomes increasingly recognized, and as the costs and risks of new brand development escalate, brand owners are starting to pay far more attention to the exploitation of their brand assets and are thus seeking novel ways in which to use branding to gain a competitive advantage in the marketplace. The result is that the branding landscape is becoming altogether more varied and lush, and the ways in which branding is used are becoming more complex and imaginative.

Clearly there is no 'ideal' structure for the use of branding within a corporation. In practice, the ways in which companies have adopted branding vary enormously and are constantly changing. 3M, for example, one of the world's most successful and innovative businesses, treat the 3M name, as well as powerful sub-brands such as Scotch, as corporate assets available to all divisions with only a minimum of control. The company organizes itself into small specialist groups and encourages and rewards entrepreneurial activity and innovation. It sets standards as to the precise ways in which the valuable corporate brands are to be used but generally, as long as these standards are met, it is not concerned as to the products upon which they are used. The Scotch brand has, therefore, been used on a whole host of products including adhesive tapes, photographic films and fabric protectors.

Whatever system of branding approach is adopted, however, clear branding rules and strategies need to be established. It must also be recognized that each of the brands, be it at a corporate, divisional or product level, has its own values and attributes which need to be clearly understood and precisely communicated. If the brand owner does not clearly understand the values and attributes inherent in each of his brands it is quite certain that the various target audiences will have no understanding of them either.

IMPLICATIONS FOR BRAND VALUATION

The profusion of ways in which branding is used can at times present the valuer with particular difficulties, especially with regard to the valuation of corporate brands. Usually, however, these difficulties can be satisfactorily resolved. Take, for example, a brand such as McVitie's, the leading brand of biscuits in Britain. As mentioned earlier, McVitie's is a major umbrella brand within the United Biscuits group and a very wide range of biscuit products is sold under the brand. But within the McVitie's range are a number of individually branded products which have such clear brand personalities that they qualify as freestanding brands despite the fact that they carry the McVitie's umbrella brand. These include Hob-Nobs, Fruit Jaspers and Boasters. If one were valuing the McVitie's brand it is probable that the freestanding brands would merit their own separate valuations and that the McVitie's valuation would apply only to the non-specialist products which do not bear their own brand names.

Similarly, if one were valuing a corporate brand like Jaguar, now part of Ford, even though the brand is applied to a range of different products including sports cars, saloon cars, spare parts and accessories, in practice the products sold under the brand are so homogenous that the valuation would be a relatively straightforward one.

The major problems arise with diffuse corporate brands such as ICI or Philips where it may be difficult or impossible to establish brand strength, as the brand means so many different things in so many different markets; it may also be difficult or impossible to identify brand earnings. In such instances, however, even though it may not be possible to establish a sufficiently reliable figure to allow for a formal valuation, the very process of brand evaluation and review can be helpful in identifying brand strengths and weaknesses and in improving brand management procedures.

Problems arise too in valuing such corporate brands as those of advertising agencies where, it might be argued, the most valuable intangible attributes of the corporation are not really captured in the brand but rather are vested in the people who comprise the corporation. While a corporate brand in the services sector such as Hertz has, undisputably, value which is separable from that of the management team, this is much less true of brands such as J Walter Thompson or Ogilvy and Mather.

CONCLUSION

The elements of value which make up the value of a business are many and comprise tangible assets such as plant, machinery, cash, office equipment, freeholds and leases, plus intangible assets. The intangible assets are usually many and range, at one end of the spectrum, from specific, identifiable assets such as names and trade marks, patents, copyrights, designs and licenses through skilled management teams, information systems and trained workforces to, at the other end of the spectrum, relationships with suppliers and similar non-proprietary business assets. Indeed, we recently came across a situation where the company's major asset was not its stocks, machinery, freeholds, trade marks, patents or even its management team but the fact that the managing director was married to the daughter of the company's major customer.

Clearly, when valuing a corporate brand it is particularly

important to ensure that it is not the business itself which is being valued but the corporate brand, and particular care must be taken, as discussed in Chapters 3 and 4, to remunerate the capital employed in the business and ensure that brand strength is properly assessed and brand cash flows or profits properly identified. But even though valuing corporate brands presents special difficulties, in most cases a reliable valuation can be computed. Moreover the process of valuation, which focuses on the positioning of the brand, its strengths and weaknesses, its appeals, cash flows, risk elements, etc, can be exceptionally useful in assisting management in the development of corporate strategy.

Chapter 16

DEVELOPING BRAND STRATEGY

John Murphy

From the earliest times farmers have been aware that certain basic rules of husbandry need to be followed in order to produce good, consistent yields. However, those rules were by no means widely understood or adhered to and it was not until the eighteenth century that the basic rules of husbandry were drawn together into a set of principles which transcended individual prejudices and preferences. Once the need for crop rotation, seed selection and good fertilizing methods were widely understood, productivity increased enormously and the risk of crop failure was much reduced.

Similarly, the curse of all early long-distance sea voyages was scurvy. However, in certain 'pockets' it was understood that citrus juices prevented scurvy and some ships' captains were able to enjoy major success by insisting that their crews drank citrus juice on long voyages. Indeed, for many years the British Navy supplied its crews with lime juice, a major source of vitamin C, and this was so well-known to others that British sailors earned the nickname 'limeys'. Yet it took 50 years for other navies to recognize the benefits and follow suit.

We would argue that a similar situation exists today in respect of brands. The general nature of brands is well understood and certain companies – Procter & Gamble, Unilever and Mars are examples – have developed particularly good methods of brand husbandry. Moreover, these methods are being constantly appraised and updated. But though the broad techniques of good brand management are widely understood, this by no means prevents the frequent adoption by brand owners of policies which weaken brands and, perhaps, in the longer term lead to a much reduced brand 'yield'. Consider the following:

- A major international foods group was under threat of takeover. For two successive years brand budgets were drastically cut and the much reduced spend was directed primarily at 'quick hit' below-the-line promotions. The company's brands operate in highly competitive markets and in the space of just two years massive damage was done to the market position and strength of all the major brands. Two of the four key brands, for example, slipped from a strong number two position in their markets to an indifferent number three position and both of the company's market leaders, which had previously been virtually unassailable, came close to losing market leadership

- A major European consumer products company had operated for many years with a highly divisionalized structure. Each of the individual units had its own brands and local autonomy. In the 1970s the corporate structure was centralized and the units became responsible only for production; centralized marketing and brand management was introduced. However, the director of marketing was mainly charged with maintaining relationships with 'the trade' (ie retailers) and brand managers were largely left to do with the brands what they wanted. In fact, the job of brand manager was mainly seen as a training role for young high-flyers, and the culture quickly developed whereby each new brand manager, who tended to spend two to three years in the job, sacked the old advertising agency, appointed a new one and immediately changed the communications programme, the positioning of the brand, even its packaging. For almost 20 years the brands followed wild zig-zag paths and it says much for the robustness of the brands and the loyalty of consumers that the brands survived this extended period of abuse, albeit with impaired market positions and substantially reduced market shares.

In these instances, and blessed with the gift of hindsight, it is clear that both companies broke the basic rules of brand husbandry. In the first instance the company tried to take out more than it put in – the result was brand exhaustion, the branding equivalent of soil exhaustion; and a subsequent management team had to invest heavily over an extended period to restore the position. In the second instance, there was no clearly agreed understanding as to what each brand was, what personality it had, how it was different from competitor brands, what satisfactions it delivered and so on. Each brand manager was left to make up his mind on all these points and on what messages to communicate to the consumer.

Secondly, the brand managers were isolated within the company; they were provided with little operating information, received little supervision and quickly came to feel much more loved and appreciated by the ad agencies than by their own superiors. In effect, they defected to the more glamorous world of the agency. Thirdly, the company had adopted a brand management system without the slightest notion of how it should work and how it should be structured.

What, then, are the rules of good brand husbandry?

BRAND-CENTRICITY

Once it is accepted that, for many companies today, their most valuable and important assets by far are their brands, it becomes clear that an organization should develop a style and structure which recognizes this fact and which focuses the organization on the proper management, development and exploitation of these assets. We refer to this focus as 'brand-centricity'.

Thus, and as discussed in previous chapters, the accounting function will need to organize itself to produce financial information on a brand-by-brand basis and not merely on a geographical, divisional or production unit basis. Similarly, investment in brand-building needs to be treated just as carefully and analytically as any other major corporate investment decision. The switching of resources out of brands or between brands needs to be analysed and the differential performance and sensitivity of brands should be carefully monitored.

But it is not just the accounting function which needs to be 'brand-centric'. The corporate structure also needs to focus more explicitly on brands. While it might be appropriate to retain a conventional organization structure (for example: marketing, sales, manufacturing, research and development, financial, personnel) brand management needs to be closely integrated within the corporate structure; should be subject to detailed scrutiny; and should operate at a senior level.

In other parts of the organization, too, the role and importance of brands needs to be explicitly recognized. In research and development, for example, a clearer understanding of each brand's positioning, appeals, strengths, weaknesses and threats may well lead to a more focused R&D programme.

In recommending the adoption of a brand-centric approach we are not, however, seeking to deny or subordinate the role of the sales force or of the production or development departments. Rather, if a company's most valuable assets are its brands and if its most potent weapons for securing and maintaining market share, achieving distribution, gaining sales and earning margin and profits are its brands then the brands must permeate that organization. The accounts department must account for brands, R&D must help to develop new and improved branded products and so on. Brand-centricity therefore merely recognizes the actuality of the situation in many companies.

CONSERVATIVE MANAGEMENT

It is massively expensive to establish a new consumer brand; even in a single geographical market like the UK a new brand generally needs a launch budget of several million pounds before major retailers can be persuaded to stock it. It also takes a long time (several years minimum) before the brand achieves any certainty of longer-term survival. It may also be at least five years before the brand gets into the black. Finally, launching new brands is exceptionally risky – the vast majority of new brands fail. Once a brand is established, however, it is normally a robust asset and one with the likelihood, if properly cared for, of a sustained life.

The reason why it is so costly and such a long drawn-out process to establish a brand, particularly in consumer markets where the physical characteristics of products are increasingly similar, is that a large number of others are competing for the consumers' loyalty and attention and, at the same time, the brand owner is seeking to establish an emotional, non-rational bond between the consumer and the brand where the consumer, initially at least, has little interest in the brand and has more than enough other things with which to be concerned. However, once 'bonding' takes place between the consumer and the brand it can be very strong.

But as in any relationship each side must keep its part of the bargain. It is often the case however that consumers (who initially are often so reluctant to embrace a new brand) are frequently more constant in their loyalties to a brand, particularly in such stable sectors as food, drink and toiletries, than are brand owners. It is frequently the brand owners who tinker with their brands, reposition them, change the message, change the packaging, change the formulation, often without, it seems, good reason and without reference to the preferences of the consumer.

We therefore advocate the conservative management of brands. Brand owners must recognize that brands are rare and precious assets and that they deserve to be treated with care and consideration. In our experience the danger signals which indicate that brand management is out of control, and that the essential values and qualities of the brand are not clearly understood and communicated, include: frequent changes of advertising agency, frequent changes of communications message, radical packaging changes (where the old 'visual equity' in the packaging is discarded), inappropriate brand extension, 'stop-start' promotional budgets and strong swings from above-the-line to below-the-line promotions.

We are by no means suggesting that all brand re-positioning exercises, all changes of agency, all line extensions and all package re-designs are causes for concern because clearly they are not: brands like anything else must adapt or die. Rather, change for the sake of change or because the brand manager is bored, is inappropriate: if the change is unsuccessful the brand manager will simply leave it off his CV and it is the brand owner who will have to pay the price.

An essential pre-requisite, therefore, of conservative brand management is to define the precise identity of the brand, its critical point of difference and the satisfactions the brand delivers. We believe that a brand 'blueprint' should actually be written down, discussed and agreed. It should then be circulated to all those involved in the management of the brand including the brand manager, the R&D department, the advertising agency and the package designers. Naturally, this blueprint will be subject to challenge and will need constant updating. It will nonetheless serve as a fixed point for all brand-related decisions.

All too often, in the absence of an agreed brand blueprint and subsequent brand strategy, we find that those involved in the management of the brand have attitudes and plans for a brand which are by no means in step: the brand manger wishes the brand to be positioned as fresh, contemporary and up-to-the-minute, and briefs the advertising agency to achieve this positioning; the sales force, on the other hand, perceives the brand as a 'staple', a product which any retailer must stock and which affords the brand owner the opportunity to sell his other brands; the finance department sees the brand as a 'cash cow' and is loathe to spend money on brand development.

But what of the consumer? Consumers do not like 'their' brands being 'fiddled around with' – witness the Coca-Cola/Coke/Classic Coke problem in the United States when Coca-Cola tried to reformulate the product to meet the increasing threat from Pepsi-Cola. This is not to say that brand development is undesirable – it is in fact essential – but we argue that it must be handled conservatively and sensitively.

Having crystalized and agreed the brand blueprint and, at the same time, installed programmes for reviewing this blueprint, the opportunities for erratic brand management policies and subsequent brand abuse will be much reduced. Managers who wish to alter any element of the brand will need to justify their action on grounds other than mere hunch, fashion or anecdote.

LINE EXTENSION

Line extension has three main advantages for brand owners:

- It helps keep the brand contemporary and interesting

- It exploits the latent equity in a brand

- It permits new product introduction at a much lower cost and greatly reduced risk than through the launch of totally new brands

Unfortunately, in many instances brand extension has turned out in practice to be brand dilution – the extension does not enhance the original brand but, rather, harms it. So what are the 'rules' of good brand extension?

The over-riding requirement is to recognize the essential personality of the brand and what it stands for, and only consider line extensions which are consistent with this. Is Nescafé essentially a brand of instant coffee or could it be extended to embrace 'real' coffee? (Clearly the answer is at minimum a conditional 'yes' to both as Nescafé is now used on ground coffee, albeit by way of a house mark or corporate endorsement.) Does the brand HP stand only for savoury sauces or could it be extended into the other sauce areas, for example, ice cream toppings? (Apparently not: it was tried in the 1970s, without success.) Any line extension must be compatible with the essential personality of the brand and credible to the consumer.

It is also important to recognize that even though line extensions must be undertaken in short, credible, steps, a series of such steps can take the brand to a position which would be unthinkable in a single move. Consider the Benson & Hedges cigarette brand, a massively powerful brand which has received large, sustained investment over many years but which, no doubt, is under threat from changes in attitudes towards smoking. Why not extend the brand into male toiletries – Benson & Hedges After Shave? Initially the notion seems absurd, even a little unpleasant: who would wish to smell of stale cigarettes? However, a major competitor brand, Dunhill, is now firmly established internationally as a highly successful brand of sophisticated, up-market products, mainly for men, including clothing, accessories such as briefcases and belts, male toiletries, etc. Millions of men around the world have no problem with the notion of using Dunhill After Shave.

Dunhill's success has been achieved through extending the brand by degrees, using each brand extension as a new stepping stone to reach the objective of a broadly based, sophisticated, luxury products brand. This brand extension started with products closely related to cigarettes such as smokers' accessories and lighters; it then moved on to belts, briefcases, luggage and related products; and then to clothing, toiletries and other luxury items.

It is also clear that, given the high costs and risks of new brand development this should only be contemplated if it is quite clear that line extension is not feasible.

However, in many instances it will be clearly impractical to attempt line extension, for example when the new product, if treated as a line extension, could hazard the existing brand – Guinness brand fruit-flavoured soft drinks, for example. In such instances development of a new brand may be the only feasible option.

BRANDING STRUCTURES

No ideal model exists of a system for the best use of branding for all organizations – companies use branding in a variety of different ways and each company must develop a branding strategy to suit its particular needs. (See Chapter 15 for a discussion of alternative branding structures.) What is clear is that whatever system a company adopts – 'simple', 'monolithic' or 'endorsed' – it should be as a result of a conscious management decision after a careful review of the alternatives. Certainly, companies should be careful to guard against constant tinkering with brand structures with uncontrolled line extensions, sub-brands and endorsements as the result can be the destruction of brand identities.

INTERNATIONAL BRANDS

In Swift's *Gulliver's Travels*, the hero is shipwrecked on the island of Lilliput where the inhabitants are divided into two opposing camps. In one camp are those who break their eggs at the rounded end, in the other end are those who attack the pointed end. Swift's purpose in 1726 was to satirize English political parties and religious dissensions, yet his satire has its parallels in the world of branding and marketing today which often seems to have become divided into the 'global branders' and the 'local branders'. Not surprisingly, the main advocates of global branding have been advertising agencies like Saatchi and Saatchi with strong global networks and the ability to service international clients. In the other camp are the 'local' agencies who have argued that brands must be intimately developed to suit the particular needs of the local market and that branding requires local precision and focus, not international bluster and the indiscriminate spending of large, international advertising budgets.

As in all such debates each side has a legitimate point of view. To treat an Italian beer drinker exactly the same way as a Scottish beer drinker or a Korean housewife the same as a Mexican housewife is clearly asburd. On the other hand, to assume that the aspirations, interests and objectives of a teenager in Tokyo are light years apart from those of a teenager in Paris is equally absurd.

What is clear is that the last 20–30 years have seen a remarkable coming together of tastes and expectations across the developed world. An urban teenager in Tokyo may well have more in common with a teenager in Paris than with his or her rural equivalent in Hokkaido. Which is not to suggest that we are all the same – raw fish is still not widely appreciated outside Japan and British ale is clearly a minority taste, at least on an international basis. Nonetheless the opportunities for world brands are growing strongly for a number of reasons:

- There is a marked convergence of tastes and expectations worldwide

- Media and other overlaps (eg, satellite TV) are encouraging the development of international brands

- Increased travel and other influences (eg, the teaching of English) are leading in the same direction

- Barriers between countries are being removed (eg, the EEC's 1992 initiative)

The result is that no brand can maintain a strictly 'local' orientation. If it does it risks being overwhelmed by a more potent and appealing international foreign brand.

The implications for brand husbandry are clear: all brands are potentially under threat from others and all brand managers should constantly seek opportunities to 'internationalize' their brands through export, distribution agreements, licensing or overseas manufacturing. But the international brand should then be positioned sensitively at a local level and take account of local conditions and preferences. In other words, brand owners should 'think global, act local'.

BRAND DIFFERENTIATION

Most new brands fail. The new brand is carefully developed, tested extensively, discussed with retailers, promoted in the trade press and heavily advertised. So why has it failed? Often the reasons can be identified: the brand failed to achieve adequate distribution, or consumers preferred the taste of the brand leader, or the range was not wide enough.

But in many cases the reason for failure is unclear. After all, the new product looked right, tasted right and was priced and distributed right, so there was no obvious reason for failure.

In such cases the reason for failure is often simply that the brand is insufficiently differentiated from existing brands already on the market. The new brand is simply a pastiche, an accurate copy of existing brands which the consumer knows and buys. The consumer recognizes what the new brand is seeking to achieve, but why switch from a tried and tested brand to a new one when the new brand is no different from the existing brand?

Clearly, it is important that any new brand is appropriately differentiated from existing brands so that the consumer has a reason to switch and stay switched. This is not to suggest that the nature of such differentiation needs to be dramatic. Indeed, only in such areas as fragrances are wild, eccentric brands likely to be acceptable to consumers. Also, it should be recognized that in many product sectors the opportunities for differentiating the product itself, or its pricing, or even its physical packaging, may be slight. Frequently the major opportunities for brand differentiation lie in the brand's detailed market proposition or positioning or in its name, packaging, design or distribution system. After all, even if it is not possible to produce a mainstream beer brand which is dramatically different in its physical characteristics, price, taste or packaging from existing competitive beers, it should nonetheless be possible to develop a brand with a personality which is appealing to consumers but which is clearly differentiated from competitor brands.

BRAND VISION

Brands are specific intangible assets which, over time, can develop highly distinctive 'personalities' which differentiate them quite clearly from all others. Indeed, the owners of brands such as Dunhill regard the personalities of their brands as so clear and pervasive that brand strategy and all brand-related decisions are virtually made by the brand itself – what is right or wrong for the brand is unequivocally determined by the brand's personality and attributes.

This clear vision of what a brand is, of its core values, attributes and objectives, is essential to long-term brand success and is clearly present in brands such as Coca-Cola, Mars, Hertz and Porsche – all brand-related decisions take place within the context of a clear brand vision and a clear, concise and widely communicated strategy which all those involved with the brand subscribe to.

An essential part of good brand management is the development of such a vision for the brand and, subsequently, the translation of this vision into a workable and appropriate strategy. Even though this process is projective and relies in part at least on imagination and flair it should, nonetheless, be based upon an intimate and detailed knowledge of the brand itself, its performance, attributes, appeals, history, market, competition, prospects, regulatory environment and so forth. An essential first step is, therefore, a detailed brand audit, using brand valuation and evaluation techniques such as those described in this book.

A brand audit, however, no more prescribes future brand strategy than a financial audit prescribes future financial strategy – it provides a 'snapshot' of brand performance and helps to identify strengths and weaknesses yet the way in which the brand is developed in the future is essentially judgmental, tempered by knowledge, insights and understanding.

Having thus conducted a brand audit the next task is to identify key issues and then to explore the range of plausible alternative futures confronting the brand. When these are matched against the characteristics of the brand, its strengths and weaknesses, the prospects and structure of the markets in which the brand operates and the skills and resources of the brand owner it is possible to identify a brand vision or future which is based upon current realities, is achievable and plausible and which provides the brand with focus and direction. Arguably, the development of a brand vision is one of the most important but most frequently overlooked tasks of those charged with the management of these most rare and valuable assets.

LEGAL PROTECTION

Finally, it is important to protect one's brands, preferably through registration. The costs of trade mark registration are modest, defending trade mark rights is relatively straightforward and the rights afforded by registration are powerful. It is also sensible to seek protection on an international basis, even for essentially national brands. If a brand is protected internationally it will be possible to exploit that brand on a wider scale in the future. If there is no international protection, the brand owner is quite likely to find, should he decide at a later date to develop internationally, that the trade mark is anticipated by a third party and that international exploitation under the brand name is not possible.

Brand owners should regard the cost of trade mark protection as basic brand insurance – and any owner of a valuable asset who does not insure that asset is being foolhardy.

Chapter 17

THE IMPORTANCE OF INTANGIBLE ASSETS IN ECONOMIC ACTIVITY: THE JAPANESE INFORMATION CAPITAL PARADOX

Terry Oliver

INTRODUCTION

In the post-war era, Japan has developed to become one of the world's largest economies, with a GNP second only to that of the United States. Japan has consistently maintained world-leading growth rates, with real GNP growth in 1990 of 4.9 per cent. The most remarkable thing about Japan's economic success is that it has been achieved with virtually no domestic natural resources. The Japanese economic miracle has been built on a foundation of hard work and knowledge.

Corporate assets can be broadly divided into two types: information capital (or intellectual capital) – including software, management systems, know-how, brands and designs – and financial capital – including plant, equipment and other tangible resources. From the beginning of the industrial revolution until just recently, the ability to generate 'added value' or 'worth' resided largely in financial capital, and a company's tangible assets – plant, freehold land, mines etc – represented its value. Recently, however, information capital (or, more accurately, intellectual capital) is playing the key role, with the productivity of financial capital being controlled by the quality of the information capital brought to bear. Moreover, the underlying worth of such businesses is often not 'captured' in tangible assets but rather in the value of its intangible assets. Japan is instructive in understanding the workings of companies and markets which are information based rather than mainly capital based.

The United States has what is known in the industry as a $149 sewing machine market. In Japan, however, the biggest selling machines cost over $1,000, with more functions than could ever be used in the average three hours per year that the Japanese housewife actually uses her sewing machine. In Japan, brand names are critically important and have a highly influential role in consumer decision-making – one Japanese girl, on being questioned as to why she was willing to pay an extravagant price for a Louis Vuitton brand bag made of vinyl, replied with conviction that she was sure only the best vinyl was used!

In the Japanese factory, the ability to manage information is a key element in reducing inventories, and thus in increasing the company's stock turn and its return on financial capital. Strategic information systems are now linking information from the market place to the R&D centre, allowing Japanese companies to remain competitive by investing in more successful products ahead of competitors and by marketing their products only to the people most likely to buy them.

While these principles hold true in all the advanced nations, they are particularly true in Japan, where the lack of natural resources has created a national obsession with the expansion of 'added value' as a means of economic survival. In this chapter, we will examine how Japan is capitalizing on information and knowledge to maintain its economic success and competitiveness and the emphasis that the modern Japanese corporation puts on its intangible assets such as brands, patents, information systems and know-how. We will also look at some areas where Japan has failed in the information game and the paradox this creates of strong information capital at the national and company-wide level but with primitive information flow at the ground level.

BRANDS

Louis Vuitton, Chanel, Pierre Cardin, Burberry, Tiffany – once these brands would have been exclusive to Paris, London or New York, but now they are equally at home in Tokyo, Osaka or any other Japanese city. Not only do Japanese manufacturers rely on intangible assets but their consumers rely on the appeals of intangible brand assets as well. Indeed, the Japanese consumer is the world's most voracious consumer of branded goods and, for some luxury brands, Japanese consumers account for as much as 70 per cent of worldwide annual sales.

Mitsui & Co, a leading general trading company in Japan, alone handles more than 60 international luxury brands, including Pierre Cardin, Burberry, Balenciaga, Paco Rabanne, Marie Claire, Austin Reed, Scotch House, Bill Blass, Paul Stuart, Valentino, Gianni Versace, Basile and Etro. The Japanese consumer has developed a taste for the sophisticated and price is no object. Indeed, some manufacturers have gone so far as to say that price is no longer a valid tool of differentiation, unless of course you are talking about making it higher. Above all, it is the brand image which counts.

In Japan, fickle, discerning consumers have led manufacturers to create vast product ranges with many different products in overlapping product categories. Ajinomoto, a major food products manufacturer, for example, boasted a product range of 4,000 different items at its peak, though it still lagged behind QP Corporation, which boasted 9,000 products sold under its brand name.

The Japanese consumer is ever in search of something new, and Japanese advertisements are speckled with the word *'shinhatsubai'* – 'newly released'. As a result, many new product brands are often developed to last just six months. *Fuyumonogatari* (A Winter's Tale) is an example – it is a beer just for the winter season.

While the diversity and sophistication of brands in Japan is unquestioned, their management is much looser than elsewhere. In fact, brand managers do not exist as such in Japan. Also, a brand name, once developed, may well be pirated at will by other divisions of the company. A name created for a soft drink might therefore next appear on hard candy with no particular person or group of people in the company directly responsible for approval.

Responsibility for brand and product marketing tends to be loosely structured with one subsidiary in charge of product development, a manufacturing company that handles production, and a number of sales companies with overlapping responsibilities.

BEER AND CHOCOLATE: JAPAN'S BRAND WARS

In Japan, fierce competition in certain areas has led to the rapid proliferation of new brands. The introduction of Asahi Super Dry beer in 1987, for example, gave Asahi a 50 per cent share of the domestic beer market, sparking what has come to be known as the 'beer wars'. Manufacturers have released a flood of new brands in an effort to compete. Thus Kirin Brewery countered with Ichiban Shibori, a beer that supposedly uses the first pressings and it now has a line-up that includes Kirin Fine Draft, Kirin Fine Pilsner, Kirin Lager, Kirin Premium and others. Sapporo Breweries also entered the war, offering Fuyumonogatari and Ginjikomi, in addition to its line of Sapporo Original, Black Label, Sapporo Nama Draft Beer, Yebisu, Sapporo Malt 100, Sapporo Black, Edelpils, Cool Dry and Hardy. Suntory Limited has lagged behind though it recently launched Ginjo Karayaburi, a beer that purports to improve beer taste by cracking the malt.

Thus, Japanese brewers try to differentiate their beers by reference to the manufacturing process used as opposed to differentiation by lifestyle segments. Furthermore, as bars in Japan generally stock only one beer brand, brand loyalty counts for little when a Japanese consumer is out on the town, though it is fiercely exhibited in the home.

This flood of brands is notable in that since the launch of Asahi Super Dry, subsequent brands have been little differentiated. The proliferation of brands has, however, spurred consumption of beer, giving it a higher share of the alcoholic beverage market than ever before.

Another stunning instance of brand proliferation in Japan is the recent 'chocolate wars'. Chocolate has not been a traditional part of the Japanese diet and until just recently most stores carried only a few kinds. This was changed completely with the launch of Lotte V.I.P. Fresh Cream Chocolate. The success of this new product has made chocolate a daily habit with many Japanese, particularly young women. Lotte immediately backed up its success with Fresh Cream Doubleberry, Fresh Cream White Chocolate, Super Fresh Cream in Chocolate, Tiramisu Fresh Cream Cheese in Chocolate and DIOS Beer. When added to such products as Crunky, White Crunky, Ghana and Vessel in the Fog, this vast line-up has allowed Lotte to dominate store shelf space, with Meiji Milk Products and Morinaga struggling to respond, though Morinaga in particular has had some success with its new line of Solid Bar products, which includes Cheese Cake and Peanut Butter flavours.

MANAGEMENT SYSTEMS

One area where information capital and know-how have paid big dividends for the Japanese is the area of management systems. In Japan, there is currently a major movement underway to develop strategic information systems as a means of securing market share and improving corporate performance. This trend has been particularly noteworthy in the distribution industry, with the number of stores with point of sales (POS) systems expanding from just 4,212 stores and 12,196 registers in 1985 to 70,061 stores with 183,497 registers in 1990. To assess the benefits that accrue from this information intensive approach, let us examine some cases in Japan.

Distribution

The case of 7-Eleven Japan is instructive. In Japan 7-Eleven opened its first store in 1974, with the number of stores expanding to about 3,700 by 1989. The chain introduced POS terminals in all of its stores in 1982. These terminals monitor information for each sale, including the product, number sold, type of customer, time of sale, relationship of products purchased, and price. This information is used first of all to re-order products sold. Wholesalers make several deliveries each day, so that the company is able to stock 3,000 to 3,500 products in a store with just 100 square meters (1,000 square feet) of floor space. The turnover on capital is phenomenal and has made 7-Eleven consistently one of Japan's most profitable retailers. The information is also used to determine product line-ups, with roughly half of the store's products being changed every six months. (Interestingly, the increased number of daily deliveries by convenience stores in Japan, while increasing inventory turnover and thus return on capital, has had its adverse effects as well. Japan is now, for example, suffering from a severe truck driver shortage.) In addition, 7-Eleven has used information systems to offer new services, such as receipt of utility bill payments, acceptance of express packages and others. The remarkable success of 7-Eleven Japan led its owner, the Itoyokado retail chain, to purchase 70 per cent of Southland, the operator of 7-Eleven in the United States, for $430 million so as to apply the company's information capital to the restructuring of the failing business, which had spent four months in the bankruptcy court.

Manufacturing

In the manufacturing sector, Toyota Motor Corp has shown the world that information capital can pay huge dividends even in industries that require vast amounts of financial capital.

Toyota's *kanban* production system is a management system aimed at eliminating unnecessary inventories and reducing production lead times. The system makes use of a placard called a kanban, which is affixed to materials and intermediate products. When the inventory is used up the placard is detached and sent to the previous production process where it serves as a production order. As a result, the amount of work in process never varies. Inventories at each stage are reduced to minimal levels, so if a faulty product is identified at any stage of production or if any delay occurs the entire line stops, making it easy to identify production problems and line balance inefficiencies.

In addition, the company has developed techniques to reduce die exchange times. The reduction of these lead times from hours to just a few minutes allows Toyota to run many different model types with varying options on the same production line.

As a result of this systematic implementation of knowledge capital, Toyota has risen to become Japan's most profitable company, with profits of almost $3 billion on net sales of over $60 billion in 1990. The company now boasts of being able to manufacture and deliver a car to buyer specification in less than one week, and Toyota has expanded its product line-up from just two passenger car models, the Crown and the Corona, in 1960, to 22 models in 1990.

The important role of management know-how and management systems was further underscored by Toyota's joint venture with GM. The joint venture began manufacturing in Fremont, California in 1984, and the success brought about by Toyota's management capabilities has led to plans to expand production by 100,000 pickup trucks per year beginning August 1991.

The high value of the yen following the Plaza Agreement has in fact caused many Japanese companies of all sizes to move some or all of their manufacturing operations overseas and such companies are increasingly realizing that their only real assets are their knowledge and information. This has created something of a boom in what are called development imports, products which are developed in Japan, manufactured overseas and then imported back to Japan. Thus the most knowledge-intensive, high-value-added work remains in Japan, with the lower value-added manufacturing processes being moved to a location where production can be undertaken inexpensively.

Delivery services

Another well-known example in Japan of an innovative information-based business is Yamato Transport Co, which has used information strategically to restructure Japan's delivery industry. The company currently has 40,000 employees, 1,500 offices and 20,000 trucks. Yamato's 40 per cent market share is supported by 240,000 agents who accept packages for delivery, with the service area extending to 99.9 per cent of the nation's population.

The company's system is built on a POS system for information on package collection, an information network named NEKO net, which feeds information to the database, the database itself, which also supports accounting operations, a package tracking system that allows every package in transit to be located and progress reported, and a sophisticated communications system. This integrated system allows Yamato to provide an exceptionally reliable next day delivery service throughout Japan. The services offered by Yamato include the special delivery of golf and ski equipment so that enthusiasts can go to the golf course or ski resort unencumbered by luggage, and the refrigerated delivery of packages, a service which is used extensively by people in rural communities to ship local delicacies to relatives in the cities. The ability of Yamato to handle and process information has created a new industry and provided its pioneer with an overwhelming market share.

Failure in the office

While the Japanese have shown great skill in implementing large scale management information and POS systems, at the ground level information flows slowly, if at all. For example, in one major Japanese computer company, sending a facsimile message to one of the company's overseas offices requires the approval of a supervisor, a manager, a division manager, and the chief engineer. The document will run through this circle of approval three to four times until everyone is satisfied. While this process makes sure that everyone is informed and prevents mistakes, it also stifles the development of any new information.

While the *ringi* or circular system described above has been praised overseas as a means of getting everyone involved, its real purpose in Japan is to prevent anyone from being able to, or having to, make a decision. The sheer effort involved in getting everyone's seal on the same piece of paper prevents change. A company dealing in government procurements may well spend half of its working time searching for proposals that have already been approved in the past and old answers to old questions will be cut and pasted into the new proposal. Any notion of providing new information will be banished by anxieties as to the complexities involved in getting approval of anything new. Indeed, in some businesses approval processes can be so complex that it may require six weeks to process an acquisition for a few folders and, as a result, many employees actually purchase their own stationery supplies.

Another area where information inefficiency is painfully evident is in the endless meetings held in Japanese companies. In one recent case, 20 middle managers were called to an eight-hour meeting to consult on the use of one word in a press release. Endless discussions were held, but no decision was made. It was finally decided to leave the decision to the advertising agency.

The Japanese company is characterized by the absence of anyone with the authority or the will to make a real decision. Serious decisions can only normally be made by the president and in meetings bright young employees are discouraged from speaking up for fear they might contradict the opinions of their superiors. Everyone sits, a few talk, cigarettes are smoked, endless cups of green tea are drunk, but nothing gets done. Some companies in Japan, in an effort to combat this modern corporate meeting disease, have taken stern action, such as removing all chairs from meeting rooms so that everyone has to stand up or forbidding smoking and tea drinking in conference rooms. Such measures have had some success in cutting down unnecessary meetings, but companies taking these measures are still a tiny minority.

Trading relationships

Another area where intangible assets are critical to business success is the corporate groupings and trading relationships that characterize Japanese business. Companies do not establish trading relationships easily and existing patterns of supply are very difficult to alter. This has given rise to extensive vertical marketing systems (VMSs) and manufacturers in Japan often serve as channel leaders, dictating pricing and other policies, a practice which is questionable in anti-trust terms but extremely common.

Matsushita, for example, has tens of thousands of sales outlets throughout the country that, while not directly owned or controlled in any way, carry only Matsushita products. These valuable distribution groupings are not in any way recorded on the company's books, but are the major reason for Matsushita's continued leading market share in many product categories.

Corporate groupings are another example of embedded trading relationships. In Japan, corporate groupings usually consist of a central bank and a trading company at the group's core, and various manufacturing and service companies around the periphery. The trading company and the bank will often serve as stable shareholders and financiers and will help to put together deals and create new trading arrangements for group companies. While such groupings are by no means universal, and much business takes place within more conventional trading relationships, they are an important aspect of Japanese business with mutual shareholdings also serving to prohibit unfriendly takeovers.

Mitsui & Co, for example, the trading company at the centre of the Mitsui group, has 354 subsidiaries and 217 affiliated companies. The trading company will typically provide a variety of information and marketing services, bringing companies together to work on joint projects and taking an equity position in new ventures thus created.

Information processing in Japan

One measure of a nation's competence in the use of information capital is the level of its information processing systems. These systems are the tools with which information capital is produced, distributed and applied. In 1990, the Japanese market for computer equipment exceeded $7 billion and in 1992 the Japanese are expected to purchase nearly two million personal computers, in addition to sales of office computers, mainframes and supercomputers. These figures place Japan as a major computer power. However, the numbers are not what they seem. Japan has been a late-comer to office automation (OA) and while nearly a quarter of all Japanese companies have special OA promotion projects, by and large they lag far behind other advanced nations. As recently as five years ago one subsidiary of a major computer manufacturer had just two personal computers, both outdated models scrapped by other divisions, for a staff of nearly 100 employees. Proposals had to be sent out for typing and any changes required complete retyping. Recently, however, considerable improvements have been made to Japanese-language word processors and sales of such word processors reached almost three million units in 1989, well outpacing sales of personal computers.

Software

In addition to increased use of computers, the use of certain application software has grown markedly in recent years. Computer aided design (CAD) applications, communications, data base software, scientific programs, and artificial intelligence (AI) software are all on the increase though well over half of all package applications sold in Japan are games, reflecting the belief in Japan that the computer is still in some way a toy rather than a tool.

Networking and communications

Japan's efforts to take leadership in information systems is perhaps most notable in integrated services digital networks (ISDN). In April 1988, Nippon Telegraph and Telephone Corp (NTT) became the world's first company to commercialize ISDN and Fujitsu released its first ISDN system at the same time. The Fujitsu system allows the connection of existing computers using an ISDN service port and ISDN-compatible public telephones complete with modular jacks for attaching other equipment have been installed in locations throughout Japan.

Nevertheless, only one company in ten in Japan is connected to any kind of network and networking in Japan is still very limited, with few companies actually performing computer communications at all.

Artificial Intelligence (AI)

Japanese expenditures on AI-related software have increased rapidly and the Japanese have been leaders in the development of AI, with the Institute for New Generation Computer Technology (ICOT) being formally launched on 14 April 1982 to bring private and public sector resources together. As a result of this programme and other efforts, the Japanese have developed a substantial number of expert systems, ranging from semi-intelligent Japanese language word processors to sophisticated systems for monitoring production.

RESEARCH AND DEVELOPMENT LEADS KNOWLEDGE DEVELOPMENT

R&D is the key driving investment in the development of knowledge. In 1989 Japan spent about $7 billion on research in science and technology, about 70 per cent of which was spent by companies. These expenditures have shown constant growth, indicating steady expansion in the development of knowledge. As a result, Japan has recorded higher annual real growth in R&D expenditures than the United States, France or Germany every year since 1985, with a ratio of R&D expenditures to GNP of 2.85 per cent leading all but Germany, which invested 2.87 per cent of GNP in R&D activities.

The largest portion of these resources was spent by companies in the manufacturing industry, particularly in electrical machinery, communications, chemicals and other key industrial products. In addition, 80 per cent of all R&D in Japan is conducted by private-sector companies, thus enhancing these figures when viewed in the context of information capital formation.

Intellectual property rights

As a result of these activities, Japanese companies have filed a vast number of applications for industrial ownership rights, with 336,232 patent applications in 1988. Overseas as well, the Japanese have emerged as leaders in the procurement of patents and other intellectual property rights, particularly trade marks. In 1990, the four winners in the race to receive US patents were all Japanese: Hitachi Ltd, Toshiba Corp, Canon Inc., and Mitsubishi Electric Corp.

To speed up the processing of patent applications, Japan's Patent Office recently installed a system that allows patent applications to be filed by computer. This on-line system will undergo further improvements and is expected substantially to reduce application processing time.

In the field of trade marks, too, Japanese businesses have been remarkably active in securing powerful, registered, international rights, often based upon brand names taken from Western languages. The Japanese term for words borrowed from other languages is *gairaigo* and such words are absorbed into everyday use, defined and written in the syllabic alphabet *katakana*.

R&D and competitive advantage

The competitive advantage offered by knowledge and the results of R&D are graphically illustrated by a look at the market for personal computers in Japan. NEC Corporation released Japan's first 16-bit computer in 1982. When Fujitsu released its first 16-bit computer two years later, the damage was already done: all of the software suppliers had already adapted to the NEC standard. In addition, Fujitsu opted to use the CP/M operating system, which failed to attract the necessary software support. As a result, NEC has remained predominant in the market, with a domestic PC market share estimated at 90 per cent in 1988.

NEW MEDIA

As information comes to play an increasing role in society, new media are being developed to meet the challenges of communicating that information. New media currently attracting attention in Japan include videotext, video response systems, cable television, home shopping, home banking and home trading of securities. Moreover, in Japan, CAPTAIN videotext systems have been installed in a variety of locations, providing users with information on shopping, leisure and other activities.

Cable television systems are also taking on a unique scope in Japan and encompass viewer polling, security and other information services.

Home shopping and home banking are two sophisticated information services that are expected to make rapid headway in Japan, though one of the main problems with implementing such systems is the need for standard terminals. In Japan, game computers that have wide distribution are expected to cover this role, and soon it will be possible to check bank balances, electronically transfer funds, trade securities and purchase products based on CATV and videotext presentations all from a terminal conveniently located in one's own living room. Home-use game computers are already present in over 13 million homes in Japan and are well suited to this type of application. However, one major problem which stands in the way of cable TV systems in Japan is the cost of cabling – the cost of securing rights of way can be staggering.

ACCOUNTING FOR INTELLECTUAL PROPERTY

Despite the unquestioned importance of information capital, brands and other forms of intellectual property in Japan, there is at present no concerted effort to reflect their value on the corporate books. For tax purposes, however, software and R&D expenses are treated as deferred assets in Japan and the cost of registering brands can be recorded on the balance sheet though brands themselves cannot be valued.

This, however, is hardly surprising. Japan is seldom a leader in innovations of the kind required for brand valuation and since the concept of brand valuation and the valuation of other intellectual assets is new even in the UK and the United States, it will require considerably more time for Japan to accept such practices. Still, there are signs that Japan's companies are beginning to take an interest in this new movement to account for information capital. Increased M&A activity in Japan, which has accelerated in recent years, is likely to provide the impetus needed to bring about changes in generally accepted accounting principles there. In addition, several of the major Japanese trading houses and companies have used brand evaluation techniques to appraise brand-based acquisition candidates in Europe and North America. Indeed, such is the Japanese fascination with luxury brands, in particular, that in recent years Japanese companies have shown a strong interest in acquiring such brands. As the 'worth' of these brands is largely intangible, brand evaluation techniques have been used to choose between alternative candidates and also to help fix a fair price.

INFORMATION FOR THE PRIVILEGED FEW

In Japan, information is often reserved for the privileged few. Large government projects lay the infrastructure for large companies to implement systems at the company-wide or factory level to raise competitiveness, but at the ground level information flows slowly if at all. Indeed, in some cases, conscious efforts are made to prevent information from being revealed.

Shareholders and disclosure

One excellent example of this is the state of corporate disclosure of information to shareholders. Japan's disclosure rules give shareholders a minimum of information with which to make decisions and cautious investors often find themselves having to read annual reports issued overseas to meet foreign reporting requirements to get the data they require.

Japanese companies also strive to make their annual shareholders meetings as short as possible, usually under 30 minutes. They are, however, opposed in this goal by the *sokaiya* mobsters who blackmail companies by threatening to disrupt the formality and tranquility of their meetings and keep the meetings going by asking all kinds of questions. To combat this, almost all of Japan's listed companies hold their shareholders meetings on the same day and at the same time, thus making sure there are not enough *sokaiya* to go round.

Non-investigative reporting

The Japanese media are another example of how information is controlled in Japan. It is amazing for foreigners who come to Japan to see that all of the major newspapers print almost exactly the same stories each day. Television news is even more incredible – at 6.00 pm, flipping through the channels, one finds all of the channels presenting the same stories at the same time and sometimes in the same order.

This homogenization of the news is coordinated through the *kisha kurabu* or press club system, where Japan's media meet to discuss what will get aired and what will not. Investigative reporting is strongly discouraged and reporters learn not to fall out of favour with the politicians and companies which feed them carefully diced nuggets at press conferences. Indeed, Japanese companies do not hesitate to bar reporters from press conferences if they print a scoop on the company's products before they are released.

CONCLUSION

Japan has demonstrated a remarkable ability to handle information capital at the strategic level, but shows serious failings at lower levels. This is perhaps rooted in the country's heavy emphasis on long-term vision and planning, while at the same time largely ignoring short-term issues, such as whether anyone in the office did anything useful today. Furthermore, while the Japanese exhibit tremendous diligence in creating and analysing information, much of this is ignored in the actual decision-making process where gut feeling is relied on.

Japan is a paradox to observers, even to those who have lived and worked in the country for many years and know it well. But for a country with few natural resources, a critical shortage of labour, an ageing population and only a tiny usable land area it is remarkably prosperous, innovative and dynamic. Central to its success is the generation, transmission and application of knowledge and, for many reasons, Japan could be considered as the world's first true post-industrial society. Japan clearly demonstrates that 'added value' can be created by information, know-how, copyrights, patents and brands, and challenges popular Western conceptions as to the prime rôle of tangible assets in the creation of wealth.

Chapter 18

THE FUTURE OF BRANDING

Paul Haftke

Until relatively recently the term 'brands' was restricted to fast-moving consumer goods. However, while the process of branding found its early expression in relation to tangible products, changes in the nature of economic activity, particularly in the growth of the service sector, have given rise to new kinds of brands outside the established frame of reference. As we move towards a wider definition of branding, what opportunities and challenges does the brand owner face?

NEW KINDS OF BRANDING

Much of the recent debate about branding has focused not just on the value of brands themselves but on who is best placed to exploit the powerful benefits they confer. Though the idea of branding has been around almost as long as organized economic activity itself, the modern concept of branding has its origins in the Industrial Revolution. The desire of manufacturers to capture and make specific to their products the more generalized demand for goods by a growing population led to the adoption and promotion of individual brand names and identities. Many of these brands have survived and indeed flourish in the marketplace today, among them Heinz Baked Beans, Pears Soap and Quaker Oats.

To some extent, and particularly for manufacturers' packaged goods, these early examples of branding still hold good today in providing an understanding of what branding is. Without a concentrated retail sector, only mass market, national brands could yield the scale economies on which, together with a lead in technology and product quality, the competitive advantage of the major manufacturers rested. However, early branding does not prove helpful in explaining why, in a recent survey of the UK's top 500 brands by media expenditure, eight out of the ten top brands, including the first six, were not products but retailers; nor why the leading brand-category was financial services. A similar survey, conducted as little as 15 to 20 years ago, would have yielded a quite different set of results. What has occasioned the rise of these 'new branders', and what are the implications for the traditional concept of branding?

What might be regarded as the first of the new generation of retail own-label products developed in the UK during the 'supermarket wars' of the 1970s. Against an economic background of recession and rising inflation, the own-label proposition was primarily price-led. Such products were designed, quite deliberately, to be cheap and generic by comparison with manufacturers' brands, making few pretensions to comparable quality. Their primary purpose was to capture market share from other retailers. As such, if they posed a competitive threat to established brands, it was invariably only to the weakest among them, those whose equities in terms of quality or brand personality were sufficiently marginal to make vulnerable the pricing premium they had historically commanded.

The changing social and economic conditions of the 1980s brought a profound shift in this attitude to own-label products. Though price competition remained an inherent part of the own-label proposition, it no longer dominated the product. Instead, quality became the crucial benchmark for comparison with manufacturers' brands. Though the retailer could not compete across the full range of own-label products with the advertising expenditures of individual manufacturers' brands, the consistent proposition of comparable quality at a lower price became a compelling one for consumers. It is possible to see, for example, in some of the blatantly imitative packaging of the period how retailers sought to effect a transfer of equities from the leading manufacturers' brands to competing own-label products and thus to leverage own label into brand label.

If the concept of branding is to be drawn sufficiently widely to encompass labels such as J. Sainsbury – and by any reasonable standard it should – it clearly cannot in future be based on the traditional manufacturing paradigm. Where retail brands now compete head-to-head with manufacturers' brands, and in many cases are now considered superior to them, it can be argued that scale economies in terms of increasingly concentrated buying power, integrated distribution and umbrella promotion, accrue predominantly not to the manufacturer, but to the retailer. Similarly, while a sustainable lead in manufacturing technology is increasingly hard to protect, the potential value to retailers of proprietary electronic data generated at the point of sale is only just beginning to be exploited. Even in the area of a brand's emotional appeal, the point of slavish imitation of manufacturers' brands has long since been passed. Today's retail brands are among the best packaged and promoted of all brands and often bear any comparison with manufacturers' brands. Indeed, in some food sectors in the UK, for example chilled and frozen meals and ready-prepared dips and snacks, retailers' brands quite clearly lead the field.

GROWTH IN SERVICE BRANDS

In analysing the shift in control of the benefits of branding away from being the exclusive preserve of manufacturers, the experience of retail brands is instructive but by no means exclusive. Recent estimates have put the figure for service sector output and employment in the world's advanced economies at 50 per cent, rising to 70–80 per cent by the year 2000. In the EEC alone some 16 million jobs in agriculture and industry were lost between 1960 and 1988, while 19 million were created in a services sector now accounting for 57 per cent of the EEC's workforce. This structural change in economic activity has brought with it explosive growth in the nature and variety of services available to the consumer, and thus in the need to distinguish one sector from another.

The financial services sector provides a particularly interesting example of the growth of branding in a tertiary economy. The recent interest shown by major institutions in applying branding techniques to a host of different 'offers' to the consumer – for example in savings accounts, current accounts, mortgages and pension plans – results from a number of factors. In what has become a highly complex market, in which intangible products can appeal to none of the conventional senses, brands clarify, simplify and provide reassurance. Faced with a bewildering stream of technical information, it is not surprising that the consumer gravitates towards the powerful appeal of a strong differentiated brand identity.

Indeed it is the absence of hard 'deliverables' that has brought about the new emphasis on corporate identity, and on quality and customer care programmes within financial services organizations. Perhaps following the lead of the airlines, they have realized that a key influence on a financial brand's personality is that of its corporate parent, and often this is most powerfully expressed to the consumer in the attitudes and behaviour of people who are frequently the company's most junior staff, for example bank clerks, stewardesses or receptionists. It is in this context, and only half-jokingly, that the company chairman is sometimes referred to as the 'corporate brand manager'.

The introduction of behavioural criteria to the concept of branding does not sit easily within the established manufacturing-led model of branding. If our understanding of branding is to be re-drawn in such a way as to accommodate not only the manufacturer's brands with which we began, but also service brands such as hotels, insurance companies and airlines, what common properties do they share and what is the future for brands as a marketing tool?

SUCCESSFUL BRANDING

Brands, whether manufactured goods or services, must offer consistency, credibility and protectability. Though they exist largely in the mind of the consumer, and appeal in a way that is both rational and non-rational, they enable him to judge with confidence the relative value they confer. In order to do this a successful brand must offer benefits, real or perceived, which distinguish it from other goods or services.

There is a considerable number of products and services which arguably would not pass such a test. Though they may, over their lifecycles, have developed about them a formidable and expensive superstructure of brand management, market research and promotional expenditure, the value they confer relative to competition is slight. Such brands are characterized by their failure to deliver a sustained competitive advantage to their owners, and the absence of any incremental benefit to consumers.

It is these products which will in future prove most vulnerable to continuing retailer encroachment and to being marginalized by the competition. And this threat is by no means confined to manufacturers' goods: the success of Marks & Spencer's debut unit trust product took many in the financial services sector by surprise. Nor will the edifice of brand management which has developed around such products provide effective insurance. On the contrary, it is precisely these superstructures which are stripped away with relish by predators seeking to liberate cashflows.

For those brands which can deliver to their owners a sustainable competitive advantage, based on a differentiated consumer proposition, what future opportunities and challenges can be anticipated?

BUILDING INTERNATIONAL BRANDS

Theodore Levitt has maintained that 'the world's needs and desires have been irrevocably globalized'. With accelerating consumer choice and the growth of modern communications, brand owners will increasingly be forced to look beyond their own national boundaries for a viable franchise. Only by aggregating carefully segmented products and services on a global basis, it is argued, will the critical mass necessary to launch and sustain a major brand be built. While 'globalization' has proved one of the marketing consultancy watchwords of the 1980s, it is not essential to swallow the argument whole in order to appreciate the growing challenge. A number of critics have observed in Levitt's vision of globalization a failure to distinguish products (which may or may not be capable of transcending national boundaries) from brands. However strong the local franchise a brand enjoys within its natioanl market, it may prove virtually impossible to globalize if the underlying product is of only limited appeal (British beer, for example).

Yet whether such brands will automatically fall prey to competing global brands remains very much open to question. One commentator was moved to describe the application of the concept of globalization to food as 'globaloney'. *The Economist* pointed out that, even at the pan-regional, developed country level, 'Europe is still far from being one homogenous market', and went on to detail examples from the personal products, brown goods, chemicals and household products sectors in which the attempt to aggregate consumer needs across even *two* national markets had proved unrewarding.

None of the foregoing effectively falsifies the globalization argument, though it does serve to remind the observer that world brands are built, rather than imposed.

Internationalizing, still more globalizing, a unified brand proposition will demand particularly acute judgments about brand positioning and strategy. The structure and organization of brand management will need to be orientated towards maximizing efficiency and responsiveness, and this may demand change on a scale which many companies will be reluctant to contemplate. Yet the rewards are potentially enormous.

The Single European Market of 1992 will have a population exceeding that of the USA and Japan combined, with GDP approximately seven times greater than that of the UK. Quite apart from the attractions of the sheer size of the market to brand owners, there may be other powerful stimulants to the internationalization of brands. In the search for growth, brand owners facing a saturated domestic market are pushed inexorably towards foreign markets. In these new markets the reflex defensive response of local competitors can often mirror their own. The reduction of trade barriers, and simplification of border control procedures facilitates distribution, resulting in a wider range of products becoming available in local markets. The brand-owner who can identify the need for a harmonized brand identity will find the prospect of exponential growth in demand a compelling reason for market entry. The brand owner who cannot will face the threat of being marginalized in his domestic market.

CHANGES IN THE MARKET

At the level of demographic and technological change, Professor Jagdish Sheth has identified a number of 'Marketing Megatrends' which are likely to have important implications for the future of branding.

The 'greying' of populations in the developed countries, with rising median ages, and the decline of the traditional family and growth in both dual-income and single households, will mark a fundamental shift on the demand side. These demographic trends will manifest themselves in changes in lifestyles and social values. Patterns of consumption will become increasingly personalized, suggesting a splintering of demand across a greater variety of products. Attitudes and values will shift away from the 'youth cult', on which many of today's brands rely for their positioning and towards a more adult frame of reference. Moreover the rise in affluence and maturity will exacerbate the gap between discretionary income and discretionary time: those with the greatest spending power will be those who have the least free time (and with whom, therefore, it may be most difficult to communicate via conventional media).

In terms of technological change, the dominant theme will be the profound impact of the electronic age on business, in the form of lowered barriers to market entry and exit, an increasingly global marketplace, lowered unit costs and enhanced standards of quality. These developments, it is argued, will result in a heightened responsiveness to change in the marketplace as transaction times and geographic distances are shrunk. Market-entry and unit-cost conditions will stimulate niching strategies, with a further fragmentation of the mass market.

Against this background of demographic and technological change, seven 'megatrends' have been identified by Professor Sheth, from which some tentative conclusions about the future for brands may be drawn:

- The rise of 'dual mass-consumption', affluent two-income households without children. In the battle for the spending power of these groups, premium value-added brands will be at a considerable advantage relative to commodity or mass market products

- Increasingly personalized per capita consumption, in which buying decisions are made according to individual (rather than household) preferences. Opportunities for impulse purchase and for premium product selection can be expected to escalate

- A blurring of established vocational and domestic roles. Stereotypes such as 'the housewife' will be rendered progressively less appropriate in targeting and promoting brands

- A breakdown of the compartmentalization of life into activities and locations such as home, work and shopping. Thus there may be a need to re-examine the established categories into which brands are grouped

- The increasing dominance of wants over needs in the psychology of consumer motivation Thus there needs to be an

202

increasing emphasis on creating a distinctive and attractive personality on which a brand's emotional appeal can be based

- Declining social homogeneity, with divergence in values, attitudes and beliefs. This trend will find expression in a variety of lifestyles and will give rise to an increased number of smaller market segments

- A preference for one-stop shopping (and ultimately perhaps for electronic home shopping) resulting from the high marginal utility of discretionary time. Thus there will be an increasing level of 'background noise' as more brands fight for even shorter spans of consumer attention

CONCLUSION

The rapid rise of quite new forms of branding will continue to mirror the structural shift towards a more complex, tertiary economy. These developing forms of branding cannot easily be accommodated within the traditional branding model, based as it is on the concept of manufacturers' goods driven by the need to capture economies of scale. The competitive environment in which brands operate will, in future, nevertheless be one of heightened complexity, dynamism and opportunity. It would perhaps be unduly optimistic to expect the attrition rate among brands old and new to be anything other than high under such circumstances. The potential rewards for those brands whose power can be sustained and extended have, however, never been so rich.

BIBLIOGRAPHY

Burgleman, Robert A. and Sayles, Leonard R., *Inside Corporate Innovation: Strategy, Structure and Managerial Skills*, Macmillan Inc., New York, 1986

Bureau, J. R., *Brand Management: Planning and Control*, Macmillan Press Ltd, London, 1981

Buzzell, R.D. and Gale, B.T., *The PIMS Principles: Linking Strategy to Performance*, New York: Free Press, 1987.

Catrer, Peter and Hatt, Roz, *How Far Does Advertising Protect The Brand Franchise?*, Admap, London, 1983

Davidson, J. Hugh, *Offensive Marketing: Or How To Make Your Competitors Your Followers,* Penguin Books, London, *1987 (second ed.)*

Davis, Ian, *Does Branding Pay?*, Admap, London, 1986

Interbrand, *Brands: An International Review by Interbrand*, Mercury, London, 1990

King, Stephen, Has Marketing Failed, Or Was It Never Really Tried?, *Journal of Marketing Management*, London, Vol. 1, No. 1

Murphy, John M. (editor), *Branding: A Key Marketing Tool*, Macmillan Press Ltd, London, 1987 and McGraw-Hill, New York, 1987

Murphy, John M. and Rowe, Michael, *How to Design Trademarks and Logos*, Phaidon Press, London, 1988 and Northlight Books, Cincinnati, USA, 1988

Murphy, John M., *Brand Strategy*, Director Books, London, 1990 and Prentice-Hall, New York, 1990

INDEX